THE COMPLEAT SWINDLER

THE COMPLEAT
SWINDLER

by Ralph Hancock

with Henry Chafetz

The Macmillan Company, New York

Collier-Macmillan Limited, London

FIRST PRINTING

The Macmillan Company, New York
Collier-Macmillan Canada Ltd., Toronto, Ontario
Printed in the United States of America

To the Gullible American

May his numbers never dwindle

Contents

Preface

No one reads a preface, but like the choirmaster who needs a tuning fork to set the pitch for every tune, we need this place to make our pitch for a tune rarely played before.

With education being upgraded in every field and with every field expanding into countless specialties, we are amazed that this one is so universally neglected. In an age of fast-buck philosophy, where the emphasis in education is on the material rather than the spiritual, where even education itself is big business, it is amazing to find no Chair of Swindling, no Professors of Fraud. Do not our boards know that swindlers make more money than all the doctors put together (MD's, PhD's, LLD's, LittD's, and DD's) and that fraud is a practice more common than fornication? So, we ask, is it not time that some attention be given to an examination of the subject?

Introduction

When intelligent, alert, prudent Americans sink $1,000,-000 into an oil-stock operation whose major asset is a cow, or when promoters of a charity can raise $3,978,000 for a children's welfare association and then pocket $3,252,000 for themselves, or when a man can make $1,000,000 on a useless nostrum between his first police citation and his final "restraining order" (with enough left over to pay a sharp lawyer), then one must doubt whether honesty really is the best policy.

Nor should our sympathy weigh heavily on the side of the gullible and the duped. Swindlers and professional con men all admit that it is difficult to cheat an honest man. Which is another way of saying that but for the larceny in the gullible heart, there would be no dupes. And the more larcenous the heart, the less likelihood that the duped will admit he was swindled or complain to the authorities.

That is why the public estimators say that for every swindle exposed by press or public prosecutor, hundreds never see the light of publicity. Indeed, there are more ways to make a dishonest buck than there are to make an honest one, because for every honest trade or profession, there are endless fraudulent ways to do the same thing.

This is the story of how swindlers do it, but rarely why, with no complaint and only a little criticism, for this is not a book with a message. Had we written it thirty years ago, we might have sought out the theme that "crime does not pay," and the villains in the end would have received their just desserts. Even twenty years ago, when serious young men were returning from a war to write the truth and nothing but, we might have slanted this whole book as a piece of bitter satire on a society that could countenance such things as wars abroad and swindles at home. Ten years ago, we would have been influenced by the same factors that produced the scattershot exposés that were intended to spur thinking and public action. But we have seen the futility of that approach too. Anyone who criticizes with conviction is sooner or later called an alarmist, a calamity-howling Cassandra, a prophet of doom. And, in all conscience, we have always felt that the sanctimonious were suspect, the satirists suffered from grudges, and the exposers were hypocrites.

No, today we think there is a growing body of book readers who read for the hell of it. They suspect the motives of moralists, satirists, and crusaders. They take pride in their intellectual freedom, diverse tastes, and uninhibited reading habits. This book was compiled with them in mind.

The sources that provided most of our material—the police files, the records of mutual protective associations, the Better Business Bureaus, and other law-supporting agencies—cooperated because they were convinced that we would treat the material with objectivity and no bias. This approach is reflected here, hopefully, as restraint and understatement. On the other hand, there was such an immense body of available material, we could not have squeezed it into a hundred books. Obviously, we could pick only those pieces that, in our judgment, were the most exemplary, if not the most extraordinary, swindles ever perpetrated.

Of course, this got us into history, because some of the experts today have not been able to improve on those of former times. But we have been frugal with our history and in the main used it more for its comparative value or as background for the present.

There was another yardstick for selection of material. There were thousands of examples in closely parallel fields —theft, blackmail, burglary—but, in the end, we decided to disqualify anything to which we could not apply the common dictionary definition of a swindler: "One who obtains money or property from another by fraud or deceit; one who practices imposture for gain."

Ralph Hancock
San Diego County
Henry Chafetz
New York City

Swindler: One who obtains money or property from another by fraud or deceit; one who practices imposture for gain.

—Webster's Dictionary

THE COMPLEAT SWINDLER

1

THE ART OF DECEPTION

We cannot speak of deception and say that one age in history knew more of it than any other, only that each succeeding era discovers refinements on the accomplishments of the older. The art of deception began long before man's concepts of morality became fixed in his consciousness. Succeeding eras perfected the art, found new resources on which to use it, and like amoebic multiplication, it expanded to its present limitless potential. Indeed, its very vastness restricts our own treatment to one form of deception—the art of swindling.

The hoax, which is another popular and closely related form of deception, might have been a more entertaining field for us to cover, since it frequently involves overtones of humor, caricature, or burlesque, but the ultimate purpose of a hoax does not appeal to us.

It is the purpose and the effect that distinguish one form of deception from another. The swindler wants to get something—money, power, prestige, or revenge—and he may use any deceits within his power to attain his end.

The hoaxer may use any deceits within his power too,

and he may even duplicate those used by the swindler, but the purpose and the effect distinguish a hoax from other forms of deception. The hoaxer intends his work to be a satirical comment or a reinterpretation or a criticism or perhaps no more than a practical joke. Only when the hoax is used to obtain money or some material advantage can it be called a swindle.

An examination of the art of hoaxing might therefore be of questionable service. It would stimulate the imagination, perhaps, and entertain, but the only practical use that could be made of it would be as a supplementary work in the training of a swindler. We shall keep it in mind, however, and should the demand for such a supplementary work prove that it would be of more than limited service, we shall comply.

Our emphasis here, therefore, will be on the more practical applications of deceit and those examples that best illustrate the practices of the successful swindler.

Although we shall cover a wide range—horizontally by various fields and vertically by money levels—swindles, it should be remembered, are cyclical phenomena. They may originate in the minds of clever fellows, or they may be modern adaptations of old ideas, but whatever the game, they appear to rise to a peak at certain times, with profit to many, then they seem to drop into disuse and obscurity. But they never entirely disappear. They are part of the fabric of civilization, and sooner or later other swindlers will try them. The con men will dust them off and revise them to fit the times, develop new angles and new gimmicks, and use them to fleece a whole generation of suckers who have never heard of them.

Our material is presented on the basis of a two-part assumption: that the reader is (1) objective and (2) ambitious. To make the best possible use of this material, the student should be able to weigh it against a moral concept that is fair and unbiased, and he should desire with some intensity to make a fast dollar.

SWINDLER VS. SWINDLED

Any serious study of swindling must assume that a little bit of larceny exists in everyone. Some of our fellow academicians, perhaps holier than we, contend that swindling is the natural evolution of conduct that begins with pathological lying. Pathological liars become impostors, swindlers, and other kinds of criminals, they say. We have no clinical polls, laboratory charts, or learned theses on which to base our theory, but we shall state it anyway: lying is merely one of the many talents that the adept swindler must have at his command. If it is pathological, then he lies for the sake of lying. He enjoys the fantasy world he creates around himself. He is more impostor than swindler. The shrewd swindler, on the other hand, lies for the sake of some material gain. He is practical where any fantasy is concerned, for should he wish to indulge in fantasy, he knows he can buy it if he has the money.

The most likely pigeon, or victim, of any swindle is the man who is himself basically dishonest. He is looking for easy money, bites on anything that looks like a sure thing, and if it is a little shady, so much the better. He is in the same frame of mind as the swindler and has no more conscience. The only difference between them is that the pigeon plucker is in command—it is his game, he is experienced, and he has confidence in his own talents. Further, the accomplished swindler understands enough about the workings of an avaricious mind so that he rarely makes a mistake or misjudges his quarry.

The gullible are not restricted to any race, creed, or economic condition. Nor has any period of history been known for more easy marks than any other. Gullibility is a trait common only to the thinking animal, and one cannot delve far into the folklore of any ethnic group without some encounter with this purely human peccability. Indeed, more often than not, the hero image in tales of the gullible may be given to the swindler or the impostor. An excellent example is the anecdote—presented in nearly every collection of folklore, with variants to fit particular backgrounds and environments—about a peasant who is so poor that all he owns in the world is a hen (or a pig or a burro). Nearly starving, he tells his wife to take the hen to market and sell it.

"How much shall I ask for it?" the woman wants to know.

"Ask as much as they'll pay, of course," the man says.

So she takes the hen and sets out. Coming to a village, she meets a merchant.

"Good morning," says the merchant. "Where are you going with that hen?"

"I'm going to market to sell it for as much as they'll pay me."

The merchant weighs the hen in his hand, purses his lips, thinks a moment, and says, "You better sell it to me. I'll pay you three pennies for it. . . . Yes," the merchant says, more firmly now, "three pennies is as much as I'll pay."

So the peasant's wife sells the hen for three pennies. Then she buys a pretty paper bag with one of the pennies and a piece of ribbon with another penny. She puts the third penny into the bag, ties the bag with the ribbon, and then, feeling that she has made a very good bargain, she returns home to her husband.

There, when he hears the whole stupid tale, he flies into a great rage and at first threatens to beat her. "Was there ever such a foolish woman in the world?" he shouts angrily.

The poor woman, who by this time is snuffling and weeping, whimpers, "I don't see why you find fault with me. I'm sure I'm not the only gullible person in the world."

It is a good point and an opportune moment to bring it up. Anyway, it starts the peasant to thinking that perhaps there are people in the world as gullible as his wife. He decides to go out and see whether he can find them. "If I do, I won't beat you," he promises.

She escapes the beating, of course, because the farmer finds that nearly everyone can be tricked by one fraud or another. When he perceives how easy it is, he pyramids his take through a series of adventures and returns home a wealthier and wiser man.

Though the nonprofessional will be interested in the glossary of terms that we have appended at the end of this work, some differentiation of terminology should be stated here. Criminologists classify swindlers as thieves, but our premise is simply that it takes more intelligence and talent to be a swindler. Professional thieves include the cannon (pickpocket), the heel (sneak thief who operates in stores, banks, and offices), the booster (shoplifter), the pennyweighter (steals jewelry and small objects by substituting worthless items for valuable ones), the hotel prowler (steals from hotel rooms), and the con (specializes in confidence games).

These rackets are all related, since they involve manipulation of suckers by nonviolent methods. Futhermore, the skills required in each have many similarities. Salesman-

Salesman

ship, acting ability, a sense of timing, ability to judge character, dexterity, and sleight of hand are common to them all, but not all racketeers enjoy all these skills. Only the expert con will have the intelligence and the talent to develop all those skills and graduate from the College of Cons with a BS (Bachelor of Swindling). And not all persons can be successful swindlers. The master swindler generally must have a winning personality, shrewdness, agility, and great egotism. He must, first of all, be a good actor. The whole con game is a matter of acting. If he cannot put on a veneer of culture, he cannot make a go of it. A confidence man, the compleat swindler, must live by his wits.

Therefore, our premise, within the framework of these assumptions, is that the means should justify the end. Any lout with gun in hand can rob a bank for a few dollars, but he is a scholar and a gentleman who can take it for a few million. No deceit is necessary for the petty robbery, while deception's greatest perfection is demonstrated in the $1,000,000 embezzlement.

Why, then, since his goal is the biggest possible haul, does the robber rob instead of embezzle? Because he can't do anything more than rob. He knows nothing of the arts of deceit and even less about the talents he needs to practice it. Every exercise in deception—indeed, even the quality and quantity of deception involved—depends on the education of the individual. Whatever his talents, his earning power depends on how well these talents are cultivated.

Frequently a swindler pulls off a large haul and the public is amazed that he could do it. When the news of it suddenly appears in the newspapers, people are surprised that a "pillar of the community" could be so deceitful. What they never realize is the fact that for the swindler this may or may not be a climactic use of his talents for deception. It is only the public's sudden discovery of a talent he has been cultivating for years. No one, certainly not the really talented swindler, can recall all the day-to-day deceits he has practiced and in time perfected.

Assuming that we are all born equal and equally inherit that little bit of larceny, how, then, can it be developed, educated, to the point where it is capable of swindling someone or some company out of $1,000,000?

In order to develop any talent, one must begin at the beginning. And the beginning, as we have said, is the assumption of a student with both an open mind and the ambition to develop his latent larceny. If you can look at yourself and honestly confirm this assumption, then you have completed your first lesson in the art of deception. In the practice of this lesson, you will continue your day-to-day activities in a completely normal way. However, you will know that the more "normal" they seem, the more gyp artistry you are practicing.

NO LAW'S DELAY

The inexperienced, the timid, and the rare one who may really be honest will question at this point whether the laws against swindling do not inhibit anyone planning or pulling off a swindle. The timid novice and the really honest may be inhibited, but the professional knows that even if he is caught, there is a public attitude that motivates courts to decide in his favor.

There are hundreds of historic cases to prove this point.

Weapons from Congress

Indeed, the pride Americans express in the *nom de commerce* "Yankee trader" or "Yankee ingenuity" is based on historic patterns of what might be good business practice for Americans but is swindling to anyone else. The first line in the text *Crime Is a Business*, an academic treatment of buncos, rackets, and confidence schemes by John C. R. MacDonald, former police inspector and lecturer, is this: "Swindling, or bunco, is nothing more or less than high-pressure salesmanship."

Only the American, with his famous sense of fair play and sportsmanship, can appreciate the values involved in this case, for example. Attorney for the defense was lawyer and politician Ichabod Bartlett, who was a contemporary and a neighbor of Daniel Webster. Though the latter gained more fame, Bartlett, in his day, was just as brilliant in court. As attorney for the defense, he frequently matched wits with Webster and others equally capable, and in the art of gaining verdicts, Mr. Bartlett was the superior of any of them. In an article published in an obscure and long forgotten publication (*Green Bag*, 1894), there is a report of a typical case of Yankee trading. In this case, two distinguished lawyers of New Hampshire had bought a horse from a farmer in Hampton for $30. They managed to get the steed as far as Exeter, where they lived, a distance of about ten miles, but the animal proved too weak to stand up even to eat his oats and soon collapsed, a total loss. The irate purchasers brought suit against the farmer for fraud in the sale. Bartlett was retained for the defense. He began his argument somewhat in this fashion:

> Gentlemen of the jury, before we consider the testimony that bears on the circumstances of this sale, let us for a moment see who are the parties to this suit. Whom have we here as plaintiffs? Two able, astute lawyers. Who is here as defendant? A plain farmer. One of these

plaintiffs, gentlemen, is James Bell! A lawyer of talent and experience, a gentleman of such shrewdness that when the rich corporations of Massachusetts were hunting all over the state of New Hampshire for the right kind of attorney to protect their enormously valuable interests at Lake Winnipesaukee, they selected *him*. Amos Tuck, another lawyer, gentlemen, of such marked success and distinction at the bar that the people of this district have just chosen him to represent them in Congress. These two keen-witted men, as if not content to trust their own sagacity and skill, proceeded to call in a third party to help them. They selected none other than Stephen W. Dearborn, gentlemen, the High Sheriff of this county, who is sitting in yonder box, a man known all this region roundabout as the sharpest horse jockey to be found anywhere. And now, gentlemen, with this combination brought to bear on the subject, you are seriously asked to believe that they were cheated in a horse trade by my poor, simple old client!

The more astute swindlers are familiar with the laws of the state within which they operate, and most know the extent of protection to which they are entitled. Though they may enjoy more or less freedom in different states, some generalizations at this point may be helpful.

The courts generally recognize the necessity that adults of competent understanding should have complete liberty to contract, and that contracts, when entered into freely and voluntarily, should be held good and should be enforced by the courts.

"Liberty to contract" is a phrase that rings fair in the ears of businessmen and jurists alike. But the swindler, whose contract may have defrauded a victim, may encounter certain limitations on this liberty. If he has to protect his contract in court, he may very well find that what seems fair to one individual seems blatantly unfair to another.

However, there have been cases where the swindler proved that both he and his victim acted in good faith, that what the plaintiff claimed was a swindle was actually nothing more than a shrewd business deal.

Thus, the climate in certain courts is highly favorable to swindles and fraud, and this climate may be influenced quite effectively by the kind of legal eagle that specializes in this field.

When one considers that we are only a few centuries removed from common law, when the victim of fraud or even of his own mistakes got little or no relief in court, one can see how little the law has changed. A fact unknown to most is that the Statute of Frauds, an act for the prevention of frauds and perjuries enacted by the English Parliament in 1677, has been incorporated virtually unchanged into the law of every state in this country.

In ancient times, the prevailing standard of business morality was based upon what the academicians call "extreme individualism," or, more simply said, "every man for himself." The idea that each person was obliged to protect himself from fraud was expressed in the rule *Caveat emptor* ("Let the buyer beware"). When a trader deceived his customer and profited in a one-sided bargain, it was considered commendable. Naturally, in the primitive economy of an uncomplex society, the parties to any transaction were usually well acquainted, the subject of the transaction was familiar to all.

Contrast that condition with the situation today. Today we buy many quite complex and unfamiliar items from people we have never seen before. The law, meanwhile, has continued to reflect much that was only common law in ancient times. Add to this the fact that the population level is higher than ever before and one can understand how swindling has become the most profitable of professions. If a sucker was born every minute in Barnum's day, a hundred years ago, that maxim's figure should now be updated, in accordance with today's population explosion, to six every minute.

In such a "market," even the sky is no limit. A Memphis entrepreneur has worked out a slick stock-promotion deal that he calls "Shares in Space." What with the government's fabulous expenditures for space exploration, someone like George was bound to come up with a good swindle in this field. But we shall discuss Shares in Space and George's *modus operandi* in the proper place. It is enough, for the moment, that we add this simple summation: the art of deception is practiced today by more people in more ways for more profit than ever before in the history of the world.

2

THE SHORT-CHANGE SWINDLE

THE small-time con whose daily take may average no more than a few hundred dollars is not in a class with the bank embezzler or the crooked stock manipulator, but his profession is swindling just the same.

The ambitious novice, with his eye on bigger things, may start with a short-change exercise. Many, once they perfect a system at this level, never go on to bigger and better things but are content to work their specialty year in, year out. That is why each year there are more and more practitioners in this field. And despite all the "Count Your Change" signs hung on cash registers and the frequent warnings broadcast by authorities, the annual take by the short-change artists is variously estimated in the hundred millions of dollars. Counting the swindlers on both sides of the cash registers, that amount may be nearly doubled.

The most amazing fact behind all this is not the haul, but the number of people who are careless in handling money. The average citizen loses more from being short-changed than from taking counterfeit money, and yet bogus bucks get the more sensational headlines.

THE SHORT-CHANGE ARTISTS

This carelessness on the part of the public, as well as the press's general emphasis on other small swindles, creates a climate tailored to the advantage of the short-change artist. Within the limitless boundaries of this field, he soon perfects his own routine, and though it may be classified under one of a dozen general headings, he imparts to it his own particular characteristics.

Though a little more involved and complicated than some routines, that presently practiced by a character named "Nick" of Chicago and Miami Beach (and points in between) is one of the smoothest. Nick's stock-in-trade consists of two bank notes, a $20 bill and a $1 bill. He is a good talker with a ready line of conversation, generally prearranged and on a topic that is bound to interest the sucker. He dresses neatly but not ostentatiously, and his appearance always conforms to the average in the immediate area. He works the cash registers that are placed near exits, which provide opportunities for hasty departures where necessary. But Nick never runs, for a chase would declare his guilt. He depends on sheer nerve and his ability to feign innocence should the victim become aware of the trick.

Restaurants are classed as good marks for Nick's routine, for there is generally only a girl cashier to handle, and a little well-placed conversation ensures his success. Nick is good-looking, so he seldom worries over the average girl cashier, for a smile and a few remarks about her beautiful eyes or attractive hairdo eradicate all thoughts of the swindle in progress. Should she exhibit any evidence of experience with such routines, a hasty apology adjusts the matter, the change is corrected, and Nick evaporates in the outside crowd. Or he may compliment her on her sagacity and with some choice chatter smile his way right out of the fix.

To work his routine, Nick enters a restaurant and purchases only a sandwich or a cup of coffee (which he barely touches, for he eats only in the better restaurants). He approaches the cashier with the check, which should be less than $1, and tenders the $20 bill for payment. He immediately begins his canvas (*i.e.*, his pitch, his talk), and his subject is shrewdly chosen to interest the girl. Something in the day's news, a local event, or some topic he is pretty sure she will have thought about within the past few hours. Whatever the circumstance, this pitch must divide the girl's attention between the matter of making change and his topic.

She places the $20 note in the register and lays the change on the counter. Nick picks up the small change but never touches the paper money; at the same time, he asks for a pack of cigarettes. While the girl reaches for the cigarettes, he extracts from his pocket the single $1 bill. As he pays the girl the exact change for the cigarettes, he holds up the $1 bill and exclaims, "That's a good one! Here I had a dollar bill in my pocket all the time and didn't know it."

Nick keeps this bill in sight all the time in one hand while reaching with the same hand for the $19 on the counter. But as his hand approaches the money, he folds up the $1 bill with a swift motion and palms it, while at the same time, with a single move, he folds up the $10 bill in such a way that it is hidden within the remaining $9. Meanwhile he is asking the girl another question and looking her straight in the eye.

He holds the $19 in plain sight, though the $10 note is secreted within the other $9. The girl, if she thinks of it at all, thinks he has placed with the rest the single bill he discovered in his pocket. Then, since change is always in demand, Nick asks whether she would like to give him a $10 bill for the ten $1 bills in change. He hands her the pile with one hand and takes her $10 bill with the other. He promptly pockets the $10 and starts for the door. He pauses to light a cigarette, thus giving the girl time to discover his error, that she has $19 instead of ten $1 bills. He stalls until she apprises him of the mistake in change, or in the event the girl overlooks the mistake or decides to pocket the extra $9 herself, Nick returns as though he had suddenly discovered the discrepancy.

If she calls him back (most cashiers will), she will show him the $19 and tell him he has shortchanged himself. He thanks her prettily for her honesty and manages to combine it with other compliments about her fine character.

Then comes the punch line. He brings forth the single $1 bill that he had palmed and tosses it down with the other $19, suggesting again that she may need the change and asking for his $20 bill in return.

Nick keeps no records, but after several years of this routine, he has rarely encountered a girl who remembers the $10 bill she handed him before. And he is understandably reticent about any exact figures on his average daily take. "Rather depends on how hard I work, wouldn't you say?" Or on how many cups of coffee he buys.

The variations on Nick's routine are endless, and ambitious hustlers register as many as twenty or thirty scores a day. Some have been known to score twice in the same place on the same day, for the shortage is seldom noticed until the count is made at the close of the day's business. And the swindle is not practiced always by men.

Several women have become quite proficient, working shops where young men handle the cash registers. A little sex appeal is added to the patter, and when some of these young ladies get through working on the boys, they haven't anything left to register but their chagrin.

The anachronism "cash register" hardly describes the complicated and highly versatile machines in use in most places today. These machines perform the first steps in the nearly complete automation of the bookkeeping departments, and anyone thoroughly trained in their use can soon figure out a dozen ways to use them to defraud. In the hands of a smart manipulator, they can advance the art of shortchanging to a science. Even in their nonuse, there is profit, for "Failure to ring up cash sales" is listed as the biggest cause of "cash-register losses." Next is failure to ring up the correct amount. Cashiers at busy supermarkets have been known to make their machines do everything but dance, and considering some of their short-change artistry, they make old pros like Nick look like bums.

The negligence of customers at the point of paying for their purchases is unbelievable—but true of the majority nevertheless. They neglect to read the register, they pocket their change without counting it, they do not request or keep sales slips or register tapes, and they never examine the bill they proffer in payment. Women have given $100 bills thinking they were $10 bills or $50 bills for $5 bills. And bartenders have been known to "accept" a $99.25 tip for pouring a 75¢ drink, and the customer wasn't drunk, just careless.

Cash-register artists still pull the old ten-to-five switch. The customer pays for something small with a $10 bill. The cashier puts a $5 bill on the counter right under the nose of the customer, then gives him change for the $5 and puts the $5 back in the register. The trick can be used with bigger denominations on more rattlebrained customers. The amount of the annual take by sweet and innocent-looking old ladies and young hopefuls behind the nation's cash registers would amaze you.*

And even if the cashiers in the joint are all honest, there is still the gimmick that supermarket managers have been known to use. Let's take, for example, a supermarket with, say, seven cash registers. Every day the seven registers are tallied. In each there is as much cash as has been rung up. Periodic inventories may disclose big shortages in stock, but detectives planted in the store will find nothing wrong. All goods going out will be accounted for on the seven registers. And if they send a vice-president out from the main office to check on the stock received, he won't find any evidence of pilfering. And the take? It will always be one-seventh of the total day's receipts, as long as the manager can get away with it, for he himself is the one who installed the extra seventh check-out counter and register, only six having been installed originally.

A slick variation on Nick's short-change routine is worked with an accomplice. Generally it's a man-and-woman team. The man enters a store or restaurant and

* Employees perpetrate some 550,000,000 swindles every year for a total valuation of billions of dollars. In all probability, it is your respectable next-door neighbor who regards his employer's money as his own ~~pork barrel~~. Though new twists on old tricks show up daily, the most used gimmicks include these: manipulating the petty-cash box with false vouchers, fake expenses, and so on; pocketing cash paid across the counter and ringing up the wrong totals; paying out salaries or commissions to nonexistent, discharged, or dead employees; sending goods to fake customers; kickbacks, split commissions, and fake billing; making "adjustments" in customers' bills; raising amounts on checks that pass through one's hands; and lapping today's receipts to cover yesterday's embezzlements.

makes a small purchase, paying the check with a $20 bill. He must be as unobtrusive as possible.

Some time later, the woman enters, makes a purchase, and pays for it with a small bill. She chooses her time for this transaction when the cashier is busy with other customers. After receiving her change, she will appear to count it and hesitate as she moves away. Suddenly she returns to the cashier and insists that she has been shortchanged. The cashier names the bill she received and assures the customer she gave her the correct change. The customer demands to see the manager.

The manager, of course, sides with the cashier, because he knows the customer is not always right. Now the woman goes into her spiel. Upon leaving home, she says, she asked her husband for some money. He gave her a $20 bill and told her it was all he had, and "so the chicken will come home to roost," as he put it, he had written their telephone number on it.

"That's the bill I gave her," says the irate customer. "Look in her cash drawer and see."

The manager, if he is wise to the trick, knows he is hooked, but there is little he can do about it. He makes the "adjustment."

The swindler blessed with dexterity can easily palm a bill while the cashier is counting out his change, then, without leaving the cash register, convince the cashier that she has shortchanged him. The racket is best worked on small stores, where the cashiers are underpaid and not too bright.

The envelope switch is an easy one. The operator enters a store and offers a handful of bills and small change "for a twenty." He takes from his pocket a stamped, addressed envelope and says, "I want to send the twenty to my mother for her birthday." Upon receiving the $20 bill, and while the clerk is counting the money, he puts the bill in the envelope, seals it, and returns it to his pocket.

But the clerk tells the operator he is short $1. The operator pretends to be flustered and embarrassed. He says he will have to go home (or back to the office or out to his car) and get the additional $1. He takes back the bills and change and gives the clerk the envelope, telling her to keep it in the register until he returns.

It may be hours before the clerk opens the envelope and discovers that it contains a blank piece of paper. She calculates her loss as $19.95, because the stamp is good.

COUNTERING COUNTERFEIT

What with all the publicity and the periodic alerts broadcast by the Treasury Department, people who handle money are aware that counterfeiting is still a popular profession in the United States. What they don't know, however, is the American currency. Despite the publicity, the alerts, and a continuing campaign to educate the public, the average American shopkeeper knows less about the currency he handles than one might think. And Americans in general know less about their currency than any other people who use money.

Such widespread public ignorance provides a ready-made opportunity for the sagacious swindler. For instance, a pair we'll call Horace and Emma have worked out a slick swindle they play on shoe-store and other merchants. Emma will drop in near closing time and try on a pair of shoes, buy them, and offer a good $50 bill in payment. "Sorry, but I just didn't have time to drop by the bank and get anything smaller." But the store takes it and gives her the change and the merchandise.

Next morning, before the store has a chance to take its deposit to the bank, Horace walks in, flashes a badge, and mumbles, "Treasury Department. Tracing a counterfeiter. Seen anyone like this? She's passing bogus fifties." And he shows a picture of Emma.

The clerks gather around, and one of them recognizes the customer who passed a $50 bill the day before. The bill is located and shown to Horace, who examines it carefully and pronounces it counterfeit. He gives the store a signed receipt for the bill and tells the manager he will hear from the Treasury Department later. The store hears from the Treasury Department, all right, but it is the news that Horace and Emma are accomplices in a slick swindle. Eighteen small shops in a Southern town were hit with this one in a single day, one of them with a $100 "counterfeit" bill (Emma had run out of $50 notes). The total take was more than $1,700 plus the merchandise.

An old-time minstrel show that we remember seeing once on the Million-dollar Pier on the Boardwalk in Atlantic City included this skit.

The Interlocutor began with the line, "Two wrongs don't make a right."

"Sometimes dey do," interposed Sam, near the end of the line.

"Now, how do you figure that, Sam, suh?" asked the Interlocutor. "It is against the very nature of things."

"Can't help that, Mr. Interlocutor. There was a fellow passed on to me once a bad dollar. Wasn't that wrong?"

"Certainly it was wrong, if he knew it was counterfeit."

"I did, anyhow, when I passed it on to another man. Now wasn't that wrong?"

"Wrong? Of course—very wrong."

"Well, suh, it done made me right," was the triumphant rejoinder. "So two wrongs do make a right sometime."

There are about as many ways to pass counterfeit money as there are counterfeit bills. And we don't include such simple ploys as the purchase of a small item with a fake big bill. That is a stupid way to do it. Anyone who has access to bogus money (the going rate is 25¢ to 35¢ per dollar, depending on its quality) can figure out his own gimmick for passing. It may be something like this for passing bogus $20 bills. The passer begins with a $50 bill, a good one, which is used to purchase some small item at a busy check-out counter. He will invariably get back at least one $20 bill with his change. He goes through the motions of counting the money while the other customers wait. He returns the bill—or, rather, the counterfeit bill he has been palming—and asks the cashier for smaller change.

Since a $1 bill (a good one) is worth only 21¢ today as compared with thirty years ago, the bogus $5 bill is becoming scarce. It doesn't pay the counterfeiter to make anything less than a $20 note today, and with inflation what it is, we rather suspect that the next flood of counterfeit money to hit the market will be copies of the $50 bill. However, should anyone be in possession of a few bogus fins, the above trick may be possible by making use of a good $20 bill instead of a $50 bill. Tender a $20 bill for a $2 item and the change will include a five-spot. Movie houses, supermarkets, busy drugstores, and soda fountains are all popular ports of profit for the bogus-buck passer.

Posing as a T-man, of course, is a pretty risky business, and anyone caught in the act is very likely to get a double rap—one for swindling and one for impersonation—but more cons are doing it than ever before. Some, though operating a Treasury Department swindle, even pose as G-men, on the assumption that the public generally is more familiar with the more publicized activities of the FBI.

They knock on any door, and when the occupant opens it, they flash phony badges and say they are from the FBI. This sudden confrontation throws the average person, conditioned by TV and the daily press, into such a state of shock that the cons can get any response they want. The swindler who poses as a T-man frequently pulls the gag that he is looking for counterfeit money. A bogus-buck passer has been operating in the neighborhood, he says, and he is just making a routine check. Do they have any $20 bills, by chance?

Most people, still in shock, are so relieved by such a simple question that they run quickly to get their purses or wallets. They are only too glad to cooperate and check their bills. If they happen to have a $20 bill or two, they show them to the "Inspector," who, naturally, immediately recognizes them as "counterfeit." He tells the dupes he must take the money to "headquarters" and gives them a receipt.

Of course, as we have said, the double risk involved scratches this one for the novice swindler. We mention it only to illustrate the wide range of swindles possible within the pseudocounterfeit category.

BANKING PRACTICES

Though check passing and bank swindles are on relatively higher planes of fraud (both are covered in other chapters), the novice swindler can practice his hand in this field with a few simple tricks.

The student swindler can begin by gaining the confidence of a bank teller, exchanging good currency for notes in other denominations. Thus a pattern of trust and friendliness is established. Any transaction that follows is accepted by the teller within this framework. Suspicion is not aroused because the first and conditioning part of the total transaction is completely legal and honest, and it is a service frequently performed by the teller.

This psychological atmosphere is necessary in working the short-change-reverse trick. The novice con requests a teller to change a $20 bill for singles and is accommodated. A moment later he returns and asks the teller to recount the bills, as there appears to be an overage of $1. After the teller recounts the bills and expresses his thanks for the return of the (planted) overage, the honest-seeming stranger presents a small check for cash with the comment, "Guess I'm just as forgetful as you are today." Within this bond of rapport, the teller obligingly cashes the worthless check. Not until the day's work is balanced does the teller find that he has an extra dollar and the bookkeeping department discover that it has an extra check, with no account against which to charge it.

The short-change artist deals mostly in small amounts, but occasionally a real pro in the business can so confuse a teller with conversation or sleight of hand or both that the profit will be a $1,000 bill or more.

Banks are vulnerable to other little tricks that effect sizable hauls. The Mexican-centavos racket is one of the swindles perpetrated on inexperienced young tellers. Recently, a man in shirt sleeves (seemingly a neighborhood worker) presented to a teller in Washington, D.C., what appeared to be three rolls of quarters. He requested and received three $10 bills in exchange for the rolled coins. Subsequent examination disclosed that each roll was filled with Mexican centavos, having a value of only 75¢ per roll.

Bank tellers exchange good currency for rolled objects that turn out to be steel bars (for dimes), English pennies (for half-dollars), and iron washers (for quarters and half-dollars). One man exchanged 194 rolls of fake quarters at two banks in New Jersey and obtained $1,816.

THE "FREE INSPECTION"

Whatever your profession or business, the "free-inspection" gimmick is the simplest come-on for a profitable fraud. TV repairmen, auto mechanics, heating and air-conditioning engineers, and insect and rodent exterminators may make the offer of free inspection by advertising or by door-to-door canvassing. Once inside the TV set or under the automobile or under the house, the most cursory examination will disclose innumerable components that need repair or parts that need replacing or termites at work.

The particular means that may be used to gain entrance to a home will vary with the operator. If a householder has mailed a postage-free return postcard on which he has indicated an interest in having his furnace inspected, a smart operator may knock on the door and intimate that he represents a city-government agency or a utility company or simply a heating engineer and request permission to inspect the home heating plant.

The typical procedure of the furnace-repair con is to

gain access to the heating plant by some such ruse, then take it apart and leave the pieces scattered about the cellar. At that point he can refuse to assemble the parts again into working condition, on the ground (his) that the furnace is in immediate danger of causing a fire or explosion or of giving off deadly gas fumes. If he is not able to talk the owners into a new furnace (and a $1,000 profit for his firm), then he will settle for new parts. A little talk about imminent danger of asphyxiation, carbon monoxide poisoning, fires, flarebacks, explosions, and the like always helps.

Those who count on public gullibility know that ignorance is the base on which it rests. Public ignorance of TV, for example, is fantastic and immeasurable. Television, a marvel of the age, is complicated beyond belief for everyone but a few electronic engineers. Some TV sets have more than twenty tubes, more than a thousand components, several thousand connections. This means that the TV has three or four times as many parts as the radio, and it deals with eye tolerance as well as ear tolerance. And TV owners expect their sets to function perfectly. The technical and electronic knowledge needed by the TV expert is of a different and much more exacting order than that needed by the radioman. But the percentage of experts in this field, compared with the actual number of people proclaiming themselves experts, is questionable. The competition between swindlers, therefore, is enormous.

Still, several million sets are sold every year, and everyone is a prospect for the "free-inspection" pitch. The opportunities are obvious, and the havoc a knowing con can create in a $500 set is almost as unbelievable as the bill he presents for "repairs and replacements."

When the "household-appliance inspector" knocks on the door, he should be equipped and dressed for the part. Coveralls with famous company names printed on the back, small tools protruding from pockets, and a generally clean appearance are helpful. No housewife wants a dirty mechanic spreading grease smudges on her furniture. A thorough "free inspection" should include all electrical outlets, plugs, cords, vacuum cleaners, toasters, lamps, hair dryers, shavers, electric toothbrushes, grills, can openers, and hot plates. Rarely will he encounter a housekeeper who knows a volt from an ampere. The average housewife will gladly shift the burden of this knowledge onto the shoulders of a bright young clip artist, who is always happy to fix any appliance so that it needs fixing. And the really bright ones pick up several hundred dollars a day at this racket.

The extraordinary corollary to the repair racket is the fact that dishonest mechanics and gadget cons as a class are as vulnerable as the suckers they trim. A debonair Detroit swindler knows this well. One of his favorite tricks is to take from a dealer a used car and drive it around the block "just to try it out." Once out of sight, he drives it to a garage to have it repaired and borrows $10 or $20 from the mechanic. "Just add it to the bill when I come for the car tomorrow," he says, and goes on to explain that it is a company car and that the company won't question a few extra dollars stuck on the bill besides the loan. It looks like a sure thing for the mechanic. Isn't he holding the car against the loan and the repair bill? Hardly—he is only holding the sack.

THE SIMPLE SWINDLE

Not everyone is born with a mechanical sense, and many never acquire it, but there are still many fields open to the swindler without any knowledge whatever of mechanics. There is a portly, businesslike man who roams the side streets where many low-income families live and goes through the tenements knocking on doors and shouting, "Collector!"

When the door is opened, often by an aged person or somebody who understands little or no English, the portly one thrusts out his hand and says, "Collecting."

More often than not, the person who opens the door goes to the sugar bowl or a bureau drawer, gets the money set aside for the rent or the installment on the TV, and hands it to the "collector." He grunts, "See you next month," and goes on to the next flat. The swindle isn't discovered until the real collector comes around. It is not surprising that so many people owe so much (the figure is available at any credit office), but that so many fall for the routine. A man named Reggie, who worked this swindle in San Francisco recently, tells us that he can "collect" $500 a day in certain neighborhoods.

The COD swindle doesn't always require a uniform and props, but they help. The uniform may be that of a local delivery service or department store, with the name in some conspicuous place. The props are packages, each addressed to names taken from the telephone directory, with printed

COD slips attached. The amounts that can be collected depend on the neighborhood and the smoothness with which the fraud is perpetrated. If there is any question by the recipient, the swindler has only to say something about the package probably being a purchase by some other member of the family. "Maybe it's a surprise," he suggests. Since the package contains wads of old newspapers, perhaps it is.

Then there is the young man who furnishes his house with air-conditioning units, valuable art objects, furniture, a color television set, a refrigerator, and so on. He telephones the store he intends to swindle and orders a specific item to be delivered COD to a particular address at a specified time. He meets the delivery truck and advises the driver that he has moved since the order was placed but has a pickup truck or station wagon nearby to take the merchandise to the new address himself. After the merchandise is transferred to his truck, he gives the driver a check for the full amount of the purchase plus a generous tip. The check, of course, is bogus.

A slogan or an idea that has been fixed in the public mind by a publicity campaign or extensive advertising can be the basis for innumerable small swindles. Take fire prevention, for example. The national campaigns put on by insurance companies and others who stand to profit from fewer fires create a climate that is particularly suitable to the small swindle. All the con needs is an identification card bearing his picture and the words "Fire Prevention Council" and, under his signature, the title "Inspector" printed on it. This will get him into the house for an inspection of fire hazards. Any canvass designed to scare the hell out of the occupant will sell gyp insurance, tin fire extinguishers, an unnecessary repair job, or simply put over a bill for a "Certificate of Inspection." The usual fee for the latter is $10, though some businessmen involved in their own swindles have been known to cough up $50 for such inspection when it overlooks obvious firetraps.

BEGGING SWINDLES

We shall show how the "flopper" swindle works in a later chapter, because the advanced techniques of feigning an accident that can be taken into court puts the operator who works this routine in a higher income bracket than that of the small-time con. At the beginning level of this racket, however, where the take averages $25 to $50 a day, we must describe a few of what the police erroneously call "begging" swindles.

Everyone is familiar with the crippled, the blind, the deaf-mute, the deformed, with their upturned hats or large tin cups and handful of dirty pencils. To the public and to the police, they are classified "beggars." The fact that most of them make more in a day than some of their donors earn in a week is more a compliment to their skill than a commentary on the softhearted patsies who patronize them.

The consummate skill with which the blind musician works the subway trains should prove our point. Note that the harmonica he plays may be played badly, with little or no musical talent, but it *is* a harmonica or some other small instrument and not a fiddle or an accordian, either of which is more suitable on a street corner than in the more crowded subway. Note too that he may have a child assistant who leads him. Pity is the emotion he wants to arouse, and everything about him that the public sees (and hears) is aimed at this bull's-eye.

The corner boys who stake out busy intersections and the skate-board paraplegics who weave slowly through sidewalk throngs have each developed individual skills that, if studied, would prove they know all the basic tricks in this so-called begging swindle. The music they dispense or the pencils they offer for sale are not a grasp at respectability and an "honest" profession, but a studied front to gain the sympathy of the public. The "entertainment" or sale item also gets them by city mendicancy ordinances and qualifies them for licenses.

The one big gripe that this swindler may have today is not that people are less sympathetic or more hardened. He knows that any average crowd will have its share of boobs in whom pity is a common emotion easily aroused. If his take is greater or less than average, then the crowd was greater or less. What he is more concerned about, and what he has always griped about, is the split in his take.

What is not known by the public, but what every con in the business knows, is the fact that the begging swindle is frequently controlled by an overlord or captain. This boss man assigns the territory, or stakeout, transports and picks up his bums, schools them in techniques, provides the necessary assistants, furnishes the tools (musical instruments, crutches, bandages, dark glasses, wooden legs, and so on), and tallies the take at the end of the day. From this, the bums are paid their share. It is a good arrangement, really, as any union or syndicate ideal is basically good, but beggars have always objected to it.

Long before Charles Dickens wrote his caricatures of London's beggars in the 1830's, there were exposés to titillate the public's scorn. None of them ever had much effect, for the same swindles practiced then are still worked today.

There is a curious similarity between shifty Proteus of ancient fable and the artful rascal of our day who wanders from city to city as a begging swindler. The only way the ancients could catch the herdsman of Neptune was to pounce upon him suddenly in his sleep, for otherwise he could change his shape in an instant to any form he chose and slip away beyond the reach of pursuit.

Like Proteus, begging swindlers are masters of every trick of disguise. One will veil his cunning eyes behind patches and grope his way through crowded streets with more profit than the public imagines. Another stuffs up a monstrous hump on his back and invokes a shuddering pity and considerable recompense for his dreadful deformity. And there are others who can counterfeit every imaginable distortion of body or limb. They swathe themselves in filthy bandages and pose as victims of every wounding from zany accidents to atomic fallout. Makeup artists could take lessons from the loathsome sores they paint on their faces and hands.

Even if he is caught and under vagrancy law is convicted, the begging swindler is never at a loss for some plausible tale of woe to palliate his offenses and shorten his sentence.

"Why should I grovel in the streets as a common bum," asked one we interviewed, "when with this arm I can con a decent living?" The arm, which he carried half-exposed in a sling, had been chemically treated and made up to counterfeit the appearance of a frightful burn.

"Soapy Sam," or someone copying his act, is still seen occasionally on city streets. The first time we saw this act, Sam himself was doing it. There was a big crowd gathered around a man lying on the pavement. The muscles of his arms and legs were drawn, his face was a ghastly yellow, and his mouth was covered with foam. A cop on the beat pushed his way through the crowd and stood looking at him for a moment. Someone suggested they call an ambulance or a doctor. "Naw," said the cop, "he'll be all right in a moment," and he propped Sam up against the wall.

Sure enough, in a moment the seizure subsided. Sam's hat was providentially lying upturned on the sidewalk near him, and someone dropped a coin into it. Even the cop, recognizing his contribution to the show, tossed him a quarter. In a moment others, shaken by Sam's foaming fit, dropped money into the hat before they turned away. As the coins piled up, Sam's fit subsided, and presently he was sufficiently restored to thank his "audience," pocket the coins, put the hat on his head, and saunter away.

A psychiatrist friend of ours, interested in Sam's motivations, thought his act could be traced back to his childhood, when his mouth frequently got washed out with soap. Sam discovered then that this was a small price to pay for the fun of fibbing. Now to the fun of faking, he adds a profit.

Drs. George M. Gould and Walter L. Pyle in their *Anomalies and Curiosities of Medicine* quote a newspaper account of one E. L. Landers, who operated a broken-leg swindle. He had actually lost a leg in a railroad accident and collected a substantial sum in damages for that loss. It proved so profitable, in fact, that he went about the country thereafter collecting damages for all sorts of breakage. His *modus operandi* was to find a defective sidewalk, stick his crutch through a hole, then fall screaming to the ground. It was a trick that couldn't easily be worked twice in the same town, but there are many towns still not wised up to such grafts. Landers made enough from this racket to live comfortably, travel extensively (naturally, in the course of business), and dress the part of a gentleman. Most towns today have a little more protection against the broken-leg swindle, but we doubt whether there has been any diminution in the ranks of those who feign sprained backs and other hard-to-disprove injuries.

As a natural tangent of the affluent society, there is the well-dressed,* white-collar beggar who begs on the strength of his affiliations, true or assumed. These are the men who exploit their memberships in fraternal groups, labor unions, and veterans' organizations. They carry paid-up union cards, wear service decorations or American Legion buttons. Whether these props are fake or real is not important. The act that the swindler puts on is. This panhandler can extract from the pockets of others as much as $50 a day without any sweat. He is distinguished from the moocher by his begging without loss of dignity. He is not docile and fawning. He appeals in a frank, open manner and frequently asks and gets a buck or two from each touch.

The moocher, on the other hand, begs for dimes "for a cupa coffee," and he looks as if he will probably spend it for booze. If the moocher takes in $10 in a ten-hour period, he has had a big day.

---

* If you see your suit walking down the street on the back of another man, don't call the police to arrest him. It just might be his suit, though again it might not. He may be employed by a cleaning establishment, where, as a sort of fringe benefit, employees are permitted to wear the clothes of certain customers who leave their clothes for long periods of time. One shouldn't be too concerned, however, for after the employee has shown off his new suit, he will put it through the plant again, so it really gets two cleanings for the price of one.

SIMPLE MAIL FRAUDS

Of course, if one really is crippled and would feel some loss of dignity in public exposure, then one should try letter writing. A good letter (*i.e.*, one couched in the proper terms to gain the sympathy of dupes) should show a nice profit for one's time and postage. The dozens of charities that use this trick work it on a large-volume basis. They mail out millions of letters, and this wholesale coverage of the nation's softies must pay off, for the old charities go on from year to year and new ones are born every month. But this is big business, and so it will be discussed in detail when we come to a consideration of that peak of development. Meanwhile, there is a place in this racket for the individual, the single swindler, the beginner.

Mail fraud is an old story. No one knows when the first such swindles were perpetrated, but fraud by mail was one of the problems Benjamin Franklin was assigned to solve in 1737. A hundred years later, Charles Dickens and James Grant were writing about "postal impostors" in England. London at that time was notorious for the number and the ingenuity of fraudulent tricks that were daily practiced. Of them all, there was no department of roguery in which a greater amount of ingenuity was displayed than in that of swindling by mail. Petty swindlers among the London tricksters had already perfected every gimmick imaginable to wring pence and pounds from the gullible, and so it was only natural that letter writing should become the art of the more sophisticated swindler.

In 1839 the Scotsman James Grant wrote a lengthy treatise on the swindling "impostors who ply their avocation by means of letters, and . . . who by the assumption of distress which they do not actually feel, endeavor . . . to enlist the sympathies of the charitable and humane in their behalf." And three years before that, Dickens was writing a series of exposés on the fraud for the *Morning Chronicle*. The columns were part of the collection published under the title *Sketches by Boz*. He wrote from personal experience with swindling letters and the messengers who delivered them:

> He has besieged my door at all hours of the day and night; he has fought my servant; he has lain in ambush for me, going out and coming in; he has followed me out of town into the country; he has written to me from immense distances, when I have been out of England. He has fallen sick; he has died and been buried; he has come to life again, and again departed from the transitory scene; he has been his own son, his own mother, his own baby, his idiot mother, his uncle, his aunt, his aged grandfather. He has wanted a great-coat to go to India in; a pound to set him up in life forever; a pair of boots to take him to the coast of China; a hat to get him a permanent situation under Government. He has frequently been just seven and six pence short of independence; he has had such openings at Liverpool—posts of great trust and confidence in merchants' houses which nothing but seven and six pence was wanting to him to secure—that I wonder he is not mayor of that flourishing town at the present moment.

Such persistence and aggressiveness paid off for some two hundred and fifty specialists in this field at that time, while their take ranged from £100 to £1,000 a year. The average, according to the available data and our guess, was about £250. That was a pretty fair wage in England in the

1830's. Indeed, London police files record the fact that some of the more successful letter writers employed clerks and sported fast horses and expensive carriages.

It paid off for a specialist known as "Blind" Williams. During his heyday, his annual income from letter writing averaged from £600 to £800. He regularly employed two clerks, at salaries of £80 and £50 a year. He also kept a fine horse and gig, which he liked to show off in the most fashionable parts of town. He kept a mistress as well, and on his death, his principal clerk, Joseph Underwood, married her and thus ensured his inheritance of Williams' business. He must have been quite successful in it, though the record does not say, for he continued in it for many years.

There is, however, a voluminous file of letters—form letters, one might call them—that illustrate Williams' extraordinary talents. All the letters are quite long, but a few lines from one addressed to the Earl of Stamford, dated July 1, 1833, will illustrate his format and typical theme. The character he assumed in this letter was that of a young lady who had been seduced from her "tender parent's" roof by a gentleman, under promise of marriage. In his best girlish hand (he had a wide range of penmanship), he wrote:

> My Lord— It is with shame, indescribable shame, I presume to address your Lordship with these lines; but from having a knowledge of your Lordship's person from my infancy, and through the report of your Lordship's sympathising and benevolent character, I am about entrusting a most unfortunate affair to your Lordship's honor and secrecy. I am really ashamed to detail my misfortunes, my Lord, but I must; I must acquaint your Lordship. I know of no other person so likely to render me some assistance in the hour of need, and to save me from perdition and a premature grave, as your Lordship, whose humanity does honor to the feelings of a susceptible heart.

There is a moral in all this history that we should not have to point out. But for those who might wonder, let us say that such letters, though written more than a hundred years ago, are not much out of date. They are just longer than the ones we get today and are perhaps written in prettier English.

A SWINDLER'S DOZEN

The most extraordinary single fact we can state regarding our subject is this: the field of fraud is absolute; fraud is a factor throughout the entire range of human endeavors. Name any profession, single out any business, mention any of the limitless activities of man and countless frauds have been designed for each one of them The random examples that can be given in a work as limited as this make our task more frustrating than fruitful. How can one describe the ocean with a bottle of seawater? Or the Sahara Desert with a few grains of sand? The following swindler's dozen (eleven, naturally) of common frauds will not end our frustration, but each may serve as further examples for the studious.

The "consumer survey" is another name for the door-opener pitch. It is used to sell overpriced TV sets, refrigerators, freezer meats, insurance, and all kinds of consumer goods. The pitch begins with the sucker's name, to personalize it, followed by an introduction designed by experts in consumer psychology.

"Mrs. Jones, we are happy to inform you that you have just won a nice prize." Or, by telephone, "Mrs. Jones, this is the John Doe Associates calling. We'd like to know your opinion of . . ." Once the swindler gets her to take the bait, he will deliver a TV set, for example. "Costs you nothing," he says. "No obligation. This is not a selling deal. We ask only that you listen to this set for one hour and then fill out a report on what you think of it. That's all. Just a consumer poll."

The hooker is in the receipt she signs, which is a sales contract. Every year several thousand TV sets that cost swindlers $200 to $350 are unloaded for prices as high as $1,400.

The obituary columns of the newspapers provide endless sucker lists for a variety of swindles. Packages of worthless merchandise "ordered by the deceased" are delivered COD to the next of kin. Or the bereaved are notified that the deceased had an insurance policy with one premium still unpaid. "Just pay the $35 premium and the insurance check will be sent to you by return mail." But it never is.

The heir hunters are still around too. People with fairly common names get letters every day telling them about the death in some distant city of a "relative" who has left a sizable estate. The suckers are asked to identify themselves and send $10 or $15 as a "filing fee" so that they can be put on the list of legatees.

Talent swindlers have a field day every time some dope appears in the movies or on TV who cannot sing, dance, or act but who makes millions doing one of these things or all three at once. So they advertise: "Girls wanted for TV roles." Or: "Does your child have talent?" Every mother thinks so. The swindler who signs himself "talent scout" is not scouting for talent; he is selling a course of some kind, taking fees for representing the budding talent in Hollywood or on Broadway, or selling ads in a "talent directory," which may or may not get published.

The so-called vanity publishers play on this same appeal to the old ego. This advertisement appeared recently in the San Diego *Union*:

> to all WRITERS in this area . . .
>
> A representative of a well-known New York publishing house will soon be in San Diego to interview writers. His purpose is to uncover manuscripts worthy of publication. Fiction, non-fiction, poetry, specialized and even controversial subjects will be considered.
>
> If you have a book-length manuscript ready for publication (or are still working on it) and would like to discuss it with this executive, please telephone 239-0330, between 8:00 A.M. and 10:00 P.M., and leave your name and address. You will be contacted, later, to arrange for a definite appointment.
>
> If you prefer, write to:
Editorial Director,

Anyone who answered it soon discovered that whatever he had written or even planned to write was "worthy of publication" by this publisher, for a fee. The quality of the work or the public demand for it was not important. What was important was the sucker's desire to see his name in a by-line. The most successful outfits in this field circulate beautiful brochures to their sucker lists that are among the best sales talks ever designed. Your novel may be senseless, poorly written, and an all-around stinkeroo, but one glance at this sales pitch and you are convinced you'll make a million bucks if you can persuade them to take your money and publish the book.

Of course, if the would-be authors haven't written anything yet, they may be patsies for the correspondence schools. Systems of "creative writing" (whatever that is) offer courses in everything from spelling and grammar to plotting and poetry writing, and some of this training is good, but as William Faulkner once told us, "Writing can't be taught—it can only be learned." How many, among the hundreds of thousands who succumb to correspondence-school ads, ever learn anything much?

Swindlers and quacks who need the "front" of a diploma to hang on their office walls can easily obtain their "doctorates" from some of these schools, for a fee—which, obviously, is a case of the swindler swindled.

Songwriters are also suckers for any publishing racket. Nobody with talent wants to be an amateur, certainly not an amateur songwriter. Just as soon as he sets some words to some music and the result sounds original on both counts (even though he probably stole every word and every note), the proud composer longs to leave his amateur status and turn pro. He wants his work published, recorded, played on the jukeboxes, broadcast by the disk jockeys, or sold to a Hollywood studio. This field for racketeers improves by the day, even if the music doesn't.

Homework schemes are advertised all over and have been around so long that one marvels that they have not worn out their appeal. Nevertheless, their gross during the swindling sixties is averaging about $40,000,000 a year, according to an advertising-association survey. "A business of your own" and "Make money at home" are the catch phrases used in most ads, and the gimmick, of course, is that the sucker must make a small investment in a knitting machine or a jeweler's kit or a box of greeting cards or mushroom kits for cellar gardens or a pair of chinchillas. The one common denominator in all these spurious homework promotions is the requirement that the prospect buy something from the advertiser, whose primary interest is the sale of goods, literature, instructions, or services to the prospective homeworker at a big profit.

The gimmick of charging fees for listings or entries in

photo mug books, directories, county or city who's who books, publicity puff sheets, and programs has been worked in every community in the nation, yet there is always an opportunity in this field because a new crop of suckers is ready to harvest every year.

And then there are the people who would be shocked if told that they were guilty of a fraud equal to any of these. Take the society matron who frequently purchases a dress or some item of wearing apparel, wears it, then returns it to the store for a refund. Imagine her hauteur and rage should we call her a swindler! Retail merchants' associations have been trying for years to get member stores to tighten restrictions on returns. The havoc created in inventories, the extra bookkeeping costs, and the added expenditures for clerical help make this one of the biggest headaches, if not one of the biggest losses, suffered by department stores.

The variations that are worked on all these small swindles would amaze you. Any one of them can put quick dollars in the novitiate's pocket and prepare him for bigger and bigger swindles.

3

PLAYING FOR A FAST BUCK

GAMBLING is a vice. Gambling is a virtue.

Both these aphorisms, though opposites, can be proved.

Gambling is a vice to the anachronistic moralist, the pious fraud, and the loser.

Gambling is a virtue to the sagacious, the sincere, and the winner.

For two hundred years in this country, the pious have preached that gambling is a vice. Reformed (*i.e.*, successful) gamblers have exposed the tricks of their trade to warn the innocent. Retired lawmen have written books exposing the "public evil" and espousing ignorance. In recent years the academicians have gotten into the act, and their books on criminology, their essays on gambling psychology, and their tomes on the science of swindling are all based on the same premise, that gambling is a vice.

The only voices opposing them are our modern moralists. They, though most often touting free sex, have the best rebuttal: "How could anything so good be so bad?"

Gambling, in the gambler's book, is a practical profession. Indeed, for the man whose motivation is the desire for a fast buck, it is as pleasant as politics, as scientific as salesmanship, and as moral as medicine. Actually, the professional gambler must have some of each of these attributes—honor, science, and honesty.

Whatever degree of honor and honesty the amateur gambler brings to the profession, it will be tempered by every bit of knowledge he acquires. In the end he will realize that gambling is a science, one of the most exacting sciences known to man. Ergo, it is knowledge that separates the men from the boys, the winners from the losers, the sucker from his money.

The beginner may start with dice or cards in preliminary games, for craps and cards are traditionally first steps. He may be a student who needs expenses for a Saturday-night date, but the crap game up in Harvey's room never seems to pay anyone but Harvey. Maybe the beginner is in the Army and a payday pirate has taken chunks out of him every month since he learned to play. Or maybe he works in an office and is resigned to charging his lunch-hour losses to "entertainment."

If he is satisfied with this situation, nothing should be done to change it. Nothing should be done to upset this balance of nature, for the gambler is highly in favor of plenty of suckers, just as the coyote favors large families of rabbits.

We should point out, however, that Harvey is paying his way through college with those bouncing bones, the payday pirate is salting away a nice nest egg for his retirement from the Army, and someone in the office who is handy with cards bought a new Cobra on a Volkswagen wage.

Harvey and the Army pirate and the office worker aren't lucky, and they don't have any faith in luck. They are realists. They know that gambling is a science, a precise art, and they have prepared to win by study and practice.

And anyone who doesn't know as much as they do, or anyone who depends on Lady Luck, will discover that it is this difference that separates them from their bankroll.

ROLL THEM BONES

The antecedents of the common American vernacular for dice games, "craps" or "crap shooting," are not difficult to trace. If one combines the efforts of etymologists and the research of historians, one discovers some conflict and a few contradictions, but mainly the story is this. Around Shakespeare's time, the English had a dice game they termed "hazard," the lowest throw of which (two aces, or today's "snake eyes") was called "crabs." The French, always good copyists if not originators, pronounced it "craps."

The French brought the game of craps to New Orleans when that colony was founded, in 1718, and it spread northward up the Mississippi River in the steamboat-gambling days.

Later, "rollin' dem bones" was a natural for many a poor Negro, to whom it provided more emancipation than any presidential proclamation ever did. And it was our colored brethren who contributed most of the picturesque jargon still in use with the game.

Later still, several massive mobilizations of men for wars provided extraordinary and fertile areas of expansion and popularity, and so today "craps" is no longer listed in our

dictionaries as slang or as a colloquialism but as standard
language.

Historically, the origin of dice and dice games is more
mysterious than the way the game has always favored certain players. Archaeologists have found crude dice in ancient burial grounds in China and Egypt, some of them
crooked, proving that swindling was practiced three thousand years ago. Empires were won on the toss of phony dice
in the legends of Krishna, the greatest Hindu deity, for
crooked dice were used to cheat a maharajah out of all his
wealth and kingdoms. Greek and Roman records show that
dice games were popular in those eras too, and their great
lawmakers didn't overlook a few edicts against crooked
dice. Shakespeare punned the local slang for false dice,
"fulhams" (because they were made in Fulham), by having his actors say "fool 'ems."

Still, no one knows who carved the first cubes, and very
few players know why one man wins more often than another, because most people still think that luck has a lot to
do with it.

The amount of money that will change hands in dice
games this year is anybody's guess. Experts variously estimate it in the billions of dollars, and we'll lay you odds that
most of it is swindled. Why? Because, again, it is all a
matter of education. The knowledgeable player wins, the
ignorant loses. And considering how easy it is to educate
oneself in such a simple and uncomplicated method of taking money from others, it is amazing that so much ignorance is abroad in the world.

What the average crapshooter doesn't know about the
game would fill several books, and does, for quite a number
of experts and professional gamblers have disclosed their
secrets. They don't always agree, however, and if one were
to read all the books so far published on dice, the result

would be more confusion than knowledge. The best advice we can give anyone who wants to add dice to his bag of gambling swindles is to read a book, any book, on dice, then practice all the tricks the writer warns you to watch out for.

Most books thus become excellent texts for the swindler. This may classify the more pious authors as hypocrites and the exposé writers as insidious instructors, but where else can you get any book learning on the subject?

Practice perfects, in crap shooting as in any other activity, and on this point we cannot place too much emphasis. The watchword is practice, and if the trick involves any sleight of hand, then the watchword is more practice. Eventually, the ambitious swindler will discover that he is more adept at one or two tricks than he is at others, and he will polish these to perfection and his ultimate profit.

To begin with, no smart craps man consistently bets with the dice (*i.e.*, with the one who is shooting or tossing the dice). The odds are always against the dice tosser, whether he plays the game in a gambling house or rolls with a friendly group in the office. Experts have figured out these odds, and they maintain that the player who consistently bets that the shooter will not make his point is the smart player. Some players, knowing this, never toss the dice, always taking their chances with or against the tosser by making side bets.

There is a further advantage in being the man who organizes the game. The house (in the case of large gambling joints) or the organizer (in the case of the small game in the office, the barracks, or the dormitory) is entitled to a cut, a percentage of the game, no matter who wins or loses.

Mathematicians have figured out the odds for every variation possible, and these are available in several books for the studious and the serious crapshooter. The expert will know them, and the swindler will make good use of them, but just to make doubly sure that he wins more than he loses, the swindler will have a few crutches to lean on.

Admittedly, it is possible for anyone with sensitive fingers to become so adept at throwing that he can shoot for any point he wants and make it most of the time. Such finesse is thrilling to watch, but rarely encountered among amateurs. The books describe how the real artists in this game can curl their fingers around the dice and toss them in such a way that they come up anything on demand. No swindle is involved in such skill, so long as legitimate or true dice are used, so we are not suggesting that you waste any time developing it—you have to be born with it. It is enough that you learn, at this point, how to handle illegitimate or crooked dice and develop a smooth switch when you must exchange them for the legitimate dice on the table, or vice versa.

There are no rules for the performance of this trick. You may develop the ability to palm one set and throw the other or to make a quick hand-to-hand change, or you may work with a confederate. Whatever the system, the only advice we can give you is to work it on a dull bunch first before you try it on any crowd of sharpshooters. We have a report from the Kansas City *Star* about a man who blew in from Chicago recently and then was blown out real fast when some of the prairie boys caught him throwing loaded dice in a legitimate game.

For that matter, the legitimacy of any crap game should never be taken for granted. Even the big houses have been known to use magnetized tables and metal-loaded dice so that the operator could control any throw. This is a simple swindle and an oldie, and most people think it is rarely used today. But the May, 1966, FBI *Bulletin* reported the seizure of "a quantity of gambling paraphernalia" from "a gambler known for many years as an expert in the construction of magnetized dice tables and other gambling gadgets," among which was a large portable dice table. "Attached to the underside of the playing surface of the table was a panel, resembling a support, but actually a concealed compartment containing a series of batteries and electronic equipment that could be activated by a miniature signaling device to control the magnetized dice." Several marked playing cards were also seized. And just to illustrate the versatility of this swindler, other items found included a quantity of metal washers similar to those being used in the area for slugging pay telephones.

Then on July 27, 1966, a UPI story datelined Tulsa, Oklahoma, reported that "marked cards and altered dice, bearing the stamped insignia of some well-known Las Vegas gambling centers have been confiscated at the offices of a Tulsa gambling equipment maker." Federal agents, according to the story, said the marked cards and dice were included in "hundreds of decks of cards and hundreds of pounds of dice." The agents also seized metal filings and metal disks "suitable for weighting dice," trick glasses, an "arm mirror manipulator" used for reading marked cards, "juice joints, magnetic coils, switches, and relays," and a "card-holdout device." Invoices found in the raid showed that there had been shipments of such merchandise to customers throughout the United States.

The FBI said the altered dice also bore stamped insignia of the Louisiana Club and the New Frontier Hotel, Las Vegas; the Riverside Hotel, Reno; the Commercial Hotel, Elko, Nevada; the Elbo Room, Wells, Nevada; the Cal-Neva, Lake Tahoe, Nevada; and numerous other establishments. Of course, this is no indictment of these fine joints or any others. Anyone could have ordered such gambling equipment and specified that the cards and dice be marked with these famous names. Nevada-inscribed dice give an air of authenticity and honesty to any gambler. For is not the public conditioned to trust the legalized (*i.e.*, licensed) gambling houses of Nevada?*

Really tricky dice are the "shapes," or imperfect cubes. Dice with one or more rounded sides (to favor the flat sides), dice with rounded or roughed edges, dice with rounded corners, and transparent dice with loaded dots are scientific wonders. Rounded sides, corners, or edges must be within a few thousandths of true cubes, otherwise they will be detected by the average eye. The dots in a transparent die are gold, platinum, or some other heavy metal covered with paint. Obviously, this is no job for the average home craftsman, but the amateur interested in such a handy crutch will have no trouble buying these technical wonders. A pair of loaded dice can be purchased for around $10 in New York and Las Vegas and for $25 to $50 in the more remote areas of the world. Their ultimate value, of course, will depend on the man who learns to use them. Once he masters them, he can renounce the old English maxim that "the best throw at dice is to throw them away."

Simple "tops and bottoms" (*i.e.*, dice that are numbered incorrectly) went out of vogue when the Army taught all

---

* Could be, of course, that the manufacturing outfit merely made them for status seekers. We saw some specialty coffee and crap tables for sale in a local furniture store for $249. Such tables were sold in large quantity (they cost no more than $35 to make), for what better conversation piece than a genuine Las Vegas Coffee–Crap Table (with green felt cover and crap layout, yet!) in the living room? And what better place for a crap game while your guests sip their cocktails and admire your status symbol?

the yokels to count. One may still see a pair occasionally, and they are still for sale, but they should be considered mere curiosities, a collector's item.

THE MATCHMAKERS

Gambling never goes out of style, and neither do the tricks that swindling gamblers use. Times change, populations shift, and wars alternate with peace, but the tricks of the gambler remain essentially the same. They may be colored by the times, adapted to the environment, or bent to the bias of war or peace, but, dissected and examined, they reveal the fact that there are no new tricks, only old ones adapted to fit the immediate present.

Take the simple game of matching coins, for instance. The Egyptians, four thousand years ago, matched slabs of clay; the Hebrews, a thousand years later, drew lots, and the kings of Israel were forever chastising the "money changers" for gambling on temple steps. The only refinements on matching occurred when the Lydians or the Chinese began metal coinage, about 700 B.C. Coins, whether clay or metal, have always had two faces, and this fact, a 50-50 chance, became the basis of money matching. Thus the tricks have always involved simple manipulations of the coin so that the odds were changed from 50-50 to a 100 per cent certainty. Dexterity in the fingers was an asset (the inveterate coin tosser for lunch or drinks *can* control his coin), naturally, and some sleight of hand was no handicap, but the really profitable swindles were and still are worked by a two-man team against one, the one being the sucker, of course.

A perusal of the old files of any newspaper will yield innumerable stories of how some visitor from the rural districts squandered his life savings matching coins with strangers. The frequency with which the story appeared forty or fifty years ago attests to its popularity among readers as well as confidence men. One wonders how anyone with common sense could have been inveigled into such a game with strangers, particularly since that racket continued to receive so much publicity.

But despite its age and the fact that every now and then some ambitious reporter devoted a column or two of space to exposing the game, it still clicked with consistent regularity. Every week brought a fresh crop of suckers who would gamble their bankrolls on the toss of a coin—of course, having been assured that they were destined to be on the winning end without fail, with their opponent marked as the chump.

But while we are laughing at the stupidity of our grandparents, let us explain how the coin-matching swindle works and show how adaptable it is to era and environment, because it is just as popular today as it was in grandpa's day.

The best of the coin-matching swindles requires two operators, one to steer the sucker and the other to play the role of a fool. The characters these two impersonate fit the neighborhood where the racket is worked. Everyone likes to think he is a trifle smarter than the next man, and working on this theory, the steerer gets his sucker to believe that he is playing the role of expert trimmer himself. At the same time, the steerer's partner assumes the part of the fool.

This team will be found today working in a bar, poolroom, bowling alley, hotel lobby, restaurant, or any place where transients are likely to be. Under most city ordinances, matching coins is classed as petit larceny, but the hustlers season their work with just a dash of intelligence, gambling on the chance that the victim will take his loss like a good sport and not holler when he realizes he has been clipped. They also figure that since he was knowingly taking part in a crooked game himself, he will hesitate before going to the police with a complaint. But should he go to the police, he will be told step by step just how he behaved from the time he met the strangers and, likely as not, shown a photograph of the pair. Consequently, police records of most cities show an average of two or three weekly raps, registered by as many unsuspecting chumps who figured they could outsmart the other fellows, only to lose their bankrolls and their new acquaintances at the same time. How many swallow their chagrin and never report to the police, no one knows.

The steerer first becomes acquainted with his mark in a routine way. He asks for the right time, requests a light, or calls him by some name, giving the impression that he believed him to be an acquaintance. Once the conversation is opened, the steerer works fast. There is a round of drinks, and then the steerer becomes more friendly. He drops a word here and there in confidence to the effect that he has just closed a big deal and is in town to have a little fun. He flashes a big roll and a most pleasing personality, and soon they are on a buddy-buddy basis.

At this point the fool enters, attired for the role. Obviously, he is a stranger in town. In other days he posed frequently as an immigrant with a slight accent, or he played the role of a small-time traveling man. Today (as in former times) he is loud and a little drunk. He approaches the other two and invites them to have a drink on him. The steerer refuses, politely but a little annoyed. But the fool insists and finally suggests that they match to see who pays for the round. Plainly he challenges the steerer's gameness, insinuating that he is too cheap to take the chance.

The steerer whispers to his companion that he will match for one drink to get rid of the pest, and they toss coins. The steerer wins, and the fool pays for the drinks.

Everything up to this point is calculated to cement the bond of confidence between the steerer and the dupe. Now, as the fool pays for the drinks, he exhibits a wallet stuffed with bills of large denomination. A new element enters the game, for this is the moment when the dupe's avarice, if he has any, will show. The fool excuses himself and retires to the men's room. His exit line is something to the effect that he will even the score when he comes back.

This is the moment when the steerer makes his pitch. "We ought to trim that loudmouth," he says. "Maybe we should teach him a lesson." The sucker agrees, and this is the steerer's cue to explain the game of odd man wins. In this game, all three uncover coins, the man with the odd coin winning the pot. Obviously, two out of three times, one or the other of them will win. The steerer exhibits his bankroll, and this confidence inspires the sucker to show his, and thus the steerer finds out how much money the sucker has. They agree on a set of signals by which the sucker will understand when to turn up head or tail on his coin, thus assuring them against any possible chance of loss. Finally, they agree to meet at an appointed spot outside after the game is over to divide the spoils.

This team, the steerer and the fool, has pulled this trick so often that it has become a pat routine. Now the fool returns, and the drinking and the matching begin again. The sucker is permitted to win several games, and then the ante is raised. The game swings from one side to the other. Meanwhile the stakes are getting higher, and the sucker is now in for the kill, but he doesn't know who the victim is.

The signals between the steerer and the dupe are working perfectly, and the steerer is gradually taking the fool's bankroll and the dupe's also. But the sucker suspects nothing. Finally the sucker's last dollar is up, whereupon the fool plunges all he has. This pot, too, is won by the steerer.

Now the next and final act begins. The fool shows his chagrin and buries his disgust in his drink. The steerer winks at the sucker and drifts away. A few minutes later, the sucker excuses himself and goes to join his partner. He waits at the appointed place for a few minutes, then returns to the scene of the game, but by then both the steerer and the fool are miles away. By then, too, the sucker may realize he has been caught in the middle of a squeeze play and taken for his wad.

There are several variations on this game that every successful coin operator knows. He also knows he can make a comfortable living as a specialist in this field without having to resort to any other swindle. And the really adept operator does not need a confederate. He has such sensitive fingers that he can distinguish heads and tails by touch, and he can arrange coins to turn up on call. He also knows that when only two persons are matching coins and the game is free from any tricks, he will win if he starts out with more coins than his opponent. This does not mean that he cannot lose, only that he will not lose as often. Suppose he starts with fifteen coins and his pigeon with five. The chances being 50-50, he will lose his fifteen coins once while the other loses his five coins three times. In other words, he has three times the chance to win all the pigeon has.

The game can be speeded up if each player holds his stack in a roll between the first two fingers and the thumb of one hand. The coins of each player are uncovered simultaneously by taking off the top coin.

In the odd-man-wins version, as explained above, the operator must have a partner. Between them and the sucker there will always be a head on each pile or a tail on each pile or two heads and a tail or two tails and a head. The latter two patterns will occur three times out of four, so the person with the odd coin wins the other two. When all three are alike, each player keeps his own. The game may look fair, but prearranged stacks of coins can be manipulated so that one of the con men will win every time. In any case, the sucker is bucking a 2 to 1 bet, and if they are matching dollars or even half-dollars, it won't take him long to lose a chunk of silver.

Two-headed coins and coins with tails on both sides are so common and so easy to come by that any dupe who doesn't know such things exist or doesn't suspect them probably isn't worth taking anyway. He would certainly be too dumb to have much money on him. But too many people are wise to this gambit. Thus has modern-day communication spoiled a good thing for the small-time swindler.

There is a variation on this theme, however, that calls for a little more finesse and so presents the necessary challenge to the beginning swindler. This is the spinning-coin trick. A notch or a slight bevel on one side of a half-dollar will cause it to fall with more control. With practice, one can spin it to fall on call.

A tossed coin caught in the palm of one hand and slapped on the back of the other provides a split second when the expert can control it. This moment is the instant when the fingers close over the coin and hold it in the palm. The experts need only this touch to know how the coin lies. Control from that point on is the simplest sleight of hand. This trick is good for a drink, a meal, or a few quick bucks almost anywhere.

THE SHELL GAME

No one knows when the shell game was introduced to America, but it probably was played on the local yokels by some of the Jamestown boys. Two hundred years later it was a popular pastime among the forty-niners in California. By the turn of the century, it had returned to the cities and was causing the police of Chicago so much trouble that they printed descriptions of the game in the press to warn the public. But this only increased the number of shell men—or "nut" men, as the press called them—and didn't discourage the suckers "from the rural districts," who never read the city papers anyway. This item, published about 1901, was typical:

> Three half-shells of the English walnut, a rubber "pea," and a soap box or small table complete the swindling outfit of the shell man. At least one "booster" is essential to the success of the swindle.
>
> The operator rolls the pea about under the inverted shells and bets the victim that he cannot tell which shell it is under. The booster steps up first, and the operator with seeming carelessness allows the pea to slide slowly under one of the shells. This motion is seen by the countryman and the booster. The latter makes a bet and of course wins. Then the victim is inveigled into the game.
>
> The operator appears to handle the shells more carelessly than before. He allows the pea to remain an instant

under the edge of one shell. The victim sees this and imagines that he has a sure thing. He makes his bet and picks up the shell, to find it empty. The shell operator, skilled in handling the pea, causes it to pass under the shell picked up by the victim and inside the next shell. This motion is too quickly made for detection.

Today the rubber is synthetic, and the operators pass the pea under the shell and palm it, so that no shell picked up by the dupe will contain the pea, but everything else about the swindle is the same.

Some of the old-time shell-game operators were real artists in the truest sense of the word. Not only were their fingers trained to a degree of deftness rarely seen today, but the spiel that accompanied their act was hypnotic in its effect on the suckers. Had they gone on the stage with these talents, many of them would have earned more fame and doubtless more fortune than they did as pitchmen and sidewalk swindlers. But swindling was their forte, and if that was more fun than acting on a stage, they should not be criticized for their choice of professions. It has been a quick way to make a buck since some hungry fellow discovered it in Greece more than two thousand years ago.

The first man probably used seashells and a little gravel. By the time the trick had migrated to England, gamblers were using thimbles and a pea. The term "thimblerigger" was a common name for these artists until comparatively recent times, when walnut shells began to replace thimbles and "shell game" came to mean the same thing it did in some village on the coast of Greece a long time ago.

Once we began to examine this swindle and realized its antiquity, its simplicity, and its fascination for the sucker, we wondered whether there were any up-to-date links in the story. We visited a certain state fair in the autumn of 1966, and this is what we saw. A small group of people gathered about an empty packing case in back of one of the machinery exhibits to listen to the cultured voice of a spieler. The scene could have been lifted right out of a Currier & Ives print except for the clothes the onlookers wore.

"The object is to pick out the shell that covers the pea," the spieler said. His voice was refined, softly modulated, and pitched to catch the ear of everyone in his small audience but not beyond. Picking the pea is easy, he said, that is, easy for anyone with good eyesight. He moved the shells and the pea slowly on the flat top of the packing case, with the pea in plain sight. Then covering the pea with one of the shells, he offered to wager that none of the bystanders could pick out the shell covering the pea.

A seedy-looking young man, whom we had already picked out as the possible capper (shill), now squinted and pointed to one of the shells. "A buck says it's under that one," he said.

It was, of course, and the operator paid off with a flourish.

The next one to take a chance was no capper, but the operator let him win three or four times. By then he had the sucker's confidence up to a pretty high pitch, and several others in the crowd were betting on his skill. At this point the operator became apparently careless and hardly glanced at the shells. The pea was seen to roll under one of the shells while the operator slowly moved them about. The sucker and the others threw their money on the table, and the sucker pointed to the shell he saw the pea roll under. The operator said, "Pick it up."

The sucker picked up the shell, but there was no pea under it. We glanced quickly at the operator's fingers. The nails were a little longer than usual for a man. He could have concealed the pea with one finger. His take for this one short pitch was about $50. Shades of our boyhood, we thought, amazed that anyone today could be roped in on such an oldie. But they were, and they are.

Some historian, to illustrate a point, once said that Sir Walter Raleigh, imprisoned in the Tower of London, there learned that a man's own eyes can bear false witness against him. It is not recorded that Sir Walter paid a bunco man to learn this lesson, but thousands annually continue to relearn it through some swindle that tricks the eye, and the shell game gets its share. They are legion, they are numberless who have such trust in their eyesight that they fall victim to this simple trick every year. The callow youth, who is surer of everything at eighteen than he will be of anything at eighty, is ready to bet his head that he can put his finger on the shell that covers the pea, for has he not just seen the covering with his own eyes? And there are others, and fairly intelligent men, too, who progress to middle age without getting the wisdom that will prevent them from staking a one-spot or two on their eyesight in this ancient bunco game. In all its variations, the one essential feature is the delusion of the eye by sleight of hand, and this is a trifling feat for an expert juggler.

The only certain assurance against loss at the hands of these small-time artists is to keep out of their reach. If an honest man or a man who does not trust his senses is occasionally thrust into contact with them, he refuses to take a hand in any of their gambling games. A common trick is to propose a simple game at cards or billiards with no stakes, but after playing indifferently for half an hour or so, the swindlers will grumble a little at the dullness of the game and suggest the hazard of a small stake, "just to give an edge to the play."

The dupes who are caught playing with them are apt to consent from their own silly dread of seeming disobliging or poor sports or mean, and the practiced swindlers have every device at their finger tips for exciting, deluding, and drawing on their victims until their pockets are emptied. Plucking a pigeon was a bunco game of hoary antiquity even in the days of our youth, and yet it is still played in every city, every day of the year, and its future seems as certain as death and taxes. It was a regular practice of professional bunco men to run up and down our river systems in the palmy days of the steamboat and to work trains and ocean liners when this era came in. And we recently witnessed a pigeon plucking aboard a transcontinental jet that would have made "Soapy Sam" foam with envy and admiration. All we can say is that anyone who can turn an innocent penny-ante game into a $1,000 clip between Los Angeles and New York (with no stopover in Chicago) may not be a big-time con, but he certainly earned his jet fare, round trip.

Probably the real heyday was about seventy-five years ago, because few con men since have equaled the finesse or the artistry of such Gay Nineties experts as Herrmann or Keller or Bret Harte's exotic Ah Sin. Our grandparents who saw these boys in action understood how foolish it was to trust appearances in bunco games, even when the performers were bunglers compared with really accomplished jugglers. An artist of the first rank can easily defy detection in the execution of his shuffling and palming tricks, even when he is standing in the midst of a crowd and challenging exposure, as Herrmann and Keller frequently did. The professional who swindles with cards, dice, peas, and other pocket games today must strive for something near their perfection or become the buncoed himself. Too often the modern swindler resorts to crutches like marked cards or loaded dice, or they get by on some flamboyant personality characteristic (Ah Sin's tapered nails and long sleeves were more functional than ornamental), or they operate with confederates or shills.

On the other hand, the hypocrisy of the sucker is phenomenal. When he loses and then squawks about it, his squawk invariably is that he lost because he was honest and the swindler was dishonest or used dishonest tricks to take his money. If the dupe were really honest, he would blame his loss on his ignorance. His lack of knowledge and perception was his handicap. He simply was no match for the con who took his roll, and honesty in either one of them had nothing to do with it. It is practically certain that the ignorant dupe has no chance of winning anything from the swindler. His vaunted honesty, after he has lost his bankroll, is the sucker's attempt to justify his ignorance. Had he been an honest man, he would not have entered into a game where he expected to profit by another's loss.

If the green one should see anyone apparently winning from the operator in a shell game or from the dealer in three-card monte or in any other bunco game, he can be sure that the winner is a capper. The sole exception to this conclusion is when the amateur gambler is suffered to win small sums once or twice in order to entice him to put up a stake that will empty his pockets.

THREE-CARD MONTE

Three-card monte may not be as old as the shell game, but it is every bit as popular. One encounters it most often today aboard buses, trains, and planes. Wherever people have time to kill, the three-card-monte operator finds enough suckers to make the time profitable to himself. This bunco is similar to the shell game. About the only difference is that three-card monte uses three playing cards instead of the shells and pea.

For instance, if three aces are used—the ace of hearts, the ace of spades, and the ace of clubs—they are shuffled around on the table in the same manner as the shells, and the operator invites the onlookers to pick out the ace of clubs. If he operates with a shill, he will allow him to win a few bets in order to gain the confidence of the crowd. Sometimes the confederate is given an opportunity to mark the card so that everyone but the operator knows which one is marked. After the shill and some of the outsiders win a few bets on the marked card, someone is induced to put up a really big bet. But when the dupe turns up the marked card, it is not the ace of clubs but the ace of spades. Obviously, this is a good example of palming, and the game should really be called four-card monte. Certainly four cards are involved, though, of course, the sucker doesn't know it.

The origin of the game is a little obscure, though the first records of it indicate that Texas and the Southwest played it first. And its name indicates Spanish origin, so it probably did-in as many American frontiersmen as the Alamo before the gringos caught on.

Three-card monte has many variations, but the best we have seen was the one worked by a lone operator who used to hang around Penn Station in New York. He used no marked cards, no shills, and paid off when he lost. After all, he had a 2 to 1 advantage, so he could figure on winning two-thirds of the time. But just to make doubly sure, he had a way of shuffling the cards flat on the table that confused any gull who tried to keep his eye on the right card.

PHONY PONY PROFITS

We wish we had a foolproof way to beat the horses, but despite a long series of costly experiments and the examination of every system propounded by the experts, we have still to find one that works more than 50 per cent of the time.

The Thoroughbred Racing Protective Bureau (TRPB) has set up so many restrictions that virtually all the old tricks that swindlers used to make a quick buck are now most difficult to pull. Bureau files contain pertinent data on everyone connected with racing, from the anonymous but important groom to the steward. A fingerprinting program, set up some years ago, now includes thousands of prints covering everyone who has anything to do with thoroughbred racing. Further, a strict check on identification does not stop with the human beings in racing. A lip-tattoo system of identification developed by the TRPB has made ringing, or the false representation of a horse's identity, an impossibility at any Thoroughbred Racing Association (TRA) track. Today some twenty thousand racehorses are tattoo-branded on the inside of their upper lip with a letter denoting the year of birth and certain digits of their Jockey Club registration number. Tracks have become so damned virtuous, it's hard to make a dishonest dollar any more. Even the touts are depressed.

The only one we know who makes any money as a tout is a free-lancer whom we shall call Mortimer Smelt. Mort Smelt poses as a prosperous track habitué, which he is, with a copy of *The Racing Form* in one hand and a diamond-studded gold ball-point pen in the other. He is affable and easy to approach, and he is always willing to pass along his hot tips, on an "if you win, pay me" basis. He may even walk with the patsie, hand on the dupe's back, to the pari-mutuel window. In any case, he will take some opportunity to make a mark on the sucker's back—chalk on a dark suit, black pencil on a white shirt—which becomes his only record. Each horseplayer gets a different tip, so in every race, one of them is bound to win. When the race is run, Mort sidles up to the payoff window and watches for his mark on the back of the mark who wins. When Mort spots him, he goes over and slaps him on the back to congratulate him and remind him where he got the tip. If he can line up enough patsies to have a winner for every race, he can count on collecting a few hundred dollars in an afternoon.

Of course, no one believes the line that doping doesn't occur any more. The Detroit Racecourse stewards and the TRPB reported (August, 1966) that a groom at the local track said he administered dope to a horse on which he had bet $100. A gentleman from Lansing, Michigan, was quoted as having made the statement after tests on the horse, Rides The Wind, showed that the thoroughbred had received phenylbutazone tablets prior to his victory in a race. Rides The Wind paid $6.60, $4.00, and $3.40. The drug cost about $5. If the man's C-note was riding on the nose, it was a nice profit.

The editor of a sports magazine had a surefire system for beating the horses. One of its attractions was a 10,000 per cent profit. And four thousand horseplayers ponied up $100,000 in four years to get the system and the 10,000 per cent profit. There was one flaw in the operation: the editor offered a money-back guarantee, and he made the offer by mail. He advertised the wonders of his system for beating the horses and assured prospective customers that a $250 "custody-account" deposit made by each of them would be refunded if the system failed. Each customer received in the mail a pamphlet on whose cover were the words: ELECTRONIC BRAIN THE LATEST SPACE AGE BREAKTHROUGH TO A LIFETIME INCOME FROM RACING. It would have been a successful racket except that a few customers found the system disappointing and demanded a refund of their $250.

Track patrons around New York are familiar with a character known as Murray the Stooper—so named because he searches among discarded pari-mutuel tickets at metropolitan-area tracks for good ones thrown away by mistake. Occasionally he finds one that looks good but actually isn't. One of these he recently sold for $1 to an Aqueduct Racetrack pretzel vendor, suggesting that it be used to play a practical joke on his friends. The pretzel man showed it to another man, who took it and showed it to another man, who took it and showed it to another man, and so on, until finally it was cashed in for $19,978.40. How could such a hand-to-hand movement make a valid ticket out of a discard? One of those hands was that of a capable forger or expert counterfeiter. It happens all the time.

U.S. Attorney Robert M. Morgenthau recently explained how the big winners are swindling the Treasury out of millions of dollars in taxes. Under U.S. Treasury Department rules, winners of daily doubles and twin doubles of $600 or more must identify themselves at the cashier's window and sign their names and addresses on a Treasury form. However, the big professionals frequently hire stand-ins to collect their winnings. They provide them with forged Social Security cards or drivers' licenses and pay them 10 per cent of the winnings. Professional stand-ins can even use their own legitimate identifications. They simply pick up also-ran tickets or buy losing tickets from guys like Murray the Stooper. It isn't hard for the professionals to establish enough losses this way to offset their winnings.

Properly organized, to assure regular winners, gamblers can make out all right in this racket. A seven-man syndicate operating at Yonkers Raceway won $5,000,000 (Internal Revenue Service estimate) in 1966. The syndicate employed a "substantial number" of cashers, who took the winning tickets to the payoff windows at the track, to split up the winnings among many people, thus avoiding the heavy income tax. The syndicate then would supply the cashers with enough losing tickets so that they would not have to report a winning income at the end of the year, according to Morgenthau. He explained how the group "consistently" won the twin by buying up winning combination tickets at the end of the seventh race. The twin double at Yonkers is based on the sixth, seventh, eighth, and ninth races. Bettors who successfully pick winners of the first two of those races exchange their tickets for a combination on the second two races.

Doping, ringing, wiretapping, and bookie shenanigans have made track history, and made it interesting. Everyone who follows the ponies has his own store of anecdotes. Few, however, know how all the colorful track lingo originated. This is how the familiar phrase "today's best bet" became part of track parlance. George Graham Rice was a reporter for the New Orleans *Times-Democrat*. His last big assignment for that paper was his coverage of the hurricane that hit Galveston, Texas on September 8, 1900, and caused great damage and the most lives lost (five thousand) of any storm in U.S. history. He also covered that catastrophe for the New York *Herald*, and it may have been his success with this contact that encouraged him to go to New York the following spring.

He was unable to find employment, however, and by March, 1901, his cash reserves had shrunk to $7.30. The dollar that is worth 21¢ today was worth a dollar in 1901, but still it was a precarious situation for an unemployed reporter, until he met an old racetrack friend, Dave Campbell. Campbell was down on his luck too, so they had a beer on Rice's money and commiserated with each other.

Beer joints were called saloons in those days, and the fancier ones sported news ticker tapes that kept the patrons aware of gambling odds and entries at all the tracks around the country. Convenient adjuncts to the news tickers were the bookies who hung about such places. It was in this atmosphere that Campbell asked his friend, "Do you still bet on the horses?"

"No, I haven't had a bet down in more than a year," Rice answered.

"Well, here's a letter I just received from Frank Mead in New Orleans, and it ought to make you some money," said Campbell.

Rice read the letter. "There's a pig down here named Silver Coin," it said, "that has been raced for work recently. I think he's fit and ready and that within the next few days they will place him in a race that he can win, and he will bring home the coonskins at odds of 10 to 1."

Rice had seen letters like that before, but his interest was aroused. He picked up someone's discarded copy of *The Morning Telegraph* and turned the pages. He noticed several tipsters' advertisements, all claiming they were continually giving the public winners on the races. "Do these people make money?" he asked Campbell, pointing to the ads.

Campbell assured him they must, for the ads had been running for months. Rice was highly critical of the ads, for they were poorly written, and the tips they offered were obviously pure guesses. A moment later the ticker began to click. Among the entries, Campbell suddenly saw Silver Coin.

The coincidence stirred Rice's imagination. "I've got an idea for an advertisement," he said. "Get me a sheet of paper." Feverishly he composed a small advertisement and drew a box line around it:

> Bet your last dollar on
> SILVER COIN
> Today at New Orleans
> He will win at 10 to 1

He faltered then, thinking of a signature. He picked up the newspaper again and turned to the page containing the entries for that day in New Orleans. A sire's name was listed as St. Maxim. "Maxim!" he said. "I'll use that, with something more to make it euphonious."

"Gay," suggested Campbell. "It's sporty."

Thereupon was created the trademark Maxim & Gay. It was to make headlines in the nation's sports pages and a pile of hay for Rice and Campbell.

The trademark was penciled in on the advertisement, then a postscript was added. It stated that the usual terms for this information were $5 per day and $25 per week and that the day after next, Maxim & Gay would have another selection, which would not be given away free.

Rice needed an address for this budding business, so he rented an upstairs office on Broadway for $15 a month, no payment required for a week. Two tin signs bearing the inscription "MAXIM & GAY" were ordered. One was hung over the Broadway entrance of the building and the other on the door upstairs. The sign painter extended credit.

It was too much for Campbell. He couldn't see how Rice was going to make any money giving out the Silver Coin tip for nothing.

"Wait and see!" said Rice.

His next stop was *The Morning Telegraph* office, which at that time was just around the corner on Forty-second Street. He ordered the ad inserted and asked for "seven dollars' worth of space," then shelled out his last cent.

When the ad appeared the next morning, Rice was disappointed. The space occupied was only one column wide and four inches long. It looked puny. Would people notice it?

At least one man did. Campbell was helping Rice to take possession of the new office (luckily, a former tenant had left a desk and chair behind in lieu of rent), when in walked a tall, booted Texan.

"Hi, there!" he cried. "Here's five dollars. It's yourn. Keep it. Answer my question, and no matter what way you answer it, it don't make no difference. The five dollars is yourn."

Rice looked at him in amazement.

"What's your source of information on Silver Coin?" he asked. "I'm a big-money bettor. If your dope is on the level, I'll pay you well for it. If it ain't, your confession will be cheap at five dollars, which will be all the money I'll lose."

Rice showed him the letter from Frank Mead.

"That's good enough for me," he said, turning on his high heel.

Silver Coin won easily at 10 to 1.

The betting was so heavy in the New York saloons and poolrooms that at post time, when 10 to 1 was still obtainable at the track, 6 to 1 was the best price that could be obtained around town. Habitués argued, "If the tip is not a good thing, what object would Maxim & Gay have for publishing the ad? If the horse loses, the cost of the ad is lost. The only way they can win is for the horse to win." It seemed like good logic, as far as it went.

But it was really sophistry. Had the horse lost, Rice would have been out his $7 advertisement and obligated for rent and signs. If he had used the $7 to bet on the horse, he could have won $70. But the way he figured it, he was taking the same risk as the bettor, but with a bigger payoff if the horse won. He was after bigger things—public patronage for a projected tip bureau.

Campbell came by the next morning to accompany him to the office. He had another telegram from Mead, informing him that the best thing in that day's race was Annie Lauretta, with probable odds of 40 to 1. "Gee whiz!" exclaimed Campbell. "If this one's as good as the other one, we ought to put some money on it."

"We may do that sometime," said Rice, "when we get a few more customers like the Texan. If we get ten subscribers as a result of that tip yesterday, we'll be in the money."

But the "if" loomed large in his mind. He was thinking that perhaps a little side bet here and there might be good insurance, when they came to Broadway and noticed a crowd of people being lined up by half a dozen policemen.

"Who's having a fire sale?" Campbell asked.

Rice said he didn't know. As they approached their office, they found that the line extended from the side street down Broadway to their building. As they climbed the stairs, they passed more people, standing in line single file, until they discovered, to their astonishment, that the line ended at their door. They unlocked the door, walked in, slammed the door behind them, and locked it.

"My God!" gasped Campbell. "What do they want?"

"Annie Lauretta!" cried Rice. "They want a tip, and we've got one for sale."

"But suppose Annie don't win," Campbell said.

"Hell's bells!" exclaimed Rice. "Do you think I'm going to turn down all those five-dollar bills? Not on your tin-type."

Campbell had no argument against that. They sent out for a typist and a box of envelopes. The typist wrote "Annie Lauretta" on slips of paper, and Campbell stuffed one slip in each envelope and sealed it. When they had got a stack of these ready, Rice opened the door and passed the envelopes out as each man handed him $5. He stuffed the money into a top drawer of the desk, and when that became choked, he stuffed it into the next one. In no time at all, the drawers were full, and then Rice put the wastepaper basket on the desk and asked the customers to throw their money into that receptacle. When a man wanted change, he was told to help himself.

For two and a half hours, or until within fifteen minutes of the first race at New Orleans, the crowd thronged in and out of the little office. After that, Rice and Campbell counted the day's receipts. The total was $2,755.

They locked the office and went across Broadway to the bar of the old Hotel Marlborough, where they ordered drinks and sat waiting for the fourth race at New Orleans. Pretty soon the ticker began. "Alpena first," it read, then, "Annie Lauretta second—40—20—10." Anyone who had played Annie across the board had won at great odds. The popularity of Maxim & Gay skyrocketed immediately.

Rice wired Mead in New Orleans to set up an information-gathering system that could be depended on and to wire him daily the name of one horse that he thought had the best chance of winning. This tip Maxim & Gay promptly labeled and thereafter advertised daily as

"The One Best Bet," or "Today's Best Bet." Soon the term became a part of track parlance, and it remains so today.

By the end of the year, Maxim & Gay had clockers and informers at every track in the country and subsidiary offices in all the major cities where their ads ran daily. By then, too, the business had grossed $1,000,000, and Rice was constantly inventing new tricks to advertise. This full-page advertisement was typical:

> YOU PAY US $5. WE REFUND $6—If the horse we name as The One Best Bet today does not win, we will not only refund our $5 fee, which is paid us for the information, but will pay each client an EXTRA DOLLAR by way of forfeit. Pay us $5 today for our One Best Bet, and if the horse does not win we will pay you $6 tomorrow. MAXIM & GAY.

How could anybody refuse a deal like that?

Here is how Rice worked it. He would select a two-horse race (a common occurrence in those days), sell one horse to his customers, and bet $1 per client on the other one. Suppose a thousand clients had paid him $5 each for the tip and the horse didn't win. He refunded $6,000 the next day. Meanwhile, however, he had bet $1,000 on the other horse at odds of say, 6 to 1. The horse won, and he collected $6,000. If his clients' horse won, he made $4,000. If the horse lost, he made $4,000. What could be simpler than that? But it was months before the bookies caught on, and the public never did.

The information service prospered, and in a hundred-day race meet the next year, Maxim & Gay took in more than $1,300,000, most of it by mail. More hands were employed in opening the mail than were in the firm's entire tip-gathering system.

What ended such a sure thing? George Rice couldn't resist plunging occasionally on his own information. The

Post Office was beginning to clamp down on such business by mail. And Rice, the old newspaper hand, thought it would be smart business to own his own newspaper; he was spending a lot in newspaper advertising and figured he could support one with his own ads. The investment was a total loss.

Three years after he began Maxim & Gay, he was out of business and broke. All he had left was the honor of having originated the phrase "today's best bet."

PROFIT IN NUMBERS

Swindlers never play the numbers game, they only run the racket. Playing is for the forty million suckers who think their weekly two-bit or four-bit contribution will someday hit the lucky number. The only people who know the score, therefore, are the swindlers who operate the numbers racket.

Students of gambling methods know that the numbers manipulators take full advantage of the small-time bettors. For his two-bit investment, the bettor gets 500 to 1 odds on a 999 to 1 shot. Numbers dealers get away with this because their clients don't have enough money to bet on a horse or a ball game, where the odds are somewhat less savage. The small bettors must take what they can get. So they get taken.

Numbers are bet all over the land, under a variety of names—numbers, policy, *bolita*—depending on the locale. There are several ways of selecting the number of the day.

The most popular source of each day's number is the published results of the pari-mutuel action at the nearest big track. Another source is the last three figures in the daily listing of the total number of shares traded on the New York Stock Exchange.

Say that the published results of some local track add up to $1,434,397. The number for that day, therefore, would be 397. Or if 4,118,485 shares had been traded on the New York Stock Exchange, that day's number would be 485. In some cities, the payoff number is based on the last three figures to the left of the cent decimal point in the U.S. Treasury balance, the statement of the government's financial position issued daily as an indication of our country's fiscal soundness.* Weather tables, bank clearings, and anything else reported numerically in three digits or more in the daily press may be the basis for a numbers game.

Numbers players are the world's most inveterate hunch players. You can be sure that should any of them read this, they will bet 397 or 485 or some combination of the two. And you can be equally sure that if very many of them guess the winning number, the bookie operating the racket will get the hell out of town. He would be a damned fool to try to pay off too many winners.

Anyone can start a numbers game. How long he operates it may depend on his competition. Syndicates now control the racket in every community, and the moment any independent operator becomes established, he will be asked to join the syndicate. The syndicate acts as the clearinghouse, or main bank. Under it are the local banks, who may have started as independents. Under the local bank are the runners, as the collectors are known in some places.

---

* The Treasury should be as sound as the numbers racket. About $5,000,000,000 is the annual take in this country, and the Treasury's bite out of this is practically nil.

The runners are the foot soldiers in the racket. They take the day's action to the bank after they have made their rounds of regular players.

Frequently, an entire community may be handled by a collector at a newsstand, pool hall, shoeshine stand, or small neighborhood store. Bettors pay their dimes, quarters, half-dollars, and dollars and play their hunches. The runner takes his cut, and the rest goes to the bank, along with the sucker's number. Should he have a winner, the payoff filters back down the same way. He collects from the local runner.

With the annual take in this field in the billions, a small-time operator may find his office, the factory where he works, or his neighborhood a veritable little gold mine.

4

THE $1,000 TOUCH

THERE are people who eat their dessert first and their steak last. Aside from the fact that this may be an unhealthy eating habit, it destroys some of the pleasure of eating steak. The middle portion of this ten-course meal in swindling is the entrée, the steak. If you are a dessert-first person, then you have already devoured our chapter on how to make a million. Let us caution you, however, against any exercise or digestion of this knowledge. It has value to you only after you have consumed the chapters that precede it. Swindling, like any other profession, involves certain talents and tools, and these are developed through sequential education. Since you would not expect to jump from high school to a medical practice, so much less should you expect to jump from penny-ante poker to a million-dollar parlay. Take it in its natural order, son, and eat your spinach next. And though anything from a C-note to a grand may not sound like spinach, it ain't hay either.

Considering the known statistic that one out of every five persons in this country passes a bad check at least once during his lifetime, it is not surprising that the total take in this field is several billion dollars annually. What proportion of this is deliberate (*i.e.*, illegal), no one knows. Our guess is that most of it represents premeditated activity on the part of so-called paperhangers, sheet passers, and penmen—professional swindlers all.

The banking interests in this country have instituted so many safeguards to prevent bad-check swindles that the novice is easily caught, so considerable practice precedes any matriculation in this field. But it is a simple matter to build up personal identification, a good appearance, and a certain amount of nerve. And there are still countless places where a check looks quite as good as cash, places where the sucker's faith in human nature hasn't been warped by warnings and personal experience with clever schemes.

Willy The Whiz was a professional penman, even though his passes seldom brought him more than $1,000. "It's not the single take that counts," he says today. "It's the day-in, day-out regularity of my system that put mink on baby and made me a pro in the business."

Wherever forgers assemble and the subject of conversation turns to their art, as it frequently does, one invariably hears of Willy The Whiz, for Willy is recognized, in the fraternity and in numerous police files, as a master craftsman in this swindle.

Willy was born in East St. Louis in 1914, when that city was notorious for its stockyards and its "Valley." It was a fitting birthplace for a wide range of professional cons. The stockyard stench has since been sweetened, so that now when the breeze from the east blows through the big sister city's new Arch, tourists aren't asphyxiated, and the whores have long since moved out of the Valley to the more prosperous environs of the fancier suburbs of St. Louis. And people like Willy, remembering their humble beginnings, have done many things to sweeten their own environs.

Willy's parents were German. They came to St. Louis in early life and moved to the Illinois side before Wilhelm was born. He was graduated from the old Senior High School as an honor student. In a district that turned out its quota of bricklayers, brewery and packinghouse workers, such a record was pointed to with pride.

In his school days, young Willy had indulged mildly in athletics, but he concluded early that the effort required was hardly worth the results and thereafter devoted his spare time to indoor sports exclusively. It was a field in which he excelled. He was graceful on any dance floor, and his skill with a pool cue was amazing.

The boys in the pool and dance halls of the Valley's environs figured that Willy was destined for a professional future, something that would provide him an opportunity to commercialize his debonair appearance and his ability to wear clothes. Equipped with a splendid physique, Willy had also been blessed with a second helping when they distributed good looks and complexion, his fine soft skin and rosy cheeks attesting to his German inheritance.

Soon after his graduation from high school, Willy left his youthful haunts for the brighter opportunities of Chicago. Al Capone was the local hero at that time, and a smart boy like Willy had no trouble finding employment in one of Al's rum-running crews.

This employment didn't last long, however, for the repeal of the Prohibition Amendment, in 1933, bankrupted the illegal liquor business. Thus, by the time he was twenty, Willy was a drifter without a racket, but with a lot of friends in mobdom. Among these were several cannon (pickpocket) mobs. (In the language of the trade, whenever two or more persons work together in a racket, they are referred to as a mob.) The members of a cannon mob are the wire, the stall, and the lammer. The wire is the nimble-fingered individual who extracts the prize from the victim's pocket; the stall distracts the victim's attention while the wire is working, and it is also his duty to interrupt pursuit by conveniently getting in everyone's way; the lammer is the chap who takes the stolen goods and disappears with all the evidence. The action is a lot like football.

These mobs were generally made up of aliens or men of alien extraction, few having much education. To them Willy was useful in his own way, composing letters to members of the gang in stir or arranging for the disposition of negotiable stocks or bonds lifted during a day's campaign on crowded trains and in elevators and hotel lobbies. When a cannon took a fall (was arrested), Willy was entrusted with the fall money to arrange for a bondsman and a mouthpiece (lawyer) to represent the defendant at trial. With no police record to inhibit his right of interest, Willy would represent himself as a boyhood friend of the man jailed and learn what he could of the evidence against him. Quite often he managed to fix a case before the date of hearing and through such activities earned the everlasting appreciation and confidence of the local hustlers.

Meanwhile, Willy was busy concocting a racket of his own. While he, like all smart swindlers, despised the thought of pocket picking, he discovered a way whereby he could use the boys of the cannon mobs to his own advantage.

Being an able penman, he selected forgery as his specialty, and he planned his periodic campaigns well in advance and worked only one day weekly, Saturday. His victims were generally Main Street merchants, and his territory stretched from coast to coast, with occasional forays into Canada and Mexico. He passed forged certified checks only, receiving in return merchandise and an adequate amount of change in cash, and palmed off as many as fifty checks in as many stores on each working day. Saturday night would find him on the fastest transportation available out of town.

His method was simple, yet it entailed many details in preparation. When a cannon mob returned to its base, the members generally were laden with a myriad of portfolios, pocketbooks, card cases, and purses of every description. Some were monogrammed with owners' initials, and the majority contained cards of identification, credit cards, drivers' licenses, membership cards, and so on. Invariably there would be something bearing a facsimile of the owner's signature. These articles were of no value whatever to the mobsters, who merely sought the cash they contained, and the presence of such items on their person, in the event of arrest, might compound the complication. But to Willy they were the vital accessories in his swindle.

Soon he possessed an assortment of such trinkets, all cataloged and carefully filed under the name of the town from which their original owner hailed. These were marked for use as identification in the passing of checks bearing the forged names of the respective owners.

Before he came to a town, Willy would post a number of letters, usually registered, addressed to the names of those he proposed to impersonate while he was in the town. He would select a half-dozen hotels in each town, and to each one would go a batch of mail directed to the name he intended to register under. He would arrive in town armed with some fifty different checks, all made out to his various aliases and all bearing forged certifications.

Willy would register at each hotel under his alias for that hotel and inquire for his mail. The several letters would be presented, after which he would saunter over to another hotel and repeat the procedure, under another alias, of course. Having registered at half a dozen hostelries, he was now established under as many names. His next move was to locate the spots for the papering and acquaint himself with the line of merchandise to be purchased.

Saturday noon would find him keyed up for action, with every number covered and his exit from the city arranged. At each hotel he had his documents handy, so that he could quickly drop the impersonation of one man and assume the role of another without delay. Then he would casually enter a jewelry store, for example, and ask to be shown a platinum watch. Affable of manner and apparently easy to please, he soon decided upon a purchase, and then he would suddenly discover that he was a bit short of the required amount in cash. Exhibiting the certified check, made out in his alias, Willy would then begin his well-rehearsed spiel, bringing forth the proper wallet or card case containing the identification cards. To make matters more convincing for the merchant, Willy extracted the check from a letter addressed to himself at a local hotel.

If the merchant hesitated after examining the documentary proof of his patron's identity, Willy would suggest that he phone his hotel to certify his residence there. If the merchant went to this extreme—and he seldom did—he generally was convinced of the genuineness of the check and readily agreed to cash it to oblige his new customer. The check always called for an odd amount, and Willy's purchase usually allowed for less than $100 difference, which he received in cash, along with the article he bought.

The same operation was repeated at the next stop, probably a block away. Under each alias, Willy would unload ten to a dozen checks, after which he would hasten to the hotel where he was known under the second alias and pick up that individual's credentials. When he had worked the second one out, he went on to the third, and so on, until he had used up all his aliases and all his prepared checks.

With the town worked to its limit, Willy would then wrap his purchases in a neat package or enclose them in a nice bag (usually his last purchase) and ship them by express to New York or Chicago or Los Angeles or Miami, to be called for at that place, mailing the receipt to himself at a drop where he received all personal mail.

Sheer nerve prevented his apprehension on more than one occasion when he had been preceded by other paperhangers working along different lines. In Baltimore he was interrupted in the midst of a purchase of jewelry when the owner of the store denounced Willy as a forger. The door was quickly locked to prevent his escape, and the police were notified. Pending the arrival of the detectives, Willy indignantly denied the accusation and, without a trace of emotion, suggested that his accusers might be courteous enough to offer him a chair.

The arrival of the officers was followed by a complete explanation of Willy's actions and his avowal that everything was true as related. He repeated his declaration of innocence and readily submitted to a search of his person. A perusal of his effects disclosed membership cards in a Rotary Club, an automobile driver's license bearing his photograph (he was a thorough craftsman), a few personal letters, and a number of credit cards all in the name of the person he had represented himself as being. There followed a whispered conference among the store owner, his clerks, and the officers, after which they decided not to make an arrest.

But Willy feigned indignation, demanded that he be arrested, and loudly threatened civil action immediately upon his inevitable vindication. The police, with no duty to perform and no desire to involve the city in a suit, left the store. Apologies followed, with the jeweler finally insisting that he be given the honor of accepting the check, which Willy, with well-staged reluctance, finally permitted. He hasn't been back to Baltimore.

Now in his middle fifties, Willy is retired and living on a portfolio of mutual funds that he acquired (legally) during his hay-making days. Somewhere along his devious route, he also acquired a wife, and they have one child, a teenage daughter. His present respectability involves no fakery—he feels he is just as entitled to this status as any of his neighbors, for who but they know how they got their gains?

PENMANSHIP

Englishmen did not originate forgery, as some historians contend, but that art did become one of the gravest menaces to the sanctity of property and the security of the ancient British kingdom.

In the Middle Ages, forgery was not considered a serious crime, chiefly because the naive penman of those days confined himself to the relatively harmless occupation of fabricating missals and other liturgical documents. Few persons could write, and until the fifteenth century most forgeries were made by good clerks gone wrong. In sixteenth-century England, a large number of land titles were undoubtedly forged, and the judges of that period must have had many a headache attempting to distinguish the genuine from the false.

Modern forgery dates from the time when bills of hand

began to be used in European commerce. A Venetian pen-man named Pascommini put several excellent forged bills into circulation, which so frightened the merchants of the time that the whole business of transferring money was temporarily paralyzed. If one sent gold coins from Ant-werp to Edinburgh, pirates and highwaymen robbed the messenger; if one sent a bill, it might be raised or altered. European countries met the challenge of the forger by making death the penalty of his art. This discouraged but did not altogether halt the practice.

Anglophiles like to say that the first bank notes were issued by the Bank of England when it was founded in 1694. The first bank notes it issued were written by hand on slips of paper engraved with: "We promise to pay Mr._____or Bearer the sum of_____," and so on, and this some historians call the first genuine paper money. But Massachusetts issued the first paper money in 1690, primarily to replace corn and cattle as legal tender and relieve the burdens (physical) of the tax collector.

We concede, however, that the first bank-note forgery appeared in England within a year after the Bank of England was founded. At once the bank ordered that all its notes thenceforth be entirely handwritten by its cashiers and that no more of the printed forms be used. It was an impossible order, because it was hard work writing all those notes by hand. The problem was solved by printing the notes on a paper specially watermarked, a trick in use right up to the present day.

But trick paper and tricky printing never really stopped the artful forger. Nor did the hangman's noose deter him. By 1797, when the Bank of England began to issue £1 notes, forgery had attained the dignity of a public industry. For six years previous to this date, there had been only one execution for forgery. During the next twenty years, there were 870 prosecutions for bank-note forgery, of which 160 of the accused were acquitted, 300 were hanged, and the rest transported for life.* During the seven years ending in 1825, more than 94,000 persons were tried on the charge of forging £1 notes! Sentence of death was passed upon 7,700 of them, but the forgeries continued until this particular series of notes was recalled.

George Cruikshank, passing one day through the Old Bailey, saw the bodies of several men and two women hanging from Newgate gallows. They had suffered, he was told, for the forging of £1 notes. This struck the artist as something less than equitable justice. He returned immediately to his studio and made a sketch that became one of the most famous cartoons of its day. It was an enlarged £1 note graphically embellished with what he had seen on the gibbet at Newgate. It was published by the courageous English political satirist and publisher William Hone, and copies were placed in his shop windows.

Cruikshank himself tells us that when the "note" appeared in Hone's windows, "it created a great sensation, and the people gathered round his house in such numbers that the Lord Mayor had to send the police to disperse the crowd."

The cartoon was sold in the streets for a penny, and soon all London was talking about it. Cruikshank adds: "The Bank directors held a meeting immediately upon the subject, and *after that* they issued no more one-pound notes, and so there was no more hanging for passing forged one-pound notes; not only that, but ultimately no hanging even for forgery."

After this Parliament revised the penal code, and *after*

* Such a "tight little island" had few facilities for the incarceration of criminals, and so they were executed, banished aboard a prison ship (transported), or acquitted.

that there were no more hanging or death penalties for minor offenses. (Perhaps not all these changes resulted from the celebrated cartoon, but Cruikshank, a man of ideals, should reap his due.)

It is a truism among historians that forgery waxes during a period of financial unrest and instability, especially when the government's money policy is considered unsound. The United States witnessed its first major wave of forgery shortly after the establishment of the state banks in 1832. The bank check as we know it today came into use about this time. The long periods that elapsed between the writing and the collection of checks offered a happy interim in which the forger could net his illicit profit and make a getaway. This advantage still exists.

High-grade scroll men had a heyday in our Eastern cities after the Civil War, and the photographs in police museums reveal that the forgers of the day were very numerous as well as exceedingly substantial in appearance. Indeed, forgery was a gentleman's crime; the lout and the muscle-man rarely attempted it. (The notorious English forger James Townsend Saward, known to history as "Jim the Penman," was a man of fine legal background and social standing. Saward never personally uttered a forged check. He confined himself to drafting false signatures and permitted the other members of his band to take the actual risk of passing the bogus paper.)

Bank-note forgery and check forgery were codified under counterfeiting, once considered treason in the United States, and the penalty for treason was hanging. Forgers were little inhibited by law. This remains true. Indeed, more counterfeit money circulates in the United States today then ever before. Although most bank-employee training programs now include and emphasize instructions for spotting the spurious, the check forger enjoys a heyday incomparable to that of any period of the past, for several reasons.

EASY MONEY

Training in the art of spotting bad checks appears to be lax if not completely lacking in many banks and most businesses. So passing fraudulent checks is still the easiest way for anyone who is not an employee to get money out of a bank or any other business. Indeed, there are more than two hundred different ways to pass bad checks, and the astute swindler can cite you a dozen variations on each one. (William Earl Rose, who has written on the subject of check frauds, says there are eight hundred ways of defrauding by check.) Thus, as in any art, with everybody doing it, forgery has deteriorated into a common crime. There are few gentlemen in the business.

Most checks, good and bad, are passed to someone en route to the bank, and so the most vulnerable breaches in the banker's wall are the bank's depositors. Supermarkets are most susceptible. They take about 30 per cent of the forger's art. Department stores run a close second place with 21 per cent. Gas stations and saloons (13 per cent each), hotels, small businessmen, restaurants, drugstores, liquor stores, and banks (about 1 per cent each) take the rest. These are our own estimates, of course. And the total take? We dare not guess, for it would be an unbelievable figure. There is no central collecting point for such data, and many bad checks are never reported to the police. Insurance companies pay off around $3,000,000 annually in bank losses, but banks cash fewer bad checks than other businesses. And, like other businesses, not all banks are fully insured against check losses. Our most conservative estimate, based on a year's research is that $150,000,000 is lost every year through check and money-order swindles.*

Since detection seldom occurs until the check reaches the bank, it would seem the logic of good business for the banks to initiate some program of education for their depositors. Except for a few large banks, this responsibility, strangely, is neglected. Banks, supposedly eager to increase the business of their depositors, do little to help them avoid the annual loss from check swindles. Any smart check artist could teach the gullible businessman all the tricks of the trade, and does, though this is an educational expense the banks might help the tradesman avoid.

The elaborate burglar alarms, safety precautions, and protections against holdup hoodlums seem a little ridiculous by comparison. The annual take by such crude operators is only a fraction of the total haul raked in by forgery. The pen is mightier than the gun, but few businessmen or bankers take sufficient precautions based on this knowledge. Thus it is a wide-open field for the bad-check artist, whatever his specialty.

Still at large is a man we shall call Wendell Nordrup, alias the infamous Walter Mitler, a "sweet old man," who has plagued banks since 1959 as the "proud-father" swindler. Mitler (or Nordrup) has defrauded banks of thousands of dollars via the duplicate-deposit-slip method of operation and its variant, the split-deposit method. He has frequently

* The American Bankers' Association (ABA) puts it at $60,000,-000, which we consider a gross underestimate, because the ABA represents few reporting banks.

thrown bank officers and tellers off guard by distributing cigars or candy while announcing jubilantly that his wife has just given birth to a baby. Considering his apparent age, this announcement alone is enough to throw the most cautious teller off guard. When last heard of, Mitler was touring the South. He defrauded a bank in Raleigh, North Carolina, by means of the same trick that has netted him thousands of dollars in Ohio, New York, Pennsylvania, New Jersey, and other states. At the North Carolina bank, Mitler passed out cigars while proudly announcing that his wife had just given birth to a baby. Then he presented a deposit slip and worthless checks for $795.65 and obtained $490 in a split-deposit transaction. The checks bore the forged signature of one of the bank's depositors and were made payable to another depositor whose name the crook had assumed.

But such a role soon earns a trademark, and this can be a handicap, because word does get around, and banks after a while do get wised up. One longtime check artist became known as "Mr. Ninety" because he always made out checks for $90. He was caught eventually because he never learned that there's an "e" in "ninety."

Actually, it isn't really necessary to put on such an act in a cash-back, or split-deposit, swindle. Hundreds do it every month the way a young lady known here as Marie, alias Daisy, alias Beulah, and so on, did it in Washington, D.C., banks. Marie (or Daisy, and so on) simply presented a deposit slip and a handful of worthless checks. The deposit slip showed the entry "Less Cash," a common split-deposit transaction. At some banks she opened accounts with small cash deposits. At other banks, however, she did not open accounts, but merely presented checks and deposit slips ("Less Cash"), as would a regular depositor, and the tellers accepted and paid without question.

Despite the general attention given this simple swindle and despite the wholesale warnings issued to banks throughout the country, it continues to be a fast way to a small profit ($30 to $150), and hence its popularity. The big disadvantage to this fraud is that it is a hit-or-miss proposition. Not every try is a hit, and, what with the banks' growing awareness, the misses are increasing. Swindlers play the law of averages, however, and in meeting with success often, they feel encouraged to continue. At least this appears to be the attitude of amateurs in the business, for about two-thirds of all forgeries are committed by novices.

Only an experienced operator uses the "account-sweetening" routine. Through some ruse or trick of his own, he discovers the name and acquires the signature of a depositor. Next he proceeds to "sweeten" the account with deposits of bogus checks. Once a teller begins to identify him with his purloined name, it is a simple matter then to milk the account for all it contains. A day's work, or three at the most, once netted one clever operator $15,465 (according to the last report we have of him). The account sweetener does not rely so much on his skill as a forger as he does on his ability to assume the identity of a legitimate customer. This calls for talents beyond the ken of an amateur.

The smart one even profits by automation. He opens a legitimate account, is given a checkbook and deposit slips that bear his account number in magnetic figures. He quietly distributes his deposit slips to the bank's counters, where innocent depositors pick them up and use them in making deposits to their accounts. But regardless of the name written on the deposit slip, the magnetic tabulating machine credits the deposit to Mr. Swindler's account, which he depletes in a few days with one of his own checks.

Bank counteraction to this dodge was to print depositors' names on the deposit slips along with the account number. It reduced but didn't eliminate this fraud.

There are dozens of variations on the deposit-slip swindle and two factors that contribute to its continued success. One is the busy hour that nearly every bank experiences almost daily. The second factor is the swindler's careful selection of a teller for his transaction. The younger women or men are preferred on the theory that inexperienced tellers are more vulnerable.

During the holiday season, still another factor contributes to the success of check frauds. In the weeks before Christmas and Easter especially, check passers work overtime to take advantage of the holiday spirit. The accelerated volume of business produces an increase in check transactions and a like proportion of bad ones.

. The swindler's success, of course, depends on his appearing to be anything but what he is. One considered a "natural" in the business is a man we'll call George G. Silver, a man referred to in the *American Banker's Protective Bulletin* as a "man's man who commands respect among bank men and attention among women tellers. He appears to be the kind of person bankers like to serve [according to his victims]." Those who recall their contacts with him say he is a clear speaker, pleasingly friendly, and, in their opinion, intelligent. The victims who cannot recall him say that his manner must have been smooth and above suspicion.

Silver's method of operation is typical of the accomplished check specialist. A report in the above mentioned *Bulletin* said: "He prefers to do his banking with women tellers, although men, both officers and tellers, also have cashed his checks. At some banks he chose a busy hour to present for cash worthless checks ranging between $195 and $400. At other banks he first requested change and gave bills in $100 and $50 denominations for smaller bills. At one bank he gave ten $100 bills in exchange for $20 bills. Following this transaction, he cashed a worthless $400 check drawn on another bank.

"The psychology of his operation, of course, lies in the impression he creates when asking for banking services that usually are not requested by other than local depositors. Some tellers readily assumed that he was a depositor. Others asked whether he was a depositor, and when he replied in the affirmative, they did not verify his claim even though he was a stranger to them." This is check passing on a pretty high plane of intelligence.

Another way an account can be sweetened is by the "genuine" forged check. This one is more easily worked on a bank with many tellers or where the employee turnover is excessive. An account is opened with the deposit of cash or good checks. It is used in a regular way for a month or so or until there is a noticeable change in tellers. One day the customer comes in with his passbook and monthly collection of canceled checks. Among the latter is one for $500 that has been charged against his account by fraud, he maintains. He displays the checks, and sure enough, the $500 one is obviously a forged job. The customer knows it is a forged check because he himself forged his own signature in such a way that anyone could see the difference, and only he could have cashed it. But the bank can't prove he forged it or cashed it, and so the bank has to stand the loss. It also loses a customer, for who could put up with such slipshod banking?

A Florida bank recently reported a loss of $362,000 in a checking trick wherein the swindler deposited and drew out such large sums that a teller was virtually hypnotized. "I thought he was a millionaire," was his excuse for paying out so much money against uncollected and uncollectable checks.

The Silvers in this racket are too intelligent to use their

own names. A familiar surname has a peculiar psychological effect upon those who see or hear it. Somehow acquaintance with it has a certain appeal to the human side. And when a banker meets a person using a familiar surname by right or by choice, he is inclined to be more than usually pleased to serve him. In banking, to be "more than usually pleased to serve," means to freely accommodate the person with banking services—principally cashing checks before collection and giving for the asking a checkbook with which bogus banking may be continued almost indefinitely.

The job of selecting a variety of surnames for use in check swindles is a serious undertaking. If for no other reason than to avoid suspicion, a swindler does not use just any name as an alias. Each name should, even though it does not always, fit the physical or racial characteristics of its user. Further, some names are not euphonious and are therefore undesirable. Try selecting five names that fit your personality and characteristics. The effort will demonstrate the difficulty of choosing names that would be suitable for use in check swindles and that would not arouse suspicion as to whether they were really yours. Check swindlers must engage in a kind of mental gymnastics when selecting names.

Names repeatedly heard and seen usually remain uppermost in the mind and become subject to easy recall. Here, for example, is a list of well-known surnames that have been used in various check operations and that have appeared in the protective bulletins circulated among banks: Daley, Dorsey, Ferguson, Ford, Hart, Hopkins, LaMarr, Marlow, Martin, Mansfield, Mellon, Payne, Robinson, Shepard, Taylor, Wilkie, Webb, Wilson. We find no difficulty, for instance, in matching Silver's picture with the name Ferguson. Neither did he.

Swindlers not blessed with an "honest" face can always

make good use of a uniform. It sets the wearer apart, almost from himself. He is no longer regarded merely as an individual but rather as a member of a group. The uniform might be that of the armed services, a civic organization, or a commercial enterprise. For several years, banks have been plagued by someone we shall call D. E. Williams, who masquerades as a filling-station employee while negotiating worthless checks. By disguising himself in an oil-stained uniform, generally bearing Gulf insignia, he leads bank tellers to believe that he is employed locally and has been sent to the bank to cash his employer's checks. These are from a number of banks, all bearing different signatures and all made out to the station that he pretends to represent. His average take at each bank is $350 to $400.

Several checks stolen from a steel company were cashed at various stores by men in work clothes and steel helmets. In another case, checks stolen from a nursing home were cashed by women in immaculate nurses' uniforms.

One might hire a uniform with a man in it, as one artist we'll call Dugans has been known to do on several occasions. He opened an account at a bank in North Carolina with a cash deposit of $80. Two days later, he summoned a Western Union messenger to a building that he claimed to be his business address. He gave the messenger a check for $13,902.81 and a typewritten note for delivery to the teller of a local bank. The note contained detailed instructions concerning the purchase of three cashier's checks, each in the amount of $4,634.27. Both the check and the note given to the messenger were ostensibly signed by a local attorney who maintained a sufficient deposit balance at the bank to cover the transaction. The teller was instructed to draw one cashier's check payable to the law partner of the attorney, another to our man Dugans, and the third to another Dugans. The checks were issued and delivered to the forger, who encountered no trouble in cashing all of them at other banks that same day. It was never reported whether Dugans tipped the Western Union messenger.

A good round figure helps. For instance, Gloria N. was a beautiful girl. The teller who cashed her $3,000 check will vouch for that. The guard saw her too, and he almost whistled out loud. The teller says she was a blonde, but the guard swears her hair was red. Her dress? Well, it was a frilly thing, and it was dark, a color like green or navy blue or black. Anyway, it was low cut in front—very low cut. That's all either remembers about her except that when she walked, she bounced. And so did her check.

COME AND GET IT

Not many years ago and within the memory of many depositors, a person who wanted to open a checking account was required to furnish references, and one of them was expected to be a bank reference. Letters of inquiry were written, and only after the references replied with acceptable recommendations was the checking account opened. Things are different today. Bankers, pressured by competition and statistics, open checking accounts without investigation of the applicant or verification of his claims to previous banking and business connections.

The pressure of competition is obvious—there are almost as many banks as drugstores, more banks than bookstores, and their advertising has changed from "institutional" and conservative to blatantly commercial, their aura from old-fashioned and trustworthy to modern and slick. They spend more money in advertising for new accounts than they lose in bad ones. What they don't take into consideration is that their advertising invites swindlers. Promoting a new low-interest rate, one bank displayed $1,000,000 in real money in its window with a sign that read: "Come and get it." Several swindlers did—and paid no interest at all.

The statistics that influence bankers most are those that indicate that the vast majority of persons desiring the convenience of a checking account are on the level and worthy of depositor status. What they don't consider is the fact that if every bank in the United States accepted only ten bogus accounts a year, about three hundred thousand worthless accounts would be opened for swindlers. And opportunities for the check specialist are limited only by the number of checks in his possession. One notorious check swindler maintains that the opening of an account without having aroused suspicion practically assures him of the success of any check operation.

It is not known how many banks freely open checking accounts and thereby grant depositor status to persons not introduced and not recommended who prove to be swindlers. The comparative number of such accounts is not high (probably about three hundred thousand), but the total take, if the data were available, we suspect would border on the incredible.

Banks repeat the axiom, "Strangers are not always crooks, but crooks are usually strangers." It's part of the training drill for new tellers. But considering the alacrity with which banks (and merchants) make blank checks available to anyone, the drill seems a little futile. New bank accounts and pass- and checkbooks have kept swindlers in business for years. We shall touch on the activities of a few of our contemporaries.

A man we'll call Odens has defrauded numerous banks in recent years. When last reported, he was still at large and continuing at a rate that yields him an estimated $36,000 annually.

Another character is said to open bank accounts rarely, but he manages to acquire genuine check forms in sufficient quantity to bring in an average of $4,000 monthly. Banks from Oregon to Massachusetts have been defrauded by him, which suggests that he spends much of his time traveling. His method of operation is simple and typical. He merely appears at a bank, presents his bogus check to a teller, and, by sheer force of personality and the skillful use of psychology, induces the cashing of the item. He even uses his true name as payee on the bogus checks, which are rubber-stamped "Jane Doe Remembrance Service." He usually adds the words "Commission sales" to give each check an authentic appearance, though apparently this touch is not always necessary.

Another operator confessed, upon arrest, that for thirty years he had opened bank accounts solely to obtain genuine check forms, with which he managed to defraud other banks and their depositors. He eked out an existence on about $40,000 a year.

Or, take the case of a lady we will call Karen Carter. This woman claimed to be an anesthetist when she opened accounts at two banks in Colorado. She made cash deposits of $150 at one bank and $100 at the other. Two days later she returned to each bank with a bogus cashier's check, made payable to her order and ostensibly issued by a bank in Alexandria, Louisiana. The check presented at one bank was for $7,550. By means of a split-deposit transaction, she "deposited" $4,050 to her account and received cash back in the amount of $3,500. At the other bank, she obtained $3,650 in a similar transaction. The cashier's check in the latter instance was for $6,650. The following Monday, she cashed checks on her accounts for $1,500 at each bank. Total take, $10,150. The weekly pay of many *good* actresses is considerably less.

One smoothie (operating under a dozen aliases) has been successful among Michigan banks since 1957. When last heard of, he was using forged or raised certified checks, and his take at each bank was averaging about $2,000.

At a branch bank in Jackson, Michigan, "smoothie" presented a deposit slip with a typewritten certified check for $4,967 drawn on the bank's main office. He listed the check with the notation "Cash out $2,967" and requested that the balance of $2,000 be credited to his account. The certification-stamp impression on the check bore the forged signature of a bank teller employed at the main office.

The same ruse was used at a number of other Michigan banks, with the same results. How did he get the signature of the bank teller in the first place? Simply by purchasing a small certified check bearing the teller's signature. And in case he needed an okay initial at the cashing bank, that was easy too.

Forging okay initials is an old and highly successful method of operation that nets plenty of profits to swindlers and plenty of losses to banks. One man approached a teller in an Alabama bank during a busy hour and requested cash for a check in the amount of $3,100. The check had ostensibly been okayed for cashing by an officer of the bank, and the man was accommodated without question. Analysis of the handwriting and the typewriter used on a quantity of worthless checks disclosed the fact that this man has foraged successfully in this pasture for ten to twelve years.

The practice of having bank officers okay a check or other item for cashing by a teller has a necessary place in banking routine. Knowing the profit potential of the fraudulent use of such initials, a smart swindler never lacks for a specimen of an officer's okay initials. By one method, the con buys a cashier's check or bank money order in a small amount. Shortly afterward, he explains to an officer that he no longer has use for the purchased item and wishes to cash it. The unsuspecting officer places his okay initials on the item and returns it. By another method, a swindler opens an account and, a little later, presents to an officer a genuine check drawn on his account in the bank and explains that the teller with whom he is acquainted is not present. The officer affixes his okay initials to the check. In each case the swindler leaves the bank without cashing the check.

The simple countermeasure that would defeat the okay-initial swindler would be to give the check to a floorman and request the person who presented it to accompany that employee to a teller to cash the item.

Swindlers are always on the lookout for carelessly written checks. One elderly lady wrote a check for $13 to pay for a subscription to a magazine. The salesman, who was an employee of a magazine sales outfit in Birmingham, Alabama, told her he was selling subscriptions because he was working his way through college. According to the police, he was not so much college student as he was ball-point bandit. The lady neglected to put in a decimal point after "13," so the salesman put it in for her, after adding a couple of zeros.

RAISE YOU ONE

Careless check writers would be amazed at how easy it is to raise a check. Anyone who writes a check for from $1 to $9 should be sure that the figure is close to the dollar sign and that the written amount begins close to the left edge of the check. Otherwise it's a simple matter to change the notation "$1.00, One and no/100 Dollars" to "$91.00, Ninety-One and no/100 Dollars." Careless people have been known to leave enough room to write in three more digits!

Habitual doodlers may be surprised at the fun and profit their daily exercises in calligraphy could give them if properly directed. For instance, there are many different ways in which a check written "$100, One hundred Dollars" can be altered to a much larger amount. It can be changed to read "$800, Eight hundred Dollars" when space has been left between "One" and "hundred." Add to the "O" the top part of an "E," dot part of the "n" to form an "i," connect the remaining part of the "n" with the "e," forming the loop of a "g" and add "ht." The figure "1" is easily changed to "8."

"Two hundred" (or "Two thousand") is easier to alter than "One hundred." Make an "F" by crossing the "T," dot the first part of the "w" to make an "i," and change the "o" to an "e." The figure "2" can be made into a perfect "5" by adding the top part of the "5" to it.

"Four" is another easy amount to alter. Extend the second part of the "u" into a "t," and add the "y" loop to the "r." "Five" can be changed into "Fifty" and "Fifteen." "Six," "Seven," "Eight," and "Nine" are easily changed into "Sixty," "Seventy," "Eighty," and "Ninety," respectively, by simply affixing the syllable "ty." A little practice makes perfect, and more doodling will disclose dozens of variations on other numbers.

The real artists, of course, are those who can forge signatures that seem more authentic than the originals. All these experts need are samples of original signatures, blank checks similar to those used by the original signers, similar pens and ink, and some identification acceptable to a teller. These accouterments are easy to come by. An expert forger once said, "Give me a depositor's bank signature and I will help myself to his cash balance." Generally, though, the loss is the bank's, not the depositor's.

If you lack the skill to forge another's signature, simply use your own, with the following variation of the split-deposit trick. At a bank in Salt Lake City, a savings account was opened with $30 for a man we'll refer to as Morgan. He returned to the bank that same day and presented a check, filled in by typewriter and checkwriter, payable to his order and in the amount of $2,125. He requested $1,000 in cash and the rest credited to his savings account. When the check was presented with the deposit slip *it had already been endorsed.* This prompted the teller to compare the endorsement with the signature of Morgan on the bank's signature card, but, being busy, he did not also check the account balance. He gave Morgan $1,000. Two hours later Morgan returned with another check but went to a different teller. Again only his signature was examined, and the teller paid. Morgan, under several aliases, has pulled off this one regularly for the past ten years. He makes more money than any of the vice-presidents of the banks he has swindled.

Although a complete catalog of tricks and check-passing swindles might be helpful to our merchant and banker readers, it might also be criticized as an aid to swindlers. However, we should like to point out that even the police have aided and abetted swindlers. For example, a man who said he was the operator of a service station in Los Angeles inquired at the police department concerning a listing of bad-check passers being sought by the police. He was referred to a firm that distributes a weekly circular describing checks passed and the check passers' methods of operation. After subscribing to this handy publication, he began passing worthless checks himself. Each week he read the circular, and as soon as one of the checks he had passed appeared in it, he would discontinue passing that type or using that method. Since there are some two hundred different variations on this game, there is no reason why he should not be able to continue indefinitely or at least until he runs out of banks.

Among the elite of the check artists, every attempt to pass a check involves a battle of wits between the swindler and the bank teller or merchant. The swindler generally has the advantage, for in developing a specialty, he also develops a keen mind and concentrates on his strategy. It takes a wilier mind to steer him, without arousing suspicion, into the hands of the law. Tellers and businessmen unschooled in deceit are no match for him.

Whenever policemen discuss the *modus operandi* (or MO—police slang for the distinctive technique of a paperhanger or check forger) of really big operators in the profession, the talk eventually gets around to a man we'll call Sam. He is serving a stretch at the moment, but before Los Angeles detectives C. W. Montgomery and John

Bengston finally nabbed him, he had rung up a total of $500,000 with bogus paper. He didn't pass it all, but he masterminded the ring of men and women who aided his efforts. A man of many talents—accountant, burglar, forger—he stole from various firms the blank checks and signatures he used in his profession. And when S.S.S. set out to paper a town, he did it with such singleness of purpose that the haul seldom was less than $40,000. His boast is that a check he passed for $14,800 was "the biggest single check that was ever passed in the whole history of forging." And that is pretty good spinach.

TRAVELERS' AID

The active swindler is the proverbial traveling man, which does not imply that the average traveling man is also a swindler. No, what we mean is simply that the swindler who actively plies his specialty must move around a great deal. Not only is the grass greener on the other side of the fence, but there's nothing like the smell of new-mown hay—or the thrill one gets in feeling it.

So how does the swindler get from here to there without spending a lot of his ill-gotten gains? The answer is that every transport facility available to the public is available without cost or with very little cost to the knowing swindler.

The daily press is filled with stories of foolish people who go on spending sprees with purloined credit cards. One young man roamed over two continents and traveled like a prince for several months before he was caught. A teenage girl took her mother's credit card and her mother's credit for a month-long spree.

The smart swindler abhors such horseplay. However he acquires his credit cards, he uses them with more discretion and never long enough to get caught. Forged tickets, counterfeit tickets, and tickets that have been kited (*e.g.*, an $8.50 train ticket can be raised to read "$18.50" if one wants or needs a longer ride) are used only when there have been no alerts about these common swindles.

The travel area is so riddled with fraud, the wonder is that the general public, which pays for it all, can travel so cheaply. Charlatans are so numerous and simple graft so common in every operation, it is amazing that one can get from here to there at so little cost. Efficiency, supposedly, is the key. But if all the fraud and all the charlatans and all the graft were completely eliminated from travel, one could get from here to there for half the present cost. Which is another way of saying that with all their touted efficiency, the nation's carriers still figure that 50¢ out of every transport dollar is being siphoned off.

5

THE FIFTY-GRAND GAFF

IF you have come this far with us and still find yourself hampered by an inbreeding of honesty or strangled in mores of morality, bear with us a moment more while we squeeze the last fallacy out of the old adage that "crime does not pay." If in this compendium of cons you cannot find one with whom you can identify or at least for whom you can experience some feeling of sympathy, envy, or emulous desire, then fraud is simply not your dish. Face it, son, and go back to the humdrum and the humble. The people in this chapter swindled the public out of $3,600,000,000. If you don't have what it takes to make a start in their direction, as we have outlined in previous chapters, don't start.

If you have never used merchandise and then returned it for a full refund; if you have never pocketed an overpayment in making change; if you have never cheated on a school test or misrepresented any personal data on a questionnaire; if you have paid all the taxes you were legally obligated to pay and have never cheated on an expense account; if, indeed, every act of your life has been

honest, fair, and devoid of fraud, you are a rare and abnormal specimen of humanity. You'll never make it big in
this world, and, what with the competition waiting for you
in the next, we doubt that you'll ever make it big there
either.

On the other hand, you may find some value in what we
have to say and want to profit from the experience of
others. If your field is forgery, for instance, perhaps you
will get the message between the following lines.

CASH FROM CARS

One of the best stories of forgery we have come across
recently involved the ring operating in Brooklyn that sold
hundreds of forged learners' driving permits for prices as
high as $230. The operators used regulation Motor Vehicle
Bureau rubber stamps and dating stamps to forge the permits. We could be more helpful if we knew how the mob
obtained the bureau equipment, for some four hundred
forged permits were sold before the operation was moved
to another place. The Brooklyn gang dealt largely with
foreign-born persons who had difficulty with English. To
get a permit in New York, an applicant must take language
and eye tests. There are plenty of people who feel they
can't pass such tests, in New York and other places.

A man we'll call Casanova of the Bronx had a one-man
operation similar to that of the Brooklyn ring. Casanova
had a bicycle- and motorcycle-repair shop, and on the side
he did a thriving business in forged chauffeurs' licenses, ac-

cording to police. They found in the shop several forged rubber stamps used to affix state markings to license forms and a quantity of chauffeurs' and operators' license applications. Obviously, anyone who needed a license had only to pay Casanova's fee, fill out the application the way he wanted the record to read, and walk out with his license.

Forgery on such a scale, however, has little to recommend it except that it is practice of a sort that might lead to bigger and richer hauls. But big-time forgery is a more advanced subject, and it will be dealt with in its proper grade. At this level there is another automobile swindle that is vastly more popular with car owners than the public realizes. And since this one also enjoys greater vogue among New York City people, we shall use that locale as our prime example.

About seventy-five thousand New Yorkers annually swindle insurance companies by inventing or inflating auto-accident claims. Insurance officials say that "some fraud taints three of every four claims filed in New York," and claims paid total about $10,000,000 a year. The insurance companies aren't complaining, really, since the loss doesn't come out of their pockets. They merely pass the loss along to the policyholders in higher premiums.

If all the kited claims were eliminated, insurance rates in the metropolitan area of New York could be sliced in half. Today the average yearly cost of a basic auto-liability policy in the city is the highest in the nation, about $150; and the local frequency rate of 115 claims for each 1,000 policyholders also is the nation's highest. (Compare this with Chicago's 65 per 1,000 and insurance cost of $110 and with Los Angeles' 57 per 1,000 and insurance cost of $105.)

How do New Yorkers (and Frisco folk and Memphis people and Philadelphians) do it? Sometimes it is the work of an organized ring. Sometimes it is the work of loners who stage accidents. But most often the swindles are perpetrated by ordinary citizens who take the attitude that insurance companies are fair game for anything. And if you still have some residue of feeling about the "innate honesty of man," let this statement open your eyes once and for all: most people, given (1) the opportunity and (2) freedom from punishment, will "taint" their claim with all the fraud they think they can get away with. Only the Internal Revenue Service exceeds insurance companies as a target for such attitudes of swindling.

Take the case of the respected young executive who seemed to be having a run of bad luck. Twice in six months his new car was involved in collisions. His car was only slightly damaged, but he and his wife filed claims for neck and back injuries on both occasions. Neither the young executive nor his wife was able to show other injuries, and the car needed only minor repairs. Yet this pair netted more than $1,000 from their claims. "It's not swindling," argued the young executive. "It's insurance money. I'm just getting back some of what I've been paying in."

The novice in this field should realize, however, that his "competition" is some eighteen million other auto-insurance swindlers, and if he plans to operate in New York, six million of these are in the metropolitan area. New Yorkers "are more claim-conscious than persons anywhere else in the country," according to N. Morgan Woods, an insurance executive and authority on the subject. Woods' file contains the name of one loner who lined his pockets with $50,000 in less than three years. This expert in the game was always on the lookout for cooperative motorists and pedestrians who would stage accidents in which the pedestrian claimed he was hit by the motorist's car. For bringing together the performers in this act, the loner took the lion's share of any settlement.

Another fraud involved five men who realized a cool $300,000 for "injuries" growing out of an invitation to a truck driver to hit their halted auto "very softly."

With everyone trying to cash in on auto accidents—claimants, lawyers, repairmen, adjusters, and just plain bystanders who want a cut for witnessing—competition for the insurance dollar is fast making this a poor field for the career swindler.

And with the costs of car insurance, car repairs, time payments, and just ordinary upkeep what they are, everyone who has a car is a potential swindler. Moralists who have made serious studies of the problem assert that no other single adjunct to civilization has caused so much change in moral concepts as the automobile. Philosophers, psychiatrists, and psychologists point to the automobile as the great revolutionizing force in society. It is redundant for us, therefore, to point out in more detail the hundreds of ways the average owner can use his car to defraud. From accident claims and padded gas bills (the latter practice takes the trucking industry for hundreds of millions every year) to Los Angeles' Zatisfaction Zack, a fictitious name for the "honest" used-car dealer, the opportunities are limited only by one's imagination.

If you have any ambition to get into Zack's class, consult the Better Business Bureau's pamphlet "Stretching Your Used-car Dollar" for supplementary text reading. For example, in this you can read how Joe Doakes "answered an ad offering an old Packard for $350. He found two Packards of this model on the lot, and signed a blank contract to buy one of them." With such gullibility, Joe was lucky he got taken for only twice what the car was worth. All the old gimmicks to get the gullible onto the used-car lot are exposed in detail in the pamphlet. The "Colossal Bargain" or "Today's Steal" (invariably a lemon) parked prominently where suckers can see it, the low prices painted on the windshields of cars that are not for sale, and the unwarranted "Ninety-day Warranty" signs are tricks any gyp dealer can improve upon with a little imagination.

But, of course, the biggest gyp of all begins with the manufacturer. All the recent hullabaloo about safety points up the fact that automobile manufacturers are perpetrating the ultimate swindle, the swindle to end all swindles, on thousands of people every year. What is the buyer getting for his money? More powerful motors, more luxury frills, more comfort, but less safety. With all this he gets a guarantee, but the only guarantee that means anything to him is unwritten: he will surely have the satisfaction of knowing that the last few moments of his life were spent in the most attractive automobile ever built. And as long as the foolish public continues to demand frills instead of safety, manufacturers will continue to disregard the pleas of safety groups.

The new cars will continue to provide more money for the manufacturer, a comfortable living for the dealer, a thrill for the driver, and more business for the undertaker, the surgeon, the ambulance attendant, the highway patrol, and the gravedigger. Auto-towing services and wreckers will benefit, and the junk dealers will expand their wrecking yards. Thanks to the ingenuity of the automobile designers, the shrewd business sense of the manufacturers, and the skilled phrases of the advertising agencies, the automobile today is the greatest swindle since gunpowder was invented.

Had the automobile manufacturers combined their skills to produce a reasonably priced vehicle that would carry human beings from one place to another in comfort and safety, they would all have gone out of business. As we have proved in other fields, it doesn't pay any swindler, whatever his specialty, to be honest or give the sucker an even break.

One operator uses fraudulent checks to buy automobiles that are advertised in the want-ad section of newspapers. He disposes of the vehicles through legitimate sales, usually in another state, where the market may be better at the moment. The trick involves a psychological gimmick. The operator is aware of the furor over bum checks, but he also knows that the average automobile owner advertises his car for private sale because he thinks he can get more money for it that way than he would from a used-car dealer. Thus, when the owner is presented with a check after only a little dickering with the nicely dressed stranger and it is for nearly the amount he expected to get, he seldom questions the validity of the check.

Despite all the publicity circulated by the Better Business Bureaus (or because of it), gyp repairmen are still in business. It is a fraud so extensive and so varied that the annual take in the United States alone probably runs into the billions. Anyone who has ever had to pay an automobile-repair bill has been swindled to some extent. The "honest" repairman may not have overcharged for his time, but through carelessness he may have used poor repair parts, through laziness and sloppy work added hours to the time card, or through pure chicanery repaired something that did not need repairing. And since less than one in ten thousand car owners knows anything much about motors, the field is limited only by the imagination of the mechanic.

THE JEWELRY SWINDLER

There is a greater relationship between automobiles and jewelry than one might think. Psychologists draw many parallels between our desires for the two and the human values we put on them. So let us now make our pitch for the jewelry swindler. The experts have more tricks than real jewels, and some of the tricks are more brilliant than the finest diamonds. As one old-timer in the business tells us, "Our pearls of wisdom must be greater than our pearls in hand, otherwise we can never make it big in this racket."

Our favorite experience in this field involved us only as bystanders, but that was close enough. It would hardly have been a favorite had it actually happened to us, for though we have been swindled many times (the basis for our authority), this particular swindle would have made us more chagrined than nonchalant. And since everyone involved is still alive and all are acquaintances, we shall tell it straight but without names or places. It will still be a profitable lesson in our course.

A golfer acquaintance of ours exhibited, during his nineteenth-hole refreshment, a diamond ring of great beauty and apparent value on his finger. In the group around him was a gentleman who had a known passion for diamonds. After much bantering, the owner consented to sell the ring for the sum of $600. As the buyer left the room, the snide remarks and suppressed chuckles of the others caused him to conclude that he had been had. He said nothing but called the next day upon a jeweler, where he learned that the diamond was paste and the ring worth about $25.

The dupe examined some real diamonds and found one closely resembling the paste in his new ring. He "rented" the diamond for a few days by agreeing to purchase it for $1,200 and putting down a $100 deposit. He took this and his ring to another jeweler, had the paste removed and the real diamond set.

His clubhouse friends, knowing how he had been imposed upon, impatiently waited for his appearance the next afternoon. To their astonishment, they found him in good spirits. He flourished his ring, boasted of his bargain, and said that if anyone present had another $1,200 ring to sell for $600, he knew where he could find a purchaser. When he was told that the ring was paste and that he had been cheated, he laughed.

Bets were freely offered that the ring did not contain a real diamond. Two men bet $1,000 each. Two bet $500. All bets were covered, and the club pro and the bartender were chosen to hold the stakes. The money and the ring were put into their hands. The referees, accompanied by all interested parties, went to a first-class jeweler, who applied all the tests and said the stone was a diamond of the first water. It was worth, he said, without the setting, about $1,200.

The erstwhile dupe quietly put the $3,000 that he had won in his pocket. He took the diamond back to the jeweler and recalled his obligation of $1,200 and, with his paste ring on his finger, went back to the club. The man who sold the ring was waiting for him. He wanted to get it back. He attempted to turn the whole thing into a joke. He had sold the ring, he said, for fun. He knew that it was a real diamond all the time. He never wore false jewels, could tell a real diamond anywhere by its peculiar light, would not be so mean as to cheat an old friend. He knew his friend would let him have the ring again.

But his friend was stubborn. He said that the seller had thought it was paste and had intended to defraud him. Finally, on the payment of $800, the seller got his paste ring back. When the whole affair came to light, everyone had a good laugh, except the first swindler.

Obviously, this little swindle between acquaintances should be classified as a practical joke, but the same trick is pulled by professional jewelry swindlers more often than one might think. The difference between these operations and our anecdote is the difference between practical swindling and friendly joking.

The jewelry swindler, if he is really expert at his trade, knows more about stones than the average store employee who handles a great variety of stones every day. Few know the difference between genuine, synthetic, and imitation, though every stone sold must be one of these three types. The expert swindler and the expert jeweler know the difference.

A genuine stone, regardless of the kind of stone referred to, is a product of nature and has only to be cut and polished. A synthetic has (or should have) the hardness, the color, and most of the general characteristics of the genuine, but it is a man-made stone. An imitation is just made to look like some other stone. The imitation (or paste) does not have the same hardness or other characteristics of a real stone, but it probably does have the same color.

In stones, the genuine is always the most valuable. Synthetics are second in value, though usually very much less valuable than the genuine. Imitations usually have no value at all, except to the swindler. They are used for costume jewelry and other very inexpensive pieces that only need to look like something else.

Synthetic rubies were first marketed about fifty years ago. They are today an inexpensive substitute for natural gems. In some respects, they are even better, for modern perfections in manufacture have developed a stone just as hard as the genuine, with a durability far above that of any imitation. Their color is now as good as the genuine, or nearly so, and they usually have fewer flaws. They are more brittle than genuine stones, and perhaps this is the main reason they are less expensive.

Synthetic sapphires were introduced shortly after the first synthetic rubies were put on the market. Both are corundum crystals, the color of which can be varied by the manufacturing process, and there is a wide range of colors with several coined names

Synthetic spinel, beryls, and emeralds are now being manufactured, and the experts in this field claim they can reproduce the imperfections for which the emerald is so widely known. Almost all the stones offered today as zircon, rozircon, aquamarine, and alexandrite are either synthetic spinel or synthetic corundum colored to imitate the other gems.

The gemologist has many ways and facilities for telling the differences between the synthetic and the genuine stone. Thus, in this age of specialization, anyone who intends to make big money in this field had better acquire a thorough education in it first.

Strangely, no one has yet produced a synthetic diamond. There are good imitation diamonds—pastes, glass, or colorless stones of little value—but no synthetics. Though man has discovered no substitute for diamonds, he, the eternal inquisitor, has tried. The ancient alchemists professed to know how to "grow" diamonds or "cook" diamonds in witches' brews or "transform" diamonds from other materials. All anyone has accomplished so far has been to waste a lot of materials and foist innumerable frauds on the public.

Stones of a given weight resemble one another too closely to admit of detection when the setting has been changed. Unless there is some flaw or peculiarity about a stone, it is almost impossible to identify it.

The three main flaws in diamonds are termed "feathers," "clouds," and "sand." Feathers are little rents or fissures in the interior of the stone. At times there may be a half dozen of these flaws that cannot be detected without the aid of a glass, and then only by those who know how to look for them. Clouds are gray, brown, or white spots, also in the interior of the stone, and are much easier to find than feathers. Sand is seedlike little bodies, usually of white, brown, or neutral tints. When sand is unusually fine and is present in large numbers, it is termed "dust." A few stones are also "chipped," that is, there are fissures on the exterior edges of the facets. A bad chip or two largely reduces the value of an otherwise fairly good stone.

In a field where not one in a thousand has any knowledge and not one in ten thousand is a connoisseur, there is opportunity for a great deal of imposition. The fraud most common in the jewelry trade is when flawed, imperfect, or off-colored stones are sold as first-water gems. There is no such thing as an absolutely perfect, flawless diamond, any more than there is a perfect specimen of humanity in the world. What are called perfect stones are gems as flawless as any found, but if a glass of high power is used, imperfections can be found in the best of them. The selling of poor stones as perfect ones takes place every day and almost every minute. The principal sufferers are would-be smart people who snatch at a "bargain" and get the worst of the deal. If people would realize that fine diamonds are the easiest things in the world to sell and that any jeweler is always willing to purchase his wares at a small reduction from prevailing rates, they would not be imposed upon so often.

The number and variety of tricks available to the jewel swindler are exceeded only by those known to the average jeweler. Any neighborhood shop can and does have at its command more tricks to make money than the public is aware of. Jewelers have a refined version of the old bean-guessing game used by drugstores. A spoonful of diamond chips is displayed in a tiny phial in the window. Suckers are encouraged to guess the number of diamonds and win a real diamond. Enterprising jewelers even send out friendly invitations to "select" lists. Strangely, nearly everyone who guesses wins a diamond. Yep! A real live honest-to-gawd diamond.

The gimmick? Well, you don't get to take the diamond right out. It's yours, all right, the friendly neighborhood jeweler tells you, only it's the rule of the joint that no jewels go out of the store unmounted. And he suggests a gold or platinum mount, for example. At only $60, it's a bargain, considering that the diamond isn't costing you anything. It didn't cost the jeweler anything much either.

The swindling jeweler knows more about people than people know about diamonds. Most people and all women firmly believe that "diamonds are a girl's best friend" and a man's best hedge against inflation, invasion, and bad investments. But their true value is known only to the expert and the swindler. If this field interests you, we suggest you acquire a copy of the Better Business Bureau's simple rules for judging the value of diamonds. It is a handy guide for the novice swindler who aims at the perfection of any of the tricks that follow.

According to the BBB pamphlet, a real diamond can't be marked with a nail file. The BBB suggests testing it in a glass of clear water: if it's paste, it will lose its luster; if it's genuine, it will keep its brilliance. Other tests are suggested, even the hydrofluoric acid test, but they all require props not readily available to the buyer, even if he were not embarrassed to bring all this paraphernalia into a shop. The BBB concludes that any jeweler who lets you clutter up his shop with all this testing apparatus must certainly be an honest merchant, while if he throws you and your apparatus out, you cannot assume he is a swindler.

The whiter the diamond, the greater its value. But jewelers know about a thin film that can be applied to yellow diamonds that makes them so white, you'll wonder where the yellow went.

Then there's the test that most people think provides the ultimate proof of authenticity. Scratch the glass on the dealer's showcase. If it makes a mark, it's the real thing. But the jeweler knows that there are varying degrees of hardness in glass and that a properly cut piece of hard crystal can scratch any soft showcase glass. He even makes sure the showcase glass is soft by replenishing it periodically—which he must, for all those scratches on it must be erased like a blackboard to make ready for the next surge of suckers.

Then again, the friendly neighborhood jeweler may very well sell only real diamonds, his gimmick being his "finance" plan. This is merely a switch on the loan shark's trade. Diamonds sold on time payments can bring in 300 to 500 per cent profit on the deal. Such dealers are really moneylending sharks, and diamonds and all the other merchandise offered on time are merely the gimmicks to hook the sucker.

The individual swindler who acquires a really fine diamond or several fine diamonds can stay in business for life. A typical professional in this field is a man we'll call Duane Hopewell. He usually works in places where a respectable-seeming foreigner might not be out of place, for he dresses the part and affects an accent. When he taps a prospect, he is furtive. Surreptitiously he pulls from his inside pocket a small packet of diamonds and exhibits them to the mark. "Smuggled in today from Johannesburg," he whispers. "Five thousand dollars for the lot."

If the mark is skeptical, Duane puts the packet in his hands and tells him to go to any jeweler and get the diamonds appraised. Few suckers can resist this bait. They take the diamonds to any convenient jeweler, while Duane trustingly waits outside. The jeweler, if he knows his diamonds, will appraise them at $8,000 and may even offer to pay that for them. The wise mark will figure they are worth at least $10,000, so when he returns to Duane, he starts to dicker. If they are smuggled diamonds, he figures he can get them for half the price offered. Duane puts on his insulted act and, with an air of hauteur, returns the packet to his pocket.

But the mark won't let him go. A little more haggling and the packet changes hands for $4,500. Or, rather, a similar packet changes hands, but it contains only paste duplicates of Duane's real stock-in-trade. How many paste copies he peddles in a year might be determined by a recent order he gave a Manhattan manufacturer: "Five hundred each of five different sizes," corresponding to the five different diamonds in his first-show packet. In that quantity, copies are cheap. Our "smuggling foreigner," who was born in Little Rock (could that have anything to do with his big-rock profession today?), averages about 2,000 per cent profit on each deal.

The secret, if one exists, of writing a successful play or

novel lies in the accurate portrayal of believable characters, whether or not they have counterparts within our circle of familiar people. Lorelei Lee may have been a character on the fringes of common knowledge, but she was an intimate in the mind of Anita Loos. And Miss Loos had at her fingertips in the daily press enough blond *femmes fatales* to satisfy the preferences of many gentlemen. One who may have inspired the birth of Lorelei Lee, or at least influenced Miss Loos, for she flourished during the childhood of Miss Loos, was Antoinette Bonner, a Rumanian immigrant girl whose father had taught her about diamonds. She became one of the leading free-lance diamond dealers of New York at the turn of the century.

Diamonds have a structure peculiarly their own. Their color, brilliance, size, and purity vitally affect their value. Even men trained to distinguish the various degrees of these qualities seldom agree, because their abilities vary. Some people never develop that extraordinary, almost extrasensory gift that enables them to appraise correctly the merits of a stone. Fewer still are those who can look into a crude stone and plan how best to divide it, cut it, and shape it for market. Antoinette could and did do all these things, and at the height of her career she was making around $25,000 a year, a good wage for a girl in her twenties sixty years ago.

Trusted, respected in the profession, and frequently in possession of valuable collections for sale, she was the subject of conjecture by many. "No man could resist the temptation of so many diamonds," they said, "how, then, can a frail girl?" Antoinette didn't. She planned her coup well, and it might have gone off without a hitch had she been more experienced in the art of swindling. As it was, she waited until she had in her possession a king's ransom in diamonds and disappeared.

She turned up in Paris, in the pose of a *nouveau riche* American lady, a not uncommon type in Paris even then. And she might easily have turned the whole escapade into a swindle rather than a theft, for there was a point at which this could have been done, but the law was more nimble-witted.

However, she was not extradited, because war intervened. The First World War swept across Europe at this time, and Antoinette and her quarter of a million dollars in diamonds were forgotten by all except those from whom she had acquired them.

One who illustrated by example just how easy it is to pull off a diamond swindle was Louisa Miles, who operated in London about the same time our Antoinette was busy in New York. Miss Miles kept Scotland Yard awake for twenty years with one trick or another, but her best was the swindle she worked on a Bond Street diamond merchant.

She appeared in the store as Miss Constance Browne, secretary to Lady Campbell of impeccable address. She asked for a "dozen or so" of the shop's finest diamonds, to be brought by a trusted employee, from which her ladyship might select a few to be set in jewelry for a niece about to be married.

At the house of milady, Miss Browne (*i.e.*, Louisa Miles) accepted the diamonds from the jeweler's messenger and courteously asked him to wait. "Milady will make her choice in a moment."

The messenger waited a moment, then several, then, in panic, tried the door to the inner part of the house. It was locked. So was the front door. He broke a window and yelled for help, but by that time, Louisa was in another part of the city. The house had been rented for a month, half of which time Louisa had used up while casing the shops and planning her strategy.

Jewelry shops are a specially fertile field for the swindler. Yields in this field are generally substantial, since jewels are valuable, and they take up little space, so that a good sleight-of-hand artist has no difficulty in palming them, or exchanging copies for real stones (pennyweighting), or simply pocketing them. However, these tricks verge on theft, and therefore they are beneath the swindler who depends entirely on his wits, intelligence, and acting ability.

The line of difference between theft and swindling is much wider than most people think. The bunco squad in any police detail can point out the difference with enough examples to fill a book. And since some of the more literate cops have done just that, the student swindler looking for supplementary texts will find such books extraordinarily helpful. However, we shall offer one example to illustrate our point, citing the swindle that every book on bunco mentions. The commodity involved varies. American books generally cite the purchase of an automobile as the gimmick on which the swindle is hung; British writers, the purchase of jewelry. We first heard of the trick in our cub-reporter days thirty years ago.

The swindler, dressed the part, enters the jewelry shop or auto showroom and indicates his interest in the most expensive merchandise in stock. He makes his selection, tenders his check to cover the total price, and then waits for the clerk or salesman to consult with the credit manager. They both return in a moment, polite but obviously concerned over the transaction. Such a large check, from a total (and unprepossessing) stranger—but the stranger exhibits satisfactory identification and suggests that the credit manager telephone his bank to ascertain his account balance.

Timing is the essence of this trick, as you will see. The

call is made to the buyer's bank only a few moments before its closing time on Friday. The bank certifies that Mr. Swindler has sufficient funds in his checking account to cover the transaction, and the credit manager and the salesman return, beaming, to hand over to Mr. S. the box of jewelry or the keys to the Cadillac. Our hero, with one eye on his watch, strolls leisurely out of the store with the gems or drives the new car out into the evening traffic.

If he has walked away with jewelry, his next stop will be the nearest pawnshop. If he has made off with a car, he will stop at the nearest used-car lot. He presents the jewels for loan or the automobile for sale. The hock-shop proprietor immediately recognizes the jewelry firm's name on the box and suspects fraud. Or the used-car dealer is alerted when he checks the speedometer and discovers the Caddy is new. In either case, a surreptitious telephone call is quickly made to the original seller. The seller looks at the clock and realizes the bank is closed. He panics. He orders the hock-shop proprietor or the used-car dealer to detain Mr. S. until the police arrive and take him into custody. The charge? Bum-check passing, and Mr. S. is thrown into the klink, where he rests quietly at city expense until Monday morning.

Early Monday morning, the action gets under way again. Mr. S. stands on his rights to hock or sell his personal possessions, and if he chose this way to raise a little cash for an evening's poker game, that was his business.

The seller, still convinced he has been defrauded, presents the check at the bank. "We know it's a bum check," he says, "but we want your NF stamp on it for evidence."

"No funds?" says the teller, going to check the account. "Why, this check is okay, sir," reports the teller, returning to his window. "How do you want it?"

The seller decides he'd better have it deposited to his account immediately, for he is beginning to realize that he is the victim of a bigger fraud than he had suspected. The payoff for false arrest in one recent example of this old chestnut was $30,000. A Cadillac really was involved in this one, so the profit was a new car plus a few extras like greenbacks.

It has been said, and bunco men all agree, that nothing produced by the industrial age offers a more versatile gimmick for swindling than the automobile.

Science has a way of catching up with fakery and exposing it, we are told by the moralists among us and by those who feel that science has the answer for everything. The accomplished and educated swindler contends that it is the other way around. Science comes up with new methods and inventions that the faker soon adapts to his own ends. It is an argument that is as pointless as the one about the chicken-or-the-egg sequence.

The con who makes a career of jewel swindling equips himself with instruments for making laboratory examination of precious and semiprecious stones, including the special microscope used to identify the properties of the stones. He knows how to measure, weigh, and evaluate stones and can establish their approximate wholesale and retail prices. Some gems have been sold for up to 800 per cent more than their actual value.

The detection of false garnets, emeralds, rubies, or sapphires is not easy. Thin slivers of such precious stones often are fused onto ordinary glass in such a way as to make the entire piece assume the quality of a genuine stone. Only a microscopic examination reveals telltale "bubbles," traceable to the fusing process. In the trade, such imitations are known as "doublets." There are also "triplets," made by inserting layers of red or green cement between the top and

bottom pieces of ordinary glass. The finished product re-
sembles a real ruby or emerald. And "genuine" green jade
is frequently a cheap mineral treated with green dye. The
stones advertised as topaz may be a yellow variety of
quartz—a very hard mineral—that is called false topaz.

Amateurs who fake a jewel robbery to collect insurance
often wind up in jail. Their inexperience in the art of fraud
is the cause of their falure. A lady we'll refer to as Romy
Burton, known to society folk as a designer of beautiful
jewelry, complained that $70,000 in gems had been stolen
from her apartment. She told police she had discovered
that the jewels were missing after she showed her house
to some prospective buyers. But police who searched her
house said they found fifty items of the jewelry she swore
she lost.

Mrs. Burton, an aristocratic lady, is the daughter of an
American mother and Russian Prince Alexander Istrivski,
last ambassador to Italy under the Czar. Finding herself in
Brazil, after two marriages, with a dwindling supply of
cash, she went to New York with $15,000 worth of jewels
she had bought. She sold them for twice that amount and
entered the jewelry-design business for exclusive customers,
among them the Duchess of Windsor. So far, so profitable,
but a 100 per cent profit is only a first step toward a 1,000
per cent markup. Somewhere between these profits, one
learns the next lesson in the art of fraud, a lesson Mrs.
Burton obviously never learned. Which points up our contention that the expert swindler takes one step at a time,
each in its natural sequence. Certainly it is foolhardy to
jump from a "legitimate" profit to an attempt to swindle an
insurance company. Insurance companies are old hands at
this game.

Maybe Macy's doesn't tell Gimbels, but posh New York
jeweler Harry Winston told Tiffany's, his competitor across

the street, when a mysterious lady in a dark suit pulled the fastest diamond switch since Yogi Berra joined the Mets. After piecing together the story from recent newspaper accounts, we concluded that this young lady knew her business. First she dumped a $7,500 ring in a Tiffany tray, plucked out a look-alike $19,800 ring, and took it across Fifth Avenue to Winston's, where she dropped it into a tray as a substitute for a similar $38,500 ring.

A Tiffany salesman witnessed part of this three-ring swindle. He told how the woman, in a charcoal-gray suit trimmed with Persian lamb, examined a tray containing a 3.69-carat marquise diamond late one Saturday. She left without buying.

Monday morning, a salesman at Harry Winston, Inc., was taking a tray of rings from a safe for display when he noticed an item that, to his trained eye, looked like a jalopy alongside a Cadillac. An executive confirmed the salesman's judgment. After all, when you find a 3.69-carat marquise diamond where you expect to see a 5.30-carat marquise diamond, you make no allowance for weekend shrinkage. Furthermore, the ring carried a Tiffany marking.

Winston's called Tiffany's, and that's when the story came to light—but only part of the story and probably only the middle part at that. What would be helpful to us would be the beginning. Did it begin as a chip of glass dropped into a Woolworth's ring tray? And what about the end? Will it be a diamond as big as the Koh-i-noor?

6

THE $100,000 HUSTLE

Pick up any magazine that contains an article warning its readers against fraud and consumer swindles. Follow the continued portions of the story through the advertising pages. It will be a rare magazine that does not pack its advertising columns with frauds equal to those it rails against.

Take, for instance, an article we clipped from a confessions-type magazine. Titled "how they take you for every cent you've got," the story relates how "crooked dealers, using bait ads and come-ons, can lure you into spending twice what you should!" This typical story of only twenty-five hundred words is spread so thin through the magazine that the reader is exposed to twelve pages of advertising. And what is the advertising about? Mostly gyp mail-order deals, "no-risk" bait coupons, overpriced pornographic materials and merchandise, and come-ons with obvious sex overtones.

The best advice we can give the novice swindler with a stock of "orginal, uncensored, unretouched photos" or "Teenie Bikini lace panties" or "Sheer Dream nighties" or "adult-entertainment products" is to advertise the goods or the mail-order swindle in the columns of such magazines.

ARRANT ADVERTISING

It would be difficult to get anyone in advertising to admit that advertising generally is a monumental fraud. What swindler would so foolishly cut his own throat? But the admission is frequently made by sideline critics. Dr. Robert O. Schulze, Dean of the College, Brown University, in a recent address before a meeting of the Association of National Advertisers, Inc., stated that one of the functions of advertising is to provide "antiinformation . . . antireality" and to create and perpetuate myths. When we consider the fact that the ANA represents nearly two hundred of the world's largest advertisers, it is surprising that Dr. Schulze was not beatified.

"We have long known," he said, "that advertising was no simple or straightforward venture. We need misinformation, we need illusion," continued the Dean, expanding on his theme. "And much of contemporary advertising addresses itself to this need, to our need to be misled not only about products and services—how superior they are—but about ourselves—how successful, popular, handsome, beautiful, good we are or may become—and about life— how simple it is, how friendly, how full of pleasure and gustos and rewards."

Advertising, Dr. Schulze said, "sensitizes us to the fact

that our world is a highly manipulative one and that getting along for many of us these days more and more involves the ability to manipulate, to sell, perhaps to con our children, our associates, our wives and husbands or subordinates and superordinates, and perhaps—most of all—ourselves." In the vernacular of the swindler, we need to con ourselves and everyone around us, and advertising is a big help.

Just don't try to play any tricks with the English language—they might backfire. Witness what happened to a used car dealer of Bristol, Connecticut. The man who was the head of the agency, advertised a 1962 Pontiac Tempest for "1,395 bananas." Bananas are okay for eating, and in conversation "bananas" may mean "bucks"—but "bananas" means "bananas" when in print and not accompanied by the dollar sign. An astute lady read the ad and brought in a down payment of twenty-five bananas. The agency refused to accept the tender. She took her complaint to the Connecticut Consumer Protection Department. She got action. Several days later, the agency accepted her payment and gave her the keys to the automobile.

There is nothing new about consumer rackets; they've been popular among swindlers for thousands of years. The main difference between the old-time swindler and the modern expert in this field is the difference in the market. In the old days, people expected the seller to be crooked. He was even admired for it, as we said earlier. Today, with every angle covered by laws and regulations, with trade and weights and quality controlled by law, the unwitting public is lulled into the assumption that all sellers are honest, if for no other reason than that they are *supposed* to be. Thus, a benevolent government has done a good turn for the swindler, one that all the con men working together couldn't have done for themselves. Uncle has lulled the gulls to sleep, and all the noise from the BBB's, the C of

C's, the business protective associations, and law-enforcement agencies only barely disturbs the siesta.

A bona fide bargain is one of the rarest things ever encountered. Generally, one pays for what one gets in this world, and the only people who get something for nothing are the swindlers. If you are in the business of merchandising anything, you know that a bargain to be a bargain must profit both parties to the deal. The seller must earn a profit; the buyer must get value or values over and above his cost. The best illustration of this fact can be found in the merchandising of household appliances.

The rebuilt vacuum cleaner advertised for $10.95 is not the bargain it appears to be. Assuming that a new one of the same make would cost about $100, the rebuilt one should, at the price advertised, give about 10 per cent of the value, service, and efficiency of the new one. And it probably would. But the customer looking for a bargain vacuum cleaner expects the percentage to be higher—nearer the values offered in the new model. If he bought it, then, he would be gypped, for the advertising leads him to believe that he is getting a bargain. However, there is more to such advertising than that.

Try to buy the "rebuilt Hoover for only $10.95" or the "reconditioned Singer Sewing Machine for $1 down." The student of swindling practices will immediately see the bait involved. The salesman will show you the machine advertised, but what he has to say about it is not very complimentary. He may even come right out and tell you it's a lemon.* "I wouldn't want to unload a thing like that onto

* One enterprising outfit rang up half a million dollars with a come-on gimmick that advertised a sewing machine for $29.50. During a nineteen-month period when this great bargain was offered to the public, 26 of the bait machines were sold, whereas 3,584 higher-priced models, averaging about $150 per machine, were unloaded on the suckers.

someone nice like you," he says. Gradually he wins your confidence and works up your desire for something better. "And we can let you have it for a price you can afford." And though you probably won't remember, what you came in for was the rebuilt job for $10.95.

A piano company in the mid-west, one of the city's oldest and most reliable houses, once hired a high-pressure crew to drag in the customers during a certain depressed period. Under a real hotshot "field manager," teen-age boys were trained to go door to door with this story and action. Each was instructed to knock politely and, when someone came to the door, to smile, glance at a paper held in one hand, and say, "Good morning. Is Mr. Harquort at home?"

"No. There's no one here by that name," the house-holder would answer (naturally, since the name was coined or picked because of its rarity).

The boy was to register disappointment, then go through the business of verifying the number of the house, the name of the street, and say, "Are you sure Mr. Harquort doesn't live here?"

By this time the occupant of the house would be curious enough to ask, "What's it all about?"

"Oh, I'm from the No Strings Piano Company, you know, the best piano made? Mr. Harquort purchased a piano from us and made all the payments but the last one. We haven't heard from him for several months, so that fine piano is about to be sold for the balance due on his contract. Some lucky person will get a piano for peanuts. It's a shame I can't find Mr. Harquort."

If the sucker showed any interest at all, the next pitch included the offer of a company limousine to take the party downtown to see the piano in question. No obligation, of course.

No Strings was not in the business of selling repossessed

or battered old upright pianos. What it did have to sell was a stock of fine new player grands, a novelty item on which the profit was enormous. So anyone who came in to see Mr. Harquort's piano would be taken in hand by a crackerjack salesman, who would lead him down a long row of shiny new pianos to a dingy storeroom at the back. There, with a supercilious gesture, the salesman would point to an old piano. "That's it," he would say. "I don't think you want anything like that." Then the hauteur would change to a polite intimacy. "You appear to be a person of taste. I'm sure you like the finer things of life. Do you by chance enjoy fine music?"

Who the hell could say no to that?

"Let me show you something I know you will appreciate. Since you've made the long trip down here, let me give you a few moments of real pleasure." A demonstration of the new electric player grand would follow, and if the prospect had any money at all the salesman would get it.

The only thing unusual about this gimmick (for it is still in use, in variations, today) was the choice of the unusual name Harquort to hang the opener on. It was not in the St. Louis telephone directory, and no one during the training period was told what to do should they actually encounter someone with that name, because it just wasn't probable.

The trick of double-talk, borrowed from vaudeville, is now part of the training in what the Better Business Bureau calls "baitvertising." Anyone needing instruction in the art of hooking suckers should read the advertisements for cheap "factory-rebuilt" television sets, "AGA-approved" gas furnaces at one-third the regular price, "refinished" furniture, and slipcover "bargains." Only the swindler or the baitvertiser knows what these terms really mean.

The old referral scheme, in this classification, is one of the easiest gimmicks to work on the gullible. A convincing salesman in this racket can disarm the most prudent buyer. He begins by telling the sucker how he can get something for nothing by participating in an "advertising" campaign. He claims that through a person-to-person advertising plan, the prospect's water softener, garbage disposal, vacuum cleaner, automobile—you name it—will be "free."

"If I can show you how you can have this equipment in your home without paying for it and even show you how you can earn extra money besides, would you take it?"

Then the salesman goes into the pitch recommended in one sales manual on "Referral Selling." He begins by quoting the total amount of money spent on advertising in the United States. He then breaks this down into the amount spent on razor-blade advertising, tobacco advertising, cosmetic and patent-medicine advertising, and so on. By the time he has broken it down to a pack of cigarettes, where "the manufacturer gets nine cents, and four cents of that covers his cost of materials and manufacturing, and the other five cents is for advertising," the dupe begins to see the importance of advertising. But, the salesman says, polls have shown that despite this tremendous expenditure, the best advertising after all is by word of mouth. One customer tells another about the wonderful bargain he got in a certain item.

"Why, it is worth the price of this product just to have you tell all your friends about it." Therefore, if the prospect will "refer" the salesman (*i.e.*, give the salesman the names and addresses of friends who might want to buy the product), the prospect will receive a commission on all the sales made through his referral.

By this time the gullible prospect gets the picture, but he doesn't see all the details, and one of these, naturally, is the paper he signs making him an "advertising agent" of the company. But the paper is a sales contract, and the "little deposit to guarantee faith" is a deposit on the full purchase price. The commissions he will get from the referral list will depend on the honesty of the company and the number of gullible people who bite the same way he did. Shades of chain-letter days!

The "sacrifice sale," "fire sale," "going-out-of-business sale," and similar distress sales, where goods are marked up two or three times their worth so that they can be "marked down to half," still fool the bargain hunter.

The swindle-minded merchant knows that in every transaction there are several stages or points at which a fraud can be perpetrated and a buck made. The obvious, of course, are the crooked pricing angles, trade-in shake-downs, and high-profit financing. The less obvious are the guarantee gyps. Assuming that a retailer is selling TV sets, for instance, who is responsible for repairs if a set breaks down within the guarantee's time limit—the store or the manufacturer? Will the dealer replace the entire set, or will it simply be repaired? Will the entire cost of repairs be covered by the guarantee or just the parts? Will the merchant make the customer pay labor costs and other charges? How dissatisfied does the customer have to be before he benefits from a "satisfaction-or-your-money-back" guarantee? If the set is guaranteed only for "normal" use, who's to say what is "normal?"

Congress is contemplating a bill that would put a slight crimp in the swindling opportunities involved in guarantees. But factions against restraint-of-trade legislation may lobby this one out of existence or at least stymie action until some compromise is agreed on. Meanwhile, appliance dealers are making hay, stacks of it, on guarantee gyps.

MODERN ANTIQUES

The real authentic antique is such a rare item in today's market that when one does actually appear, the swindling dealer may be reluctant to handle it. Unless he is able to make an exorbitant profit, he will not be interested. If he is interested, it presupposes that he discovers the antique item in the hands of someone who does not know its real value or who, because of some distress, must sell it at a very low price. But such lucky finds do not occur every day, and the average antique dealer, determined to make a quick fortune, whatever his particular line, must deal in "modern antiques." If he wants volume, then he must actually specialize in fakes. And for all practical purposes, the specialist in this business must be considerably more knowledgeable than the "honest" dealer. The swindler knows that knowledge is profit and that honesty is another name for ignorance.

And who can call whom a faker? Can the cabinetmaker who produces a perfect copy of a colonial Townsend be criticized? The fine English styles that colonial American families of means bought new were adaptations of Chippendale and Queen Anne furniture. Townsend's designs were simpler perhaps, yet they were elegant enough for colonial mansions. Modern copies are better made, and so from a practical point of view they are a better value, so where is the swindle? It is in the price people are willing to pay to be hoodwinked into thinking they have an original.

It takes considerably more art, more talent, more craftsmanship and know-how to manufacture and merchandise furniture fakes than it does to buy and sell genuine antiques. Frequently more skill is necessary in making the copy than was employed in the original. This is particularly true of eighteenth-century furniture, which brings very high prices. In former times, craftsmen used tools and materials that had no standardization or uniformity. Lumber was cut either in their own sawpits or by the local waterpower sawmill, and each sawyer had his own ideas about widths and lengths. The modern furniture maker trying to duplicate that lumber in a market that supplies only standard widths and lengths has his problems. If the old-timer needed a thirty-inch-wide board for a tabletop or chest end, he had it cut that wide. But where can a furniture maker today get such a board? He ends up joining several narrower boards together. And as for thickness in drawers, walls, and so on, the old-time craftsman never bothered to attain the uniformity that modern makers cannot avoid without considerable trouble.

Large knots in lumber are difficult to work; they are harder than the surrounding wood, and they do not season evenly with the rest of the board. The old-time craftsman, therefore, avoided them. But knotty pine is popular today, and the modern faker can get by with "antiques" covered with knots.

Finish is another problem. Old-fashioned paint and homemade varnish are difficult to copy with modern tools and commercial finishes. Patina, the tone a wood surface acquires over a period of many years, can also be a problem. But modern science has developed chemical formulas —many of them secret—for reproducing the patina of age.

One method, though not so new, calls for burying the piece in the muck under a manure pile for several months. Dug up and dried out and warped in the hot sunlight, the wood will look as if it is a century or two old.

In earlier days, rounds such as posts and legs were never perfectly round, so the modern antique maker must turn his wood with studied carelessness to duplicate the old. He must also keep in mind the fact that brasses were always put in place *before* the job was finished and painted. Only the most adroit will know how to duplicate authentic touches of wear. The stretchers on tavern tables, the front rungs of old chairs, chair legs, and chair finials, and drawer runners must all look properly worn. Duplicating wormholes is no problem, though if bird shot is used, the craftsman should remove the lead pellets.

If it is so much trouble to make a fake, why does the swindler bother? Because he has two advantages not available to the old-time craftsman: (1) modern assembly-line production methods; (2) a bigger, more gullible market. When the lords and ladies in the court of Louis XV wanted something to sit on, they bought a chair. When Mr. and Mrs. Jones want a chair, they buy a period piece. The Joneses are more interested in displaying it than in sitting in it.

The fine art of faking may be said to be developed to a very high plane indeed when the wood craftsman turns his hand successfully to the counterfeiting of "name" violins. When Antonio Stradivari died in Cremona, Italy, in 1737, he left behind him an estimated eleven hundred masterfully constructed stringed instruments. What with time's attrition, only about six hundred remain today. Yet, nearly every violin virtuoso, concertmaster, and well-heeled amateur in the world owns a "genuine" Strad. The supply, while never plentiful, has surprisingly never been exhausted. And what with Strads selling for up to $30,000, the faker is a real artist who can turn out a copy that will command anywhere near that price.

The one thing that the modern copy craftsman must always guard against, if he is to be successful, is originality. It is well known that whole tribes of American Indians make a fair livelihood from the manufacture of artifacts for the growing market among collectors and museums. And the most successful pieces, naturally, are those that most resemble those dug up by archaeologists. But when a flood of highly unusual Indian artifacts came out of Oklahoma recently, the experts became wary. Investigation disclosed that the objects did not imitate genuine tribal artifacts at all, but appeared in highly eccentric and often fantastic forms. The artist, influenced by education and inspired by the lucrative market, could not resist the temptation to originate.

Tourists have always been prime suckers for cons of every kind, particularly antique swindles. The age of tourism—that is, the period when individuals began to travel for pleasure and sight-seeing rather than in expeditions bent on exploration and colonization—began when transportation made travel as comfortable as the home environment. In the history of transportation, this occurred around the turn of the century. It coincided, too, with the birth of a large middle class, flush with new wealth and avid for culture. Since the antiquities of Europe soon were generally available, tourists came to think that antiques had to be Egyptian to be worthwhile. And when the tourist had well begun his active tours in Egypt, it was manifest that there would soon be lucre in them for the native. The reason, of course, was that the tourist wanted to buy things. He had to convince the people at home that he had really "been there," visited bazaars, penetrated into the desert, and made free with the tombs of the Pharaohs. He had heard, or he came to know, that relics were about; but the "relics" he bought were probably made when the craftsman saw him coming.

ARCHITECTS OF ARSON

In any study of fire as an instrument of swindling, one must note the ironies involved in this as in all other swindling gimmicks. Fire, the one pure element of the ancients, has always had its impure and dishonest uses. Fire, the great reagent of the ancient alchemists, by which man was to gain the secret of high fortune and lasting life, has always been as useful in the hands of Benny-the-Bake, Firebug Freddy, and all the other arson artists since Satan was invented. The educated swindler should know that the fire fraud has a history as long and as full of fateful twists as that of any other gimmick in the catalog of human deceptions. A vignette or two will illustrate what we mean.

In the fall of 1753, Captain John Lancey was ordered to proceed from Bideford, England, to the colony of Maryland with a ship well laden with bricks. He raised his hook and sail, dropped lazily down the Torridge River, and headed west toward that mysterious region of wild redskins and undreamed-of malevolence. At sundown the young skipper stood on his bridge, his knees quaking with something less than confidence. He was embarked on a swindle with no prior experience, sailing toward the Colonies, which he knew he would never see, and away from his England, fading in the distance and dusk.

At eight o'clock there was an explosion belowdecks. The upper parts of the vessel, thoroughly dried out from months in port, fired like straw. Belowdecks the sea flowed in through a great gash the powder had opened in the ship's belly. The cargo of bricks bore her swiftly down.

After some agonizing moments, Captain Lancey got the lifeboat launched and all hands safely aboard. They reached port the following day, and Lancey reported to his brother-in-law and employer, one Benson, a Member of Parliament. Benson sent his captain to a court official, before whom he swore that the firing had been accidental and that nothing could have availed to save the ship or her cargo. Benson left England for a tour of the Continent, and Lancey stayed behind.

A little later, through the tattle of some idle tongue, the captain and his rich relative became suspect, and investigation showed that Benson had laden his ship with a cargo of merchandise for America, insured the vessel and her contents for twice the honest value, and later secretly had the goods removed and the ship filled with bricks for ballast. He had commanded Captain Lancey to take her out to sea and set her afire. The young man had declined, until Benson pointed out that it was within his power to discharge and disgrace the seaman. Then Lancey had complied, setting fire to his own ship by means of an explosive mechanism that rapidly spread the fire.

Benson fled, but his dupe, the young captain, was tried, sentenced, and hanged. We mention this melancholy end to show what frequently happens to men of honor, honesty, and the other virtues common to ignorance.

The story itself shows the antiquity of arson for profit, a swindle that has always been easy, but John Lancey was not the first man to burn a ship or a house to get the insurance. Indeed, this swindle must be as old as insuring, which is nearly as old as trading. Commercial fire insurance gained headway after the great London fire of 1666, though the guilds had provided similar protection much earlier. More than likely, Shakespeare's Antonio came into dour Shylock's grip through the need of a premium for marine insurance—to cover those delayed argosies bound for Tripolis, the Indies, and Mexico.

Purposeful fires among merchants and building owners became so common in America that insurance companies eventually joined forces and set up investigative bureaus to combat the swindle. Though our daily press continually plays up the protection afforded the public by the fire marshals and arson investigators, any fire buff knows that arson is still the biggest insurance swindle in this country.

According to a recent summary from the American Insurance Association, about 20 per cent of all fire claims are possible frauds. In the New York area, for the twelve months ending May, 1965, some 758 of 3,478 fires (22 per cent) were found to be possible frauds, to the tune of $34,-500,000. How many the authorities actually suspect but cannot designate "possible," no one will say. Even the top authorities admit the impossibility of creating a valid statistical record of arson cases. The total number of fires is known, and some pretty good guesses can be made as to the number of accidental, cause unknown, origin undetermined, suspicious, and proven incendiary fires, but arson is so difficult to detect that every man's guess is his own. Our guess, influenced by a suspicious nature, is that at least 50 per cent of this nation's fires are profitable to someone, and such "profits" are rarely accidental. Our own estimate of the annual toll by torches (professional arsonists) would be more than 25 per cent of the nation's fires; another 50 per cent were set by amateurs working alone, 2 per cent were set by pyromaniacs, and the remaining 23 per cent were possible accidents.

Typical of the thousands of arson swindles that occur in this country every year was that of the grocer who occupied the ground floor of an old building on the Bowery in New York. An outside stairway ran to the second floor, where a Syrian artist lived with his wife and children. In the basement of the premises was an old-fashioned hot-air furnace, the pipes from which ran to registers in both floors.

A little after eleven o'clock on a cold night during a recent winter, the wife of the artist awoke and smelled a strong odor of gasoline. She hesitated for a few minutes, but as the odor grew in heaviness, she threw on her clothes and started for her husband, who was at a meeting in the neighborhood. Just as she opened the door, he came in and recoiled from the gas fumes. He went downstairs immediately and, not without some suspicion, forced his way into the grocery store. Just as he did so, he saw a shadowy figure retreat to the alley and drive off in an automobile, which had been parked there with the lights out.

On a shelf inside the store, the Syrian found a five-gallon water cooler with the spigot turned so slightly open that the contents dripped from it drop by drop. Underneath this device were piled two cases of matches. In the center of the floor stood two galvanized tubs half-filled with gasoline. Altogether, some twenty gallons of gasoline had been provided for the fire.

The Syrian turned off the gasoline-dripping faucet, opened the doors and windows to allow the fumes to escape, and set off for the grocer's home, a few blocks away. There, to his surprise, he found a celebration going on.

The grocer's baby son had been christened, and among the guests at the party were the local-precinct captain of police, some other city officials, and a few politicians, among whom the grocer ranked himself. The grocer tried to put the artist off, first with one excuse and then with another. Finally the Syrian's importunities reached the ears of the policeman, who decided his public duty was somewhat more urgent than his social obligations. He entered the shop and found the arrangements all set for a quick, disastrous fire.

Two errors got the grocer in trouble: (1) he planned to set fire to a building that contained people and thus became vulnerable to a murder rap; (2) his was a purely amateurish approach to pyro-swindling. The professional in such a swindle would never stoop to murder, and he would prepare his fire-setting apparatus with such care that it would not only burn down the building but also destroy all evidences of having been purposely set.

Arson swindles are the easiest to perpetrate and the easiest to hide. The tool of the arsonist is a match, the one thing most commonly found—after keys and money—in women's handbags and men's pockets. And there is no law against possession.

The matches-bound-about-a-cigarette technique, with the heads of the matches placed at a measured point from the cigarette's lighted end, is often used where the torch needs time to get away from the scene. Matches are often used in such mechanical hookups as the telephone torch. Matches are taped to the ringing mechanism with a piece of sandpaper. They can be set off by a long-distance call. Candles as a timing device and automatic fire-setting apparatus have been used for centuries.

Arsonists with a knowledge of chemistry use certain acids in a releasing device to ignite a combination of chemicals and cause "spontaneous combustion." The water-and-phosphorus ignition devices that have been invented over the years have set more fires than anyone can count. Any chemical that ignites upon contact with water can be triggered by the flushing of a toilet, rain on a leaky roof, the diversion of plumbing, or a dripping faucet.

Gas is one of the most common fire-setting agents in house destruction. Gas from an ordinary jet left open and unlit on a stove in a closed room will build up enough pressure to be exploded by the pilot light.

One arsonist, who had been an animal trainer for the Barnum & Bailey Circus, trained cats to play with the dangling chain of a gas jet. When the chain was pulled, the gas would go on or off, and the cats learned to amuse themselves with this and to use it as a signal for food. The trainer made up special shipping cases that contained a trained cat and a kit with all the connections for rigging a gas-jet explosion. He sold the cat and kit to anyone who wanted to start a fire and called the combination, appropriately, a Pyrokit.

Electrical systems, including telephone and doorbell circuits, electrical appliances, and wiring that can spark and ignite combustible material are all tools of the expert arsonist. A simple alarm clock, a little wire, and a small battery in the hands of an expert torch can work holocaustic wonders.

It is general knowledge that grass and forest fires have been caused by sunrays magnified by old glass bottles. Arsonists have used shaving mirrors, bottles, magnifying glasses, and windowpanes to rig fire-setting devices that have proved infallible in a wide range of incendiaries.

The scientific fact that fires may originate spontaneously in certain materials under special circumstances was discovered long before it became general knowledge. It wasn't until the universal acceptance of science and scientific methods of study that the term "spontaneous combustion" became popular. Swindlers were quick to adopt the term and eagerly devised a variety of fire-setting techniques to simulate the phenomenon, designed to burn up both the property and the evidence of arson. The tricks employed during the 1920's and in the depths of the Great Depression of the 1930's were frequently crude and amateurish and, in light of today's practices, often ludicrous.

One method of simulating a natural outbreak of fire was to pack an old barrel half full of oil waste and start a tiny spark burning in the middle. The pyro then packed the barrel full and tight with old clothes, greasy papers, and similar materials. The little fire in the center of the greasy waste would smolder for six hours or for sixty, depending on the density of the packing and the air vents in the barrel. Finally, however, it would burst into wild flame and set off anything within reach.

Such spontaneous-combustion barrels were often employed by dry-goods and clothing merchants. The barrel was prepared with its spark and put into the rear of the store, where windows were kept open to carry off the odor of the smudge and provide a draft for the fire. The arsonist knew, of course, approximately how many hours had to elapse before the inflammation. Usually he waited for a weekend. He closed his shop at dusk on Saturday and went about his pleasure, not forgetting, of course, to sprinkle a little gasoline about near the smoldering barrel or to hang up coats, dresses, curtains, packing cases, and all sorts of loose combustibles where the first flames would reach them. Hours later, the smudge in the barrel broke into flame, and the fire spread quickly to everything near. The store was gutted in a few minutes, generally before the fire department got the alarm.

Though there was an occasional misfire, spontaneous combustion became so popular among firebugs that the inevitable evolved: the organized arson ring. Such cliques of fire specialists soon were operating in all parts of the country, and a whole new argot came into use.

Today the arson ring may consist of the fire insurance agent, the insurance inspector, the merchant or property owner, the expert fire setter, and the insurance adjuster. The owner wants to have a fire. He contacts the crooked agent, who writes him a policy for far more than the value of the stock. The crooked inspector goes over the property and approves the risk. In a little while the professional arsonist comes along, removes the best of the stock, and rigs a device to burn the property. The owner is conveniently away on a vacation, but he returns in haste, however, once his property is gutted, and puts in a howling complaint to the insurance agent. Now the interesting part of the comedy is played.

The crooked agent, who originally wrote the policy, sends the claim to his company with the recommendation that it be paid, as the loss is complete and the owner a worthy man. The claim is passed to the adjuster, who proceeds to make an examination. His business is to find fraud if any exists, but in this case he makes it his business to overlook suspicious details. He reports to the company that the fire was bona fide, that the loss was complete, and that payment should be made. The owner gets his money promptly and divides it with the other members of the ring. Simplicity and precision are the virtues of this plan of action. It is applied to many other types of insurance.

The ring that specialized in buying up unoccupied, dilapidated tenements and warehouses and then burning them to collect big insurance payments was most successful. This ring began in New York City, and similar rings soon formed in other cities. Today there is not a community anywhere that does not have its specialists in this field or its links with the larger rings. One Brooklyn fire-insurance broker boasted to his clients that he was able to "guarantee a fire with every policy" he wrote.

It has become such a monstrous business that the Attorney General recently asked Congress to add arson to the list of Federal racketeering crimes. He said the proposal is aimed at fighting increasing interstate "fire-for-hire" operations. There is growing evidence, he said, that organized-crime groups are using arson specialists to make millions of dollars a year in insurance.

The argot common among such architects of arson is explicit. The "pyro" is the psychopathic fire setter. He sets fires "to watch the fun" or "to get even," rarely for financial profit. We do not classify him as a swindler. The "torch," the professional fire setter, understands the techniques of setting a fire without leaving telltale evidence of incendiarism. In an arson ring, it is this individual's job to set the mechanism and trigger the fire. A "touch-off" is a deliberately set fire, and a "plant" is the combustible material placed about the ignition device; together they form a "setup." "Boosters" are part of the plant; they help spread the fire. Kerosene and gasoline are typical boosters. The "brain" in an arson ring is the head swindler. The "salesman" finds the customer who wants a job done.

The professional torch knows how difficult it is to set a fire that will obliterate all evidences of incendiarism. The smart swindler today is aware of the development of laboratory facilities and techniques such as the spectrograph, the ultraviolet light, the infrared ray, and the vacuum-distillation process. Any one of these or all together can be used to find evidence of arson.

Most fire setters, however, are amateurs, with whom we

have no patience. On the other hand, to the true professional, the torch, a good incendiary job is one that destroys all evidence and enough property to pay handsomely. The dabbler and the dilettante, regardless of their profits, may set most of the incendiary fires, but they employ so little talent that one can learn nothing from them.

It is significant that arson and depression have much in common. The great waves of fires for profit that have swept across the land have coincided with the major economic depressions. All the Gay Nineties vaudeville jokes about the prosperous merchants who specialized in fire sales— before and after the fire—had their origins in fact. The depression of 1893 to 1897 was one of the worst in the nation's history. It was exceeded only by the slump of the 1930's, when all the old chestnuts about arson swindles were dusted off and retold. "Did your friend's business fail?" the straight man would ask. "No," the comic would reply. "He had a successful fire."

That was the theory—business down, fire frauds up— but economists and fire underwriters are not able to measure present trends by that yardstick. Today, in the booming American economy of the sixties, arson swindles are at a twenty-five-year high and appear to be increasing. Why this countertrend? The economists and the fire-insurance people have a variety of answers, but all of them smack of pure guesswork. Knowing swindlers and the psychology of swindling, we'd say the trend hasn't changed but business has. We may not be in the midst of a general depression in this era of the soaring sixties, but for hundreds of thousands of small businessmen, trapped between high taxes and cutthroat competition, and for some big businessmen, caught in a squeeze play between tight money and loose morals, a successful fire is the only solution. Thus the increase in fires is more an indication of a changing pattern of business than of a general economic depression.

And though business patterns have their day and problems change from era to era, a profitable fire will remain the answer as long as insurance companies are willing to gamble. That which was the solution during the depressions of the nineties and thirties is the alternative to bankruptcy in the sixties. The recent Great Fur Fire of Beverly Hills* may have been inspired by New York City's famous Dachis case, as an earlier fur fire was known in the press of its day.

One could not have picked a locale more appropriate to the plot of the Dachis story. Twenty-seventh Street between Seventh and Eighth Avenues** was badly in need of a good fire. Some of the streets in the neighborhood gave the appearance of having growing pains. They were not entirely developed, but they looked ambitious, thriving, and prosperous for the times. This particular street, however, seemed to give the impression of arrested development. It looked as though no attempt had ever been made to resurrect it from the mire of decadence.

On the Eighth Avenue corner was a mansion dating from the early 1860's, its mansard roof revealing loose tiles, with a tin chimney pipe stuck incongruously over one point. It was occupied by a Greek café on one floor and a secondhand clothes shop on another. The old private stable to the east, toward Seventh, which in the days of its glory had housed proud horses and smart phaetons and broughams, with shining silver harnesses hanging neatly on the walls, had become, by 1930, a grimy coffee shop. There were other old houses along the street, but their rooms had

---

* Since this one has been pretty well hushed up and the final settlement pending or not known, we must avoid definite labels and accurate figures.

** The area is still the fur capital of the world; eight out of ten fur garments in the United States and seven out of ten in the world are made there.

long since been converted into cheap lofts. Mostly the street was a conglomeration of five-story tenements and a few dingy taller buildings with ground floors occupied by cheap shops.

This was the scene on Sunday, July 28, 1929, for one of the biggest fire swindles in the history of New York. Business had been bad for the wholesale fur houses occupying the old building at number 213 West Twenty-seventh Street. So bad, in fact, for Louis Dachis and his brother, Jacob, that they decided to change the course of their lives. They would hire a torch to wipe out the past, collect nearly a quarter of a million dollars in insurance, which they had placed with some twenty different companies, and start life anew.

They never quite realized their ambition because of one small miscalculation: the torch they hired did not know how to destroy furs and raw skins without creating a foul odor. Joe Eisenstein, who enjoyed a long career as "Doc," was the torch hired for this job. He prided himself especially on his knowledge of chemistry. He had worked out a secret formula for a highly inflammable fluid that left no suspicious trace or odor after it had been used, but he overlooked the odoriferous qualities of burning furs. It would have been easy enough to burn down any of the old buildings on Twenty-seventh Street, but one cannot create a neighborhood stink without the neighbors' objections. And when the stench becomes so bad that it interferes with sleep, the police and the fire department are soon alerted.

The professional swindler knows that the most promising community for the expert arsonist is one in which the public has been lulled into a sense of security. For instance, new arson laws are on the books of most cities, and where law enforcement is strict and properly (i.e., favorably) publicized, the public rests assured that its agents are

awake and watchful. That the local force may be under-
staffed, underpaid, and undereducated in the field of fire
detection does not concern it. If the daily press says that
local law enforcement is adequate and efficient, that's all
the public wants to know. There's no threat of increased
taxes in applause and approbation. Only the insurance
companies are aware of the truth and the facts, and they
offset any defects by increased insurance rates. They aren't
going to say much about local law enforcement for fear
that the public might wake up to the better bargain it would
get if its money went for taxes instead of premiums.

FUR ENOUGH

Not all swindles in the fur business occur in the retail
shops (or via arson). Actually, the ultimate buyer of a fur
coat or stole or cape may be only the last dupe in a long
chain of swindles that began with the trapper or breeder.
The tricks these men pull to unload their skins on the
regional dealers and first buyers would fill a book. Pelts are
examined for quality, size, color, and primeness, and they
are paid for on the basis of these ratings. Buyers for the big
fur houses know most of the tricks, but unless vigilance is
eternal and constant they are likely to find some poorly
furred stuff has been sandwiched in among goods of first
quality. The raw-fur trade is full of stories about dyed pelts,
pelts with ragged holes, and skins with the fur worn off for
which the processing house paid top prices.

Whatever the swindle at this stage, one can be assured

that the processing house raises the ante when the furs are tanned and dyed and sold to the manufacturer. And when the manufacturer completes the article, one can be sure that enough fakery has gone into it that whatever the customer pays for it, he is really buying a piece of art as much as a fur coat.

What with the Federal Trade Commission breathing down the back of every retailer in the fur business, the ways of the swindler in this field would appear limited. But fur is a product about which the public is completely ignorant, and so long as this condition exists, furriers will have their day. Actually, the field is wide open, with plenty of room for the sharp operator to maneuver.

The FTC's Labeling Act says that any fur product that sells for more than $7 must carry a label no smaller than one and three-quarter by two and three-quarter inches that states these key facts: the true English name of the fur; whether the fur has been bleached or dyed or left "natural"; the country of origin; whether the fur is secondhand or damaged; the parts of the pelt used; alterations of the fur. To get all this within the space of a mink's ear means that one must use fine print. What matter, when the dye job is good and when a $2,000 mink coat can be made to look like a $4,000 coat? Or even when rabbit labeled "rabbit" is made to look like Arctic seal? The customer will remove the label and pass off the $2,000 coat as a $4,000 coat or the rabbit as Arctic seal. Thus is the swindle perpetuated that may have begun with the trapper.

The larcenous furrier, therefore, abiding by all the laws, still has this advantage: his customers are gullible or dishonest or both. Listen to any woman talk about her stole and you may wonder whether she means the word derived from the Latin *stola* ("robe") or the past tense of another.

Furs were prehistoric man's first real clothes, but over the centuries the craze for fur as a status symbol grew, until its practical use was far exceeded by its glamorizing possibilities. Thus has vanity, combined with gullibility and guile, produced an endless line of customers for the fraudulent furrier. If the individual merchant can't net $100,000 a year in the business, he isn't trying.

7

SEX AND SALUBRITY SWINDLES

promoting health

WOMEN are the same all over, and their ids haven't changed much since Eve. Men haven't changed much either, so the relationship between the sexes has remained a fairly constant denominator, despite refinements that beat Adam's apple munching.

An early statement of the equation was the Reverend Thomas Malthus' decorous postulate that "the passion between the sexes is necessary and will remain so." Today, 165 years after Malthus' momentous rhetoric, we can detect no deviation in the demand of either for the other. Women still adorn, compress, pad, paint, cut, and trim their bodies to conform to whatever patterns of beauty are supposed to be most admired by men at the moment. And men still play the cock, strutting their hour upon the stage for the same ends.

Thus, though the mores of love have undergone change, and more revolutions than historians have counted, the one constant factor has been that body beautification has remained the first exercise of the seduction impulse.

Swindlers have always considered this human foible

limitless in its vulnerable points, not the least of which is the fact that women spend most of the money that is spent in the pursuit of this exercise. Women may claim that the hair they pull out and the hair they pin on have nothing to do with their natural desire to attract men, that all their improvements on nature are a satisfaction of their aesthetic instincts, but the record and the psychologists prove the fallacy in their contention. The astute swindler, too, knows it for what it is—rank self-delusion; and delusion being his main resource, any self-help is welcome.

Another asset never discounted by the swindler is secrecy. Subtlety, of course, is the key to a successful projection of the sex image; and subtlety, as every swindler knows, involves the enforcement of secrecy.

Indeed, a brief analysis of the most vulnerable points should prove educational and perhaps profitable to the novitiate in the school for swindlers.

No figures are available to show the annual take in the cosmetics industry, and they would be out of date before we could print them anyway, but the total must run into billions of dollars. Surely, if we include a few items not generally considered cosmetics but classified under beautification expenses—such as hair dye, shampoo, wigs, curlers, pins, and other hair accessories; the endless list of mechanical devices used in the application and removal of cosmetics; the services of clerks, beauticians, and barbers; and cosmetic surgery on wrinkles, noses, ears, and bosoms —then the figure becomes roughly $4,000,000,000.

This would just about cover Webster's definition of a cosmetic: "Any external application intended to beautify and improve the complexion, skin, or hair." Now add to this the hidden adjuncts to beauty: the pads, the falsies, the foundation garments; the special diets, medicines, and elixirs; and all the literature on the subject. This addition alone nearly doubles the first figure.

But we can't stop there or the clothing industry will feel slighted. And the manufacturers of mechanical exercisers, the sports-equipment people, the health resorts, the million-dollar beauty resorts, and the fat-and-fortune reducing salons also get their share. Just for brevity's sake, let us round the figure off at $10,000,000,000.

To satisfy the human female's aesthetic instinct? Only the naive could delude themselves into thinking that, for little of this expenditure aids in the satisfaction of any instinct except the natural one of seduction. Nevertheless, if all this accomplished the ends toward which it is aimed and all the nation's females enjoyed a happy consummation of their sexual drives, one might consider it money well spent. But it doesn't, and they don't. Much of this is fruitless expense. Much of it is a swindle. How much would have to be another guess. However, certain details become evident after the most cursory research, and some of these are appalling.

FACE VALUES

It could happen only in America, where the commercial philosophy invites anyone with initiative to enter the marketplace and sell whatever he can—and it need not be a better mousetrap. If it can be artfully enough promoted, it need not work at all.

Considering the limited range of physical effects that

cosmetics can have, one can argue that the purposes of cosmetics are mainly psychological, that if the buyer can be convinced she is benefited by using the product, full value is received. While this reasoning may contain some truth in respect to cosmetics, it is also a justification for any kind of deception—so long as the victim is unaware of it and makes no complaint.

The ethical questions posed by the general acceptance of gross deception in cosmetics promotion need not be considered by the swindler. For his own protection, however, he should consider the physical safety of his customers. An addition to consumer-protection legislation that would require that cosmetics be tested for safety *before* they are marketed is suggested by some as probably the best solution to the safety factor. No one has yet suggested that cosmetics manufacturers be made to guarantee satisfaction or your money back. The psychological swindle, therefore, offers limitless possibilities.

There is some comfort for the consumer in the thought that a mind well supplied with reliable information is less likely to be gullible, but assuming he would take time to read them, where can an intelligent person find unbiased reports on the products he buys? The reports published by the consumer-research groups must cover such a wide-ranging selection of manufactured products that subscribers who support these admirable periodicals are limited to one or two articles on cosmetics a year. Annual surveys (*e.g., The Medicine Show* by Consumers Union editors) are more detailed and helpful, but who reads them? Not many of those who need such information. And despite the prominence of the word in the Federal Food, Drug, and Cosmetic Act, the "protection" afforded consumers of cosmetics under present Federal law is minimal.

We grant that the pursuit of beauty is every woman's

birthright. To help her achieve it, the cosmetics industry offers a dazzling array of excellent, safe products that give the ugliest duckling at least a fighting chance. Unfortunately, a small segment of the same industry has also subjected countless women to unnecessary health and safety hazards. In addition, together with a similarly unscrupulous segment of the "health" industry, it has fleeced them out of millions of dollars yearly. The smart swindler does not have to stoop to such risky practices.

Already the defenders of public morals and the Better Business Bureaus of the country are suggesting counteraction. Three steps, they say, can and should be taken to reduce these health hazards and to make it increasingly difficult for "miracle merchants" to profit from health and beauty rackets: (1) No cosmetic should be placed on the market until the manufacturer has convinced the Food and Drug Administration (FDA) that it is safe. (2) No therapeutic claims should be made for cosmetics until they have been cleared by the FDA. (3) No mechanical devices purporting to aid in the treatment of diseases or to bring about reductions in weight or enlargement of breasts should be offered for sale until the FDA is convinced that they are both safe and effective.

Every swindler knows there is just one hitch in such measures. It is one thing to get legislation passed and quite another to get it enforced. Prohibitory statutes presuppose examination, testing, and fair judgment as the obligation of the government. But we know from experience that enforcement involves many headaches. In a free society, there should be some way around this solution to the problem. Nevertheless, manufacturers are being urged to support some kind of new legislation now, at a time when no great cosmetics scares are affecting the public temper. A cosmetics tragedy of thalidomide proportions might bring on a hasty correction of deficiencies in the law. But precipitous and intemperate legislative reactions might spell disaster for many legitimate cosmetics companies.

But even assuming that all cosmetics would meet FDA safety regulations, the psychological swindle would remain the same. Herein lies the more "honorable" approach. The fakeries involved in the marketing of beauty aids begin with the advertising pitch and continue through the wholesale promotion and the retail sales talks to the final sale. Disillusionment comes only after use, but few women are willing to complain publicly that what they bought didn't make them as beautiful (as seductive) as they had hoped. Indeed, with many, the compulsion is such that they will try any new cosmetic, no matter how blatantly false its promises. It is this complusion that the swindler exploits. Next to self-preservation, the desire for sexual fulfillment is our strongest drive. No wonder it offers a lucrative multitude of inducements to the faker, the swindler, the charlatan, and the quack.

MOTIVATIONS AND MIRACLES

To a gullible and ignorant public swayed by its own desires, almost any lie can be stretched to credibility. To the woman who wants to believe that "our product gives you the effective medications prescribed by leading skin specialists, and clinical tests prove it really works," $4.95 for a four-ounce bottle of the stuff is a bargain. She believes what she desperately wants to believe. Blinded by her frantic desire to "stimulate and revive skin tone and color," she does not see the psychological impact of phrases and words like "clinical" and "medications prescribed by leading skin specialists." That "our product" may be nothing more than a perfumed mixture of cheap corn oil and alcohol is not important. She wants to believe the sales pitch. "That's what it says in the advertisements," or "That's what the saleswoman told me," and that's what counts.

Why? Not because American industry and American ad writers have established any record of honesty and scientific (clinical) tests of the products they manufacture and advertise, but because a clear skin is a fixation of erotic interest in our society, just as black smudges are considered beautiful on the cheeks of Goajiro women and white dots a sign of "availability" on Maori maidens.

The skin game may be only skin deep, but millions of dollars are being made by it. This is "the large area of fraud" recently singled out by FDA Commissioner George P. Larrick: "There is extensive, big-time quackery in the cosmetic field, generally based on the exploitation of some 'miracle' ingredient that is supposed to restore youth and beauty to the unattractive or aging skin."

The FDA recently seized shipments of a famous name brand of skin smoothing lotion because, the FDA said, the labeling gives the middle-aged woman an impression that the preparation is a newly discovered substance that "will immediately and dramatically eliminate all her wrinkles, including crow's-feet, puffy under-eye circles, laugh, frown, smile, and throat lines." The cosmetic firm's president called the government action a "test seizure." A test seizure "does not stop the further sale of our product anywhere," he said. "While this matter is in the courts, all stores now selling our product will continue to do so."

Shipments of two other antiwrinkle creams were seized in

later crackdowns. In all three cases, the government charged that the creams were drugs and were being marketed without a new drug application as required by law. The FDA also charged that the creams falsely claimed permanent change in the skin condition of those using them. Regular applications of the creams "do not provide any permanent benefits," the government charged.

Most reputable scientists would agree no lotion or cream was ever invented that will permanently "erase" or "smooth out" wrinkles in the skin. Despite the nonsense about "miracle formulas" that contain royal jelly, human placenta, plankton, pigskin extract, shark oil, orchid pollen, hormones, polyunsaturates, "biostimulins," or buttermilk, and despite their promises of rejuvenation, no ingredient or combination of ingredients can do more than soothe, smooth, and help make supple a skin roughened by exposure to weather or excessive application of soaps.

There is no such thing as a perfect figure, and no human being has ever had one, but that has not kept society in every age from setting up certain ideals toward which it strives. The ideals and the natural drive to attain them have intrigued philosophers and physicians for thousands of years. The weight-control field has always been a good one for swindlers. Pound for pound, more money is lost every year on reducing fads, formulas, and the dangerous diets dished up by quacks than the weight that all these things are supposed to take off.

The self-styled "obesity specialists" and "reducing doctors" are operating weight-reducing mills to standing room only. To meet local licensing regulations, some of these establishments operate under the pseudonym of "gymnasium"; others call themselves "beauty salons," "health resorts," and "weight clinics." Some have MD's in attendance to lend an air of respectability and confidence. Some are operated by MD's. And the advertising and illustrated brochures they circulate are aimed at a sophisticated, literate market. But the sales pitch they deliver in the confines of their "analysis rooms" smacks of fraud and chicanery. The AMA says: "These practitioners constitute a very serious and growing health menace in all parts of our country."

In the AMA files are many tragic cases. A young West Coast secretary who weighed nearly two hundred pounds took the "drug cure" and actually lost a few pounds. In the course of the treatment she became ill, and within a few days she died. The coroner's report: killed by the reducing drugs. The case has hundreds of duplicates. Dr. Norman Jolliffe, director of New York City's Bureau of Nutrition, once bluntly declared that the MD's who prescribe such treatment without adequate physical examination and proper diagnosis "are a blot on the medical profession, a scandal and a rising menace to health."

The watchful eye of the AMA may inhibit the MD's, but what of the salons and gyms and studios that sell slenderizing via massage and exercise and printed diets? Judging from the popularity they enjoy in every part of the nation, one questions whether they are inhibited by anything short of a murder rap. They offer vibrating pads, electric belts, chemical cushions, massage mattresses, whirlpool baths, and oscillating tables with claims that they will "reduce fatty spots and unsightly bulges," "improve faulty circulation to carry away fatty deposits," "melt away pounds and inches," and "reshape the figure for better health." Some outfits claim they can "correct obesity and abnormal thinness," and they do it with the same gadgets. Strangely, none offers a bona fide money-back guarantee.

Some of the advertising for dentrificies that kill "decay germs" is also misleading and is therefore a part of the great dental swindle. Doctors agree there is no germ that causes decay in the way that the tubercle bacillus, for example, causes tuberculosis. It is probable that micro-organisms in the mouth do play some role in the complex mechanism of tooth decay, but dental science still does not know.

Fluorine added to drinking water and the avoidance of excessive sweets are known to prevent tooth decay, but half the population is convinced that fluoridation of community water supplies is killing us, and the other half can't resist sweets. If the first half is right, then the promoters of fluoridation are guilty of the most fantastic hoax ever perpetrated. In any case, the confusion and the gullibility generated by the arguments over fluoridation prime the public for the hucksters who peddle dentifrices, toothbrushes, and gargles. And anyone who takes advantage of gullibility and makes a profit on a credulous public comes within the scope of our definition of a swindler.

Does anyone remember when hair was "woman's crowning glory" and hair growers were advertised like fertilizers in today's garden catalogs? Many gimmicks for growing hair have been advertised, and all of them have made more money for their promoters than hair for the suckers, but none of them ever exceeded the gimmick or the profit of the seven Sutherland sisters. Sara, Victoria, Mary, Dora, Isabella, Grace, and Naomi had among them the longest hair in the world. The combined length, when they showed it in a Barnum & Bailey act, was thirty-six feet ten inches. Photographs they used in advertising their "secret" hair grower show the seven as rather plain farm girls with luxuriant tresses that reach the ground. Their cascading hair was a freak of nature, of course, but it was the best gimmick ever discovered for selling a hair tonic that was nothing more than water, alcohol, and some coloring. They made millions on the swindle and spent it like untutored country girls would: they lived in an ornate palace and drove horses shod with gold-plated shoes. But the bobbed hair craze of the 1920's put them out of business, and hardly anyone remembered when it was long hair that made women attractive and the Sutherland process another name for "swindle."

Too much hair in the wrong places has been a problem not easily solved by women. A society that accepts as routine any shaving practice by its males prefers avoidance of the same habit by its females. Nevertheless, almost as many women as men do shave or use some depilatory method. Depilatories once offered a rich field for the profit-minded manufacturer, but a tightening of the Federal Food, Drug, and Cosmetic Act put a kink in this hair swindle. Clinical proof that shaving does not affect the rate of growth or the coarseness of hair has had some influence on feminine psychology, so society's attitude toward women shavers is changing. The invention and promotion of electric shavers for women helped. Nevertheless, a few crooks in the field still keep the FDA watchful. The reluctance of most women to prosecute, except in extreme injury cases, makes it a situation difficult to control.

Deodorants and antiperspirants are products frequently confused. Body odors generally are caused by bacterial action on secretions. Obviously, then, there are two ways to approach the prevention of body odors: (1) impede bacterial action; (2) reduce secretions. Deodorants are intended to accomplish the former; antiperspirants may do both. Antiperspirants, since they affect a body function (sweating), are *drugs* under FDA laws. Deodorants are considered *cosmetics*. Drug labels must list ingredients; cosmetic labels don't have to. So the cosmetics field offers more possibilities for the sporting swindler.

THE BOOM BEHIND THE BUST

Throughout history, mankind has accented the areas of the body considered to be erogenous zones. The hair and the skin have suffered a multiplicity of adornments and styles, hands and feet have been mutilated and deformed to change their size and shape, ears and noses and lips have been pierced and hung with ornaments, and even the head has been pressed into the current mold of beauty. Obviously, something stronger than aesthetic impulses has motivated such "improvements" on the handiwork of nature. "The passion between the sexes" was necessary, and any part of the body that could be accented by change or adornment served its erotic purpose.

But of all the erogenous zones, none throughout history has enjoyed the sensuous popularity or the erotic prestige of the mammary glands of the human female. From time immemorial breasts have been the visible, glowing symbol of the female sex and of female beauty and desirability. The bosom has been adored, worshiped, venerated, sanctified, glamorized, glorified, and exalted by every tribe, every race, and every society known to man.

Three thousand years ago, Menelaus (in Homer's *Iliad*) threatened to murder the beautiful Helen because she had been unfaithful to him. But Helen "bared the apples of her bosom" and so titillated and captivated the amorous Menelaus that he threw away his sword, clasped her in his arms, and swore never to harm her. Five hundred years later another beauty, Phryne, a Greek courtesan, accused of profaning the Eleusinian mysteries (a crime as grave as treason), not only escaped death but gained eternal fame by the same mammary ruse. In the course of her trial, her lawyer—who was also one of her lovers—was so carried away by his description of her "virtues" that he ripped off the blouse of her tunic and revealed "the most perfect bosom in all of Athens." The tribunal was so fascinated with this symbol of feminine perfection, she was acquitted, amid the applause of the spectators. The judges decided that a woman with such a lovely bosom could not be convicted, lest Aphrodite, the goddess of love and beauty, take revenge on Athens.

And Chaucer, the great English poet, wrote this paean:

> This wench both plump and well-developed was,
> With concave nose and eyes as gray as glass,
> With buttocks broad and breasts both round and high.

Indeed, one could write the history of Western sexual mores as one long quotation in praise of the female bosom; our present preoccupation with it is only today's chapter. Women have always known the unique importance of breasts and have been aware of their seductive powers. But critics recently have carped that our civilization in general is dominated by a "breast cult" and that America in particular is wallowing in a "bosom craze." It is doubtful whether the craze is stronger today than it was in Helen's day. Modern methods of communication only make it seem so. The changes that the communications media seem to be able to ring on the sex theme are a credit to the imagination but of little profit to science.

There is enough titillation in all this, however, to make sex profitable to anyone engaged in communicating ideas to the public. The quantity of erotic material being ground out daily testifies to this. It is only natural that much of it should be devoted to the erogenous zones that through the centuries have proved most provocative.

Because of the physical qualities that allow the breast to be pressed upward, inward, outward, or downward at will, women have always been able easily to flaunt their breasts or make them an object of mystery, depending on the effect they thought most likely to arouse male interest. American adoration of the breast is at an all-time high, perhaps universally more intense than it was even in the halcyon days of Greece and Rome, or the earlier civilizations when the breast was worshiped as the seat of all fertility. Girls today regard the breasts as the number one indicator of their sex potential, the most visible symbol of feminine sexual desirability. American males think the same way, and doubtless it is their ideals that influence the women or—like the chicken and the egg—who knows which comes first? The last Kinsey study observed that "American males are more aroused erotically by observing female breasts, or touching them, than they are by the sight of, or contact with, female genitalia."

But what of the nymph without them? If pulchritude is the major portion of a woman's total assets and if its most important aspect is not pulchritudinous or, worse, boyishly nonexistent, what traumas result? Plenty, if the case histories on file in the offices of psychiatrists are any indication. From these it is obvious that our bust craze poses serious psychological and emotional problems for girls and women not endowed by nature with full, well-developed breasts. Often they feel insecure, unwanted, and unloved, victimized by severe social and psychosomatic problems. They are likely to despair of achieving happiness in love and marriage because they believe that men will not desire them or want to caress them and love them. They may withdraw into a shell of despair or turn to unnatural social and sexual activities.

"Bosom inferiority is often developed among girls as soon as they reach adolescence and begin wearing miniature falsies," according to one well-known gynecologist. "In my own practice, I have had one attempted suicide and several serious and total derangements contingent upon real or fancied breast irregularities."

Several hundred gynecologists, general practitioners, and leading psychiatrists report similar experiences. The medical journals are filled with case histories that tell a shocking story of ruin and frustration. How many never reach the files in a doctor's office, one can only guess. Some estimate of the extent of the problem can be gained from the data supplied by the manufacturers of falsies. About five million young American women suffer from micromastia (immature breast development). This, say the falsie manufacturers, is the potential market for their product.

The brassiere makers are interested in this market too, since some contrivance is necessary to hold the falsies. But flat-chested females are only a small part of their market, since about three times as many women suffer from mammary ptosis (collapse or sagging of the breasts) and need the uplift and support of brassieres. Add to these the millions who don't really need support or uplift but who buy brassieres to provide a better contour to the bosom and the total is somewhere around fifty million American females more or less concerned with bosom beauty.

How many of these are potential customers of breast-developing charlatans whose blatant advertisements in brochures and magazines claim the ability to beautify the human bosom? The majority of the flat-chested girls and a large segment of the ptosis cases might fall for the come-ons.

Since bosom level has become eye level for most American males, "flat-chested" today has the connotation of "leper," while the large, finely formed bosom points up the secret of obtaining husbands, film careers, Jaguars, minks, and just plain whistles and stares. With girls in every medium of visual communication demonstrating the secret, the girl with below-average proportions soon figures this is the reason her telephone doesn't ring. Frantically she goes searching for a solution to her problem.

It is in this state of desperation that she most often meets the unprincipled exploiters of feminine credulity. These are the leeches whose extravagant promises are tempting bait. Their mechanical gadgets, creams, lotions, "correcting" brassieres, pills, and exercises convince the unwary that the bosom can be enlarged or reduced to practically any desired size or shape. The broken tissues and permanent damage that result are exceeded only by the broken dreams and the psychological traumas.

Commenting on alleged "bust developers," the *Journal* of the American Medical Association says: "Vanity is responsible for the sale of a variety of products which may momentarily satisfy the purchaser but eventually prove downright harmful."

Among the most numerous inquiries concerning bust developers that have come before the AMA's Bureau of Investigation are those about products containing estrogen, the female sex hormone. "While it is true," says the *Journal*, "that growth of the breast might be stimulated by estrogenic materials, such development is temporary only, and a return to normal size occurs immediately on cessation of treatment. The method of application involves a certain amount of risk and, if adopted at all, most definitely should be used in cases which, on examination, are found to be due to ovarian deficiency. Obviously undeveloped breasts not due to deficiency of the female sex hormones cannot be caused to develop by the use of such medication."

Attempts to enlarge the breasts through massage can be dangerous. Even physicians who admit some value in light breast massage in certain cases caution that the rubbing must be gentle. The real danger, they say, lies in the deep, heavy massage performed by quacks. These unconscionable swindlers may use the same treatment for any breast condition. Considering the fact that there are no muscles in the breast, only delicate tissues with or without fatty cells, the danger of injury is obvious. Even the slightest inflammation may be the first stage of a cancerous growth.

If all the effects of the suction pumps, massage machines, elastic garments, and other mechanical exercisers and devices on the market could somehow be tabulated, the results would add up to more damage to life and feminine appendages than could be inflicted by a mere bomb. It is a field not recommended for the respectable swindler.

Though the boyish figure and bustless busts were the vogue in the 1920's (and again in the 1960's), clairvoyants among the charlatans foresaw the later boom in busts and rushed to the Patent Office with some of the most abominable flagellators ever invented. One inventor was issued a patent in 1921 for an "improved type of a massaging machine wherein a vacuum is intermittently applied to parts requiring massaging." By 1929, a less decorous age, the machines for "parts requiring massaging" were being called "bust-developing" devices, for in that year a lady from Greenwich, Connecticut, patented a "new and useful improvement in bust massagers . . . particularly intended for developing the busts." By 1950, the age of science, a woman in Brisbane, California, was calling her patented bust developer a "passive vascular exerciser." Most of these ideas were a direct steal from the old reliable rubber plunger used to clear recalcitrant toilet bowls.*

How many of these instruments of destruction are sold every year is anybody's guess. Only the estimated incidence of breast cancer caused by them is of record. We have no estimate of the mental anguish caused by their failures or of the total in dollars thus fraudulently taken.

Agents peddling such apparatus are vague in telephone conversations, and they make guarded promises and state half-truths in their beautiful brochures. The object of many of them is to persuade the potential customer to come in for a "private personal analysis." In the privacy of their own establishments, the promoters are less inhibited.

Handicapped by our mustaches and unable personally to follow up any of the bait brochures these charlatans send through the mail, we persuaded a tomboy friend of ours, a capable young actress, to visit the "studios" of one of them. Her figure, or the lack of it, obviously inspired the saleswoman, for she pulled out all the stops in her sales pitch. First she launched into a diatribe against all competitors. She was vehemently opposed to any foam-rubber-padded bra ("It keeps the breast from breathing") and any gymnastic exercises ("The breast is made up of tissue with blood vessels, and exercise will only build up the muscle behind the breast, not the breast itself").

"My product," she said, "works on the breast itself, increasing the circulation and causing the breast tissue to grow."

* Patent Office research disclosed some interesting collateral history. Each of the dozens of bust developers patented from 1901 to 1964 is labeled an "improvement." And though the first patents were issued to men, women gradually took the lead. The bust fraud today is dominated by women inventors. Modern brassiere "improvements" also are patented mostly by women.

"What difference can you make in my figure?" our agent asked.

The saleswoman pulled out a stack of before-and-after pictures. "Look for yourself," she said.

"How long will it take?" our friend asked.

"You will notice a change in the first week," said the saleswoman. "But you must use our machine constantly to retain the size. Also, you should drink a glass of milk exactly one half hour before using. This brings the circulation up to chest level. When it hits this peak, use the machine. Thus you get full advantage of your circulation before it hits bottom." She didn't say which bottom.

Creams, the safe swindle, are no better, for it is medically accepted that despite the thousands of tons of creams and lotions sold throughout the nation, no external application can enlarge or reduce the breasts. Actually, the fantastic assertions of the cream and lotion dispensers sound like the cure-all spiels of the old-time medicine men. The cream and lotion manufacturers are not very different from the cure-all fakers who replenished their medicinal supplies from the nearest stream and added a little coloring. Tests have shown that many of the formulas they recommend for reducing the breasts are the same as those they specify for enlarging them. Only the labels are different.

Some of the products of these charlatans have an ancient history. A turn-of-the-century fashion in ample bosoms produced Bust-O-Fill. In 1905 a large catalog house offered the Princess Bust Developer, and the catalog copy told women that "if nature has not favored you, this developer will." The current bosom-conscious fad has resulted in all kinds of fancy-named devices which, says the Food and Drug Administration, "have about the same effect on the development or structure of the female breast as Smith Brothers cough drops."

What is the alternative to this fantastic and fruitless manipulation and smearing of the breasts? Are women doomed to suffer mental anguish because they cannot change their figures by these fakeries? Barring a radical change in the male adoration of the bosom, which is highly unlikely, the prospect ahead for the flat and the flaccid would seem extremely gloomy. But in a field where the financial returns are assured and the benefits to man (and woman) are guaranteed, one can always depend on science. This combination—healthier profits through healthier people—is hard to beat, so it will come as no surprise that medical and surgical science has been working on the problem for years. Only now are the results beginning to give us any idea of the beauties and benefits to come.

The history of plastic surgery is a long one, but it is the foundation on which cosmetic surgery rests. Plastic surgery began as reconstructive surgery, an attempt to return body features to normal after birth injuries, the ravages of war, or accidents. When the techniques learned in these operatons were put to purely aesthetic uses, when body features were changed to conform to some popular ideal, it became cosmetic surgery. Noses were straightened or shortened, jug ears were pinned back, chins were remodeled, and skin was stretched to take up the slack of age. Thus, it was inevitable that the female breast should demand similar attention.

Surgery to *reduce* breast size is at best a messy operation. Multiple incisions must be made, the fatty tissues severed and removed, and then the gaping wounds closed up again. The scars left by even the most skilled surgeons are often more disfiguring than oversize breasts. The first operations to *increase* breast size involved the implantation of fat removed from other parts of the body. But the tendency of the human body is to absorb fat, so the results were far from satisfactory. Other implants were tried, but none was successful until the invention of polyester. The product used was a gas-expanded foam plastic, technically a "thermoset cellular plastic material obtained through a polyester reaction," resembling sponge rubber. Cut and trimmed to the proper size and inserted between the breast and the chest muscles, it could make any woman happy and her man ecstatic. Today this operation takes only a few moments and is no more painful than a tooth extraction.

Any suggestion that any of this should be called vanity surgery is adolescent thinking. No one knows how many women are psychologically affected by some malformation or deficiency of their breasts. And no one knows how many of these would resort to cosmetic surgery if they could afford it, but it is a known fact that they come from all walks of life and every part of the nation. There is some public misconception that mammaplasty is for hopeful movie starlets, society sexpots, and bathing beauties, but if the specialists in this type of surgery depended on such women to stay in business, they would soon starve. The fact is that any woman who wants to feel the admiring eyes of men and the envious eyes of women will save and finagle and even suffer privation to pay for the operation. There are several thousand case histories to prove it.

Though bosoms by the bushel are rolling off the assembly lines of plastic surgeons, still there are millions of women trying to solve their problem with ineffective creams and lotions and gadgets. To meet this demand and to stem the traffic in bosom chicanery, science is continuing its research. Researchers are working toward a simple injection that any general practitioner could administer. Two shots of this and any woman could have two apples equal to the beautiful Helen's.

QUACK, QUACK, QUACK

When the nation's top medical and health professionals get together for a yearly congress on medical quackery to see what can be done to stop it, one might surmise that medical quackery is enjoying a fantastic renaissance in the United States. When exposés appear regularly in the medical journals and medical fakes are uncovered daily by the public press, one might conclude that quackery has become big business. But there has been no sudden resurgence of popularity, no renaissance. Quacks have been with us always, and their proportion of the GNP has been steady throughout the years. When we were talking in millions of dollars, their annual haul was in the millions. No one knows how many millions. Now that billion is the common denominator, the annual take of quacks in the United States is more than $2,000,000,000. No one knows how much more.

The quack with an array of useless electrical gadgets or bottled tap water is a lineal descendant of the spieler for the peripatetic medicine show of grandpa's day. Diploma mills still operate, and "doctors" still fraudulently practice medicine. In grandpa's day they touted the medicinal qualities of sarsaparilla, the virtues of celery. Today their commercial capers on radio and television are just as blatant. The incredible success of old-time patent-remedy manufacturers, who managed to make alcohol acceptable in a medicine when it would not be accepted in a sherry glass, is duplicated by today's hucksters, who peddle much more dangerous chemicals over the drugstore counter. The language describing the nostrums has become more scientific, the customers have changed somewhat, but the frauds are the same.

People are better educated than they were fifty years ago, and since they live in an environment molded by communications media, one must assume that they are more sophisticated. But herein lie some contradictions. Though ignorance is called the prime reason for gullibility, the record shows that despite all our vaunted knowledge and sophistication, we are as gullible as grandpa.

Indeed, we are better educated today, more able to recognize fakes, and wealthier than ever before in our nation's history. On the other hand, we spend on quacks and medical fakes about the same proportion of our income that our grandparents spent and maybe a little more. Is ignorance, then, the reason for gullibility? At most, ignorance is only a contributing factor to this common frailty, for Americans of every economic and educational level are patsies for medical pitchmen. They irradiate themselves in "uranium collars" and drink buckets of vinegar and honey to cure arthritis. Ordinary seawater at $20 a gallon is guzzled by the barrel as a preventive for practically everything. They anoint themselves with shark oil and avocado juice and take anything from potato pills to coffee enemas to cure everything from athlete's foot to eczema.

There are many factors that contribute to credulity, that make us vulnerable to medical charlatans and health swindlers, and all of them together or singly may motivate human gullibility. Avarice, anxiety, the instinct for self-preservation, mental anguish, physical pain, fear, grief, sexual impotence—the causes are innumerable.

Thus, in a world composed of stresses and strains, the

spell of that old quack magic may not be easily broken with education. We must question, therefore, whether the watchdogs of the AMA, the FDA, and the BBB are not barking up the wrong tree. Their campaigns to "educate the public" to the risks and dangers involved in dealing with quacks are futile, wasteful, and about as scientific as old Doc Whimsy's Kikapoo Indian Juice. The AMA has been at it since 1847, the government since passage of the first Pure Food and Drug Act in 1906, and the BBB since the late 1920's, yet the American people are still giving more than $2,000,000,000 every year to the false purveyors of mystic healing. Many not only have lost their money to the siren songs of modern charlatans, but have lost their lives.

Of course, those who are trying to educate the public point to what might have been had they not campaigned. Perhaps the $2,000,000,000 would have been double. But this is in the realm of conjecture, and conjecture in a scientific age is too close to fantasy. We prefer fact. And the facts, summarized, are these. The medical profession, the government agencies, and the leaders of the business community have failed to eradicate the frauds and fakes, the charlatans and swindlers, and the quacks and dangerous health faddists from our society. Noting the growth of these and the steady increment of their annual take, one wonders whether the campaigns should be called battles or incentives. The AMA calls them battles. The quacks consider them a challenge, an incentive to dream up new twists on old rheostats, new labels for seawater, new claims for common mud.

And they have been at it a long time, for quackery has a history as long as that of any other swindle. Before the American Medical Association, before America, before recorded history, tribal medicine men scratched prescriptions on the walls of caves. Archaeologists figure the life expectancy of the caveman was about twenty years, so the medicine man's percentage of cures was established a long time ago, and quacks have been batting about the same average ever since. Fortunately for civilization, we have gradually become less dependent on medicine men and more dependent on men of medicine.

The only trouble is that we still have considerable difficulty distinguishing between the two. To the gullible (from whatever motivation), the images of both are a little blurred: the quack, by his own deliberate pose; the man of science, by careless default. Whatever the image of the hardworking community doctor, the specialist, or the great man of medicine in some renowned clinic, the quack, by imitation and dramatization, can go him one better. The quack can assume his role and frequently improve upon it.

The man of science, by education and practical experience, deals only in fact and truth. To him, dramatization or misrepresentation in any form is dishonest and intolerable. This is admirable, and to the informed his impersonality is logical. But to the credulous and easily duped (again, for whatever reason), the great man of science is awesome, costly, and frequently frightening.

TYPICAL MOTIVATIONS

If you think of yourself as educated, rational, normal, how would you react under these circumstances?

Arthur Borland (though that's not his real name) is a

young director with several moderately successful off-Broadway theater productions. Scouts for the big-time stage and TV have made tentative offers. He is a young man on the way up. Only one thing stands between him and success. Arthur Borland is convinced he is losing his hearing. A slight physical defect has, through anxiety, become traumatic. No one knows about his defect, for it is really very slight. And his anxiety, which shows, is attributed to his desire that the current production be successful. He is afraid to consult a doctor for fear he will be told to wear a hearing aid. And a hearing aid, he is convinced, would broadcast his affliction and kill his chances of success.

"Hospital and clinical tests show that now you may be one of the many who can have hearing restored without having to wear a hearing aid." So reads only one of a long list of extravagant claims circulated recently by the Hear Clear Co. in New York. To "discover the joy of having your normal hearing restored," Hear Clear (also an invented name) prescribed six tablets for sixty days, at a cost of $15.

Arthur sent them $15 and received the tablets. Misrepresentation in the area of health does more than just cost people money. In many cases it can be downright dangerous. Arthur's pills were nothing more than simple aspirin, but the damage caused by their failure as a hearing cure was worse than if they had been arsenic.

The prescribing of remedies, cures, and drugs is obviously best left in the hands of the medical profession, which is qualified to do the dispensing. One must assume that Arthur was wise enough to know this; but desperate for a cure, he was vulnerable to the fraud.

To establish the basis for Hear Clear's advertising claims, an investigator from the Better Business Bureau of Metropolitan New York, Inc., tried to contact the head of the company. Two letters were subsequently mailed by the Bureau, the second being returned to that office marked "Moved, left no address." The BBB urged a Post Office Department investigation.

Swindlers, as we have noted, are most aware of the law's delay. Their fortunes depend on it. The advertising of a "hearing cure" will occur again and again, for deafness provides one of the many vulnerable areas in the perpetration of quackery.

Deafness, myopia, strabismus (cross- or walleyes), cleft palate, harelip, buckteeth, baldness, gray hair, jug ears, bowlegs, bunions, or other minor congenital or accidental physical defects afflict almost everyone, and their variety and number are exceeded only by the cures offered and the quacks who proclaim them.

From top to toe, the fake cures cover the whole spectrum of swindles. These include vitamins to "restore the original color to hair that has turned gray" and hair grower for those who have none. One of these was a compound distributed by a sharpie through a dozen aliases from as many different towns. The Post Office Department really had its troubles trying to keep up with him, and when he was finally brought to trial "to show cause why he should not be debarred from the mails for obtaining money through those channels by means of false and fraudulent pretenses, representations, and promises," a government chemist testified that hair stuff was a "hydroalcoholic liquid containing 10 per cent of mineral oil by volume and 9.5 per cent of isopropyl alcohol, colored pink."

Though the AMA frequently repeats that "there is no known drug, preparation, device, or method of treatment recognized as a cure, remedy, or competent treatment for baldness; nor as capable of growing or aiding in the promotion of growth of hair, preventing baldness, or feeding or nourishing the hair or scalp," there were enough suckers for this cure to provide its seller with a handsome income. Hair does not have "roots" like a plant and cannot be "fed" by any external application—elementary knowledge surely possessed by many of those who bit on the "false and fraudulent pretenses."

Surgery can correct crooked eyes, big noses, flyaway ears, and double chins, but several million dollars is foolishly spent every year on perfumed mud, colored mineral oil, massage machines, and trick treatments that range from a postcard with holes punched in it for straightening the eyes ($5, "with instructions") to a plastic head vise to flatten the ears ($18, "without surgery!") and a leather mold to muzzle wandering noses. Not only is the fool parted from his millions to pay for these things, but many suffer dangerous traumas from the failures.

Buying glasses by mail is an even riskier business for the afflicted, though grandpa and grandma both bought their specs from mail-order practitioners. The causes of defective vision are multitudinous, and we know that eyeglasses cannot be accurately or safely fitted by mail, and yet, surprisingly, today it is still a million-dollar business.

Denture trouble? Pick up almost any magazine and you'll find a quick and inexpensive answer—but very few of the thousands who grasp at this anchor for their floating plates find it quick or inexpensive. The difficulties involved in an attempt to obtain properly fitting dentures by mail-order methods are overwhelming, and the purchase of false teeth by mail is neither a practical nor a safe procedure.

And finally, there is no known product that will remove, "dissolve," or "reduce" bunions, but the take in this field of fakery is fantastic. "Surgery is the only avenue open to complete recovery from these bony enlargements," says an AMA bulletin, without adding that it is a pretty expensive avenue. If bunion surgery cost no more than some of the "cures" advertised, then all the sensible but economy-minded people who fall for the fakers would take surgery instead.

In between our hair (or lack of it) and our bunions lie warts, goiters, moles, acne, freckles, wrinkles, piles, and pyorrhea, and for every defect, the quacks offer hundreds of cures. For the most part, these are minor defects that most of us learn to live with or, in desperation, take to a doctor, but there are still a few million who play the fool to the fakers—to the tune of $275,000,000 annually.

In times of great mental stress, physical pain, or sorrow, the human being should be forgiven for his recantation of all that he may have learned of science and of truth. When he resorts to the abracadabra of charlatans and religious cultists, he should be given our sympathy and understanding and not our censure. He is ready to grasp at any suggestion that may be offered to him for the alleviation of his travail, never stopping to inquire as to the motives of those who would heal him or as to the basis on which their claims may rest. He is a fool, of course, but no man knows the value of a straw until he is drowning.

Newsweek, in its section on Medicine, gave the following facts in a startling and important report. At eighteen, Jerry Walsh was an all-round athlete. He had made all-state in football, and a major-league baseball scout had promised him a tryout with the Boston Red Sox. "Then rheumatoid arthritis, an excruciating inflammation of the joints, suddenly robbed him of his pitcher's arm, forced him to bed for more than eight years, and condemned him to a cripple's life.

"When doctors told Jerry's parents they had no cure and little relief for the surges of pain in his arms, legs, and hands, he turned in despair to the fringes of medicine. A charlatan sold him a pair of copper bracelets to relieve the pain; another quack used a vibrating machine to stimulate circulation; a chiropractor manipulated his spine; an elderly neighbor lady prescribed alfalfa tea. Before Walsh returned to the care of reputable physicians, he, his relatives, and friends had shelled out more that $3,000 for worthless treatments."

Jerry Walsh was forty when he recounted his frustrating pursuit for relief before the Special Senate Committee on the Aging, which was investigating the full extent of fraudulent medical practices aimed at the nation's elderly. A senator, appalled at the number of arthritic victims, gently asked Walsh how so many people could be so completely fooled. "I can guarantee you," Walsh answered, "that when you are in a bed of pain, you will try almost anything."

The agony of arthritis can make even intelligent, sophisticated people grasp at any hope dangled before them. Many write to the Arthritis and Rheumatism Foundation: "I have no interest in life. I have no job, no income. I want only to go to sleep and never to wake up again." Sufferers such as these—and they are legion among arthritics—are easy prey to dramatic promises of relief and cure.

A representative of the New York State chapter of the Arthritis and Rheumatism Foundation, made this statement to a congressional subcommittee: "From my own experience with arthritis I have been willing, when I am in particular pain, to try anything, from carrying buckeyes and horse chestnuts to wearing copper plates on the top of my head and the soles of my feet. If I am willing to try various cockeyed schemes, with my background, think what a field of suckers the untrained arthritics are for the greedy quacks."

The pain of arthritis affects more people (twelve million) than does pain from any other chronic disease. And because arthritis and rheumatism are painful and crippling and may drag on for a lifetime, despairing victims are easy prey for quacks. That is another way of stating that arthritis victims are the biggest market for questionable remedies, that arthritics are the group most exploited by quacks. Five years ago the Arthritis and Rheumatism Foundation reported that nearly one out of two victims of the disease is also a victim of the quack's extravagant promises and deceitful claims. Since then the proportion of pitiful suckers has not changed, for charlatans operating in other fields have seen the great "educational" campaigns put on by the AMA and the Arthritis Foundation and have altered their labels to include this larger list. Today six million of the nation's arthritics are being cheated of more than $250,000,000 each year by promoters who promise "cures" for the disease or who peddle misrepresented remedies and devices.

THE DEVIL'S DEVICES

Under "Devices" comes a range of objects from simple nails to machines that resemble a television set. There are hundreds similar to the Oxidouser (as we shall call it), which the manufacturer claimed would "reverse the death process into the life process" and "cure" arthritis and rheumatism. The first Oxidouser (patented in 1892 and still on the market "in more scientific form" today) consisted of a dollar-sized metal disc and a small cylinder connected by wires. The user was directed to clip the metal disc to his ankle and immerse the cylinder in water—the colder, the better. Result, zero; the cost of this phony device, $35.

Another fantastic device was supposed to cure arthritis through "magnetic induction." Two large electrically wired doughnuts were placed over afflicted areas and the plug inserted into a wall socket. Not only was this bizarre gadget of no value to the sufferer, it exposed him to the hazard of electric shock. Enough of this, of course, would stop arthritis forever.

Still another gadget was a handsome and impressive electronic apparatus. It was supposed to analyze arthritis by measuring electric currents generated by metal plates applied to areas of the body. But the only thing that its jiggling needle measured was the relative moisture of the user's skin. FDA inspectors tried this gadget on two cadavers, and the machine showed that they were in perfect health. More than five thousand of these things were sold for as much as $875 each before the FDA crackdown.

The most ingenious machine topped them all for its psychological impact. A report in the *Saturday Evening Post* gave this account: Moistened, wire-connected pads were attached to the patient's body, and he put on a pair of earphones. The machine passed a varying low current through him while he listened to "Holiday for Strings." "Fundamentally," said the accompanying brochure, "Our device is designed to transmit a controlled volume of audible sound energy . . . leaving the patient with a relaxed, intrigued attitude." The FDA was intrigued. An inspector bought one of the $500 machines and took it apart. It contained nothing more therapeutic than the recording device that played the music.

Metal devices include copper bracelets: "Greatest benefits are obtained by wearing one on each wrist to set up a curative circuit." The theory may be hokum in the extreme, but no one has yet thought up a better gimmick for selling cheap jewelry.

While uranium was a new, romantic-sounding precious metal in the public mind, swindlers sold phony uranium for "drawing" the arthritis from the body—$300. Several well-known and well-educated civic figures were among the thousands who grasped at this one.

The list of gyp gadgets could go on and on. There is a special device made of chains, a hanger, and a harness for suspension of the head.

There is a stainless-steel watchband equipped with a miniature "thermopile." Price, $22.50; material value, $3; medical value, worthless.

There is a weird applicator that produces a special ray to "expand" and "explode" all the atoms in the body. Price, $50.

There are many variations on the "chromopathic" theme —machines purported to cure by casting various colored lights. One of these was recently confiscated by the FDA. It consisted only of a plastic lampshade and a bulb. Its promoters claimed that if you put a piece of blue cellophane over the shade and bathed in the light, your arthritis would vanish.

This is therapy by mechanical witchcraft, of course, but there are still gullible people enough to make it profitable. These gyp gadgets were not brought under the authority of the Federal Food, Drug, and Cosmetic Act until 1938, so it may take the FDA a few years yet to catch up.

Most fantastic are the "treatment centers." The Ozarks of Missouri and Arkansas is a region famous for its abundance of hillbillies and natural springs. The latter are being exploited by the former as "health spas" and cure-all clinics. Considering the millions these so-called hillbillies rake in every year, all the old poverty jokes about them today sound a little ridiculous.

There is hardly a food item that has not been used at some time or other to "cure" arthritis. Recent years have brought a return to popularity of such homespun remedies as orange juice, cod-liver oil, honey and vinegar—all of no proven benefit in the treatment of arthritis. Medical science recommends a healthful diet for everyone, but it has disproved theories that particular foods have specific effects on arthritis. "Safety milk," for instance, is just another misrepresented product offered to "cure" or "relieve" arthritis. The milk, according to its promoters, gets its immunity from antibodies produced in the udders of cows injected with streptococcus and staphylococcus vaccines. Scientifically controlled studies show that this milk has absolutely no effect on the disease, yet arthritis victims are paying up to $1.70 a quart for it.

Los Angeles, the happy hunting ground for many types of quacks in medicine, religion, and politics, is the home of several hundred useless nostrums. Typical of the cures offered recently were reported in *The Journal of the American Medical Association*. There are certain arthritic remedies, "which, when taken singly or together, according to directions, in conjunction with diet charts and instruction sheets, were represented to 'go to the root of' and permanently 'eradicate' and 'cure' all forms of rheumatism, sciatica, and arthritis—this, regardless of the supposed hopelessness of the case or the fact that the sufferer had previously 'tried everything' without benefit. Further, these products were supposed to overcome high blood pressure and kidney, bladder, and prostate disorders.

"And what were these remedies? A chemist of the Food and Drug Administration certified that one was chiefly water, with less than 1 per cent each of hydrochloric and nitric acids; that another contained 36 per cent of alcohol and small amounts of Jamaica dogwood and cimicifuga; and that the third was a mixture of phenolphthalein, senna, sulfur, and cream of tartar." A physician who has had extensive experience in the treatment of arthritis and access to all the laboratory and clinical studies on the subject revealed the worthlessness of the formulas for any condition of arthritis. Only the alcohol might have given some momentary relief, and even that would have been better tasting and cheaper if bought under a different label in any saloon.

SWINDLERS' AIDS

The astute swindler, though his operations are covert, is invariably found in the forefront of medical trends and health fads. When, some years ago, tuberculosis was still being called "consumption" and the various tuberculosis associations were mushrooming as a result of public concern, the mechanical gadgets and fake nostrums offered as cures were fantastically varied and numerous. With the new associations grinding out publicity by the carload and public interest aroused to a state verging on national hysteria, TB quackery enjoyed a florescence unsurpassed before or since.

The combined efforts of the national, state, and local tuberculosis associations resulted in achievements impressive and invaluable (despite the heavy percentage of funds charged off as "staff operating expenses"). They also set the pattern for other health associations and their complement of parasitic quacks. Encouraged by the success of the antituberculosis campaigns, one after another new "non-profit" societies sprang up. The roster of these health associations today covers every part and particular ailment of the human anatomy. Let the American Cancer Society or the National Tuberculosis Association or the American Heart Association or the Arthritis and Rheumatism Foundation launch a campaign to educate the public and every quack in the nation cashes in on it. The gadgets and the nostrums don't change, but the market does—it gets better with the discovery and exploitation of every new malaise.

New Federal drug laws and postal regulations can slow up the interstate shipments of falsely labeled drugs and phony medical machines. But the widespread publicity of the health foundations creates a ready market among the incurably afflicted before the laws can be enforced.

The most effective help comes from the AMA. Its Bureau of Investigation has set up rules to help educate the public in spotting a quack. Beware, the bureau warns, if:

1. A medical "expert" uses a special or "secret" machine or formula he claims can cure disease.

2. He guarantees a quick cure.

3. He advertises or uses case histories and testimonials to promote his cure.

4. He clamors constantly for medical investigation and recognition.

5. He claims medical men are persecuting him or are afraid of his competition.

6. He tells that surgery, X rays, or drugs cause more harm than good.

Cancer, arthritis, and diseases of the heart are foremost in public concern at the moment, and every factor contributing to any of these common ailments offers a lucrative field for the quack. Smoking as a cause of cancer is an example. Many of the same publications that carried the sensational exposé of smoking's guilt carried this headline in the advertising of a quack pill: "STOP SMOKING IN ONLY 3 DAYS." (That many of them also carried tobacco advertising is beside the point.) That caught the eye of every smoker softened up by the news stories. The real punch came in the subhead: "No will power or self-control necessary." Even the fine print stated: "Proved effective beyond a question in 100% of smokers tested."

To emphasize that individual self-control is not necessary to stop smoking, the ad advised that its "safe, tested formula" would force you to quit smoking whether you wanted to or not. It then cautioned you: "Don't confuse this offer with plans, systems, books, methods, etc. . . . for these remedies require that you have enough self-control to stop smoking."

Since, insofar as medical science knows, there is no known drug, ingredient, or combination that alone and unaided can permanently cure the smoking habit, the authorities, upon investigation of the advertiser, disclosed an answering service at the address given in the ad, run by a one-man "pharmaceutical company." And the ingredient that had "proved effective . . . 100%" had little or no relationship to the problem of smoking.

The film and sound fake mentioned previously could be adapted for the "cure" of cancer by turning off the sound and letting only the "musical vibrations enter the body." Naturally, since smoking is a proven cause of cancer, the tune was changed to "Smoke Gets in Your Eyes." The tune's vibrations were supposedly carried to the cancer, causing it to disintegrate. Cataracts of the eyes and stomach ulcers also simply faded away. The quack who promoted the machine claimed he could diagnose cancer merely by running his hands over the patient's body. Whenever his hands suddenly felt chilly, he knew instantly that *there*, underneath, was cancer. Considering the fact that he invariably found cancer and his cure in all cases was that specific device ($500, remember), the field of cancer offered a rich harvest.

The real villains in the act, however, are the health cultists. The atrocities they perpetrate are usually within the law. Many operate under the guise of "doctors," others among the fanatic fringes of religion. All operate in the ignominious realm of the frenetic and the desperate. Compared to these scabrous leeches, the swindler with his electric horse collar is exemplary. And the millions poured into their voracious pockets is the least of it. As a former Secretary of Health, Education, and Welfare once said: "The cost of this problem in dollars only introduces the story. In terms of false hopes raised, in terms of delusions fostered, in terms of tinkering with human life itself, the cost cannot be measured."

Although cancer, in all its forms, actually affects fewer people than arthritis, more people fear it.* Who, reading all the publicity put out by the American Cancer Society, does not wonder or have some twinge of fear with every little pain? However, self-diagnosis is frequently disastrous, for more people die through improper self-care than are killed by all the quacks and medical charlatans. Perhaps this proves the old adage that "a little knowledge is a dangerous thing." But if a little knowledge is dangerous, who has so much that he is free from danger? It is worthy of note that the wisest doctors consult other doctors when they are sick.

Of course, there are several quack diagnosticians who

* About 71 per cent of the Americans who die each year succumb to cardiovascular diseases and cancer. Of these, arteriosclerosis and hypertension are the nation's No. 1 killers, claiming the lives of some nine hundred thousand persons annually. The No. 2 killer is cancer, which causes about three hundred thousand deaths each year.

offer a complete physical examination for only $5. Many of these "clinics" average 650 people a month. Almost everyone who avails himself of these bargain-counter examinations discovers he has some peculiar ailment. Curiously, also, they are all frightening. What would you do if you were told that you had a cancerous liver or a jellied gallbladder or a disintegrating spine or lymphoid syphilis? If you were foolish enough to pay $5 for one of these pseudo-diagnoses, you would probably consent to the treatments prescribed. Naturally, they are expensive. To reverse the disintegration of your spine, for example, you may have to pay the kindly "doctor" several hundred dollars for treatments.

So if you want to save money, self-diagnosis is the lesser of the two evils. At least you can have some control over the damage to your pocketbook if not to your health if you fill your own prescription with the drugs and advertised nostrums you can buy over the counter.

More money is spent and, as mentioned previously, more lives are lost in this self-swindle than the total take and kill by all the quacks in the country. (Americans spend more money for vitamin pills than for any other kind of nonprescription medication, but for sheer quantity they buy more aspirins. About 99 per cent of both are self-prescribed.)

Is this, then, an indictment of the American public? Hardly. The American public receives a lot of help and consolation in its sin of self-diagnosis. The big pill and nostrum makers that operate under the commercial eminence of pharmaceutical houses are the most sympathetic. Their extravagant advertising claims are strangely compelling when they call our attention to our own annoying symptoms. This is quackery at the highest level it may ever attain, for this is the old medicine-show spiel brought up to date, the voice of the old-time quack now refined, cultivated, and subtle. And with all the force of the mass-communications media behind it, it is awesome and frightening.

New laws intended to curb the patent-medicine makers are on the books, but they apply mainly to the manufacture and distribution of *harmful* drugs. They prohibit the sale of dangerous drugs without a doctor's prescription, strengthen labeling restrictions, and give the government greater power to prosecute dealers in harmful medicines.* But what protection have we against the distribution of *harmless* drugs? None. Any manufacturer can make a placebo, advertise it through radio, television, the press, and the U.S. mails, and rake in millions.

There is no question, of course, that special vitamin and mineral products serve a useful purpose when the diet actually requires supplementation. In ordinary doses, they are not harmful in themselves. But all too frequently, the unwary and the uninformed, having read somewhere of the magic contained in a "health food" or vitamin, resort to self-diagnosis, and a serious medical problem remains unchecked.

Although we admit that numerous patent medicines are effective in the symptomatic treatment of some ailments, most often this effectiveness is limited. Further, they represent a minority of the total number of remedies sold. The government's liberal estimate is that only about 5 per cent of the remedies offered have any practical usefulness. Useful or not, their effectiveness is invariably exaggerated to the point of deception in advertising, and therein lies the danger. For even the *harmless* medicine, those that are worthless or of very limited value, can be disastrous if false

* The greatest need is to speed up the action and eliminate the law's delay. Quacks have been known to make a million dollars between a citation and a restraining order. It took the FDA seven years and innumerable court battles to stop the flow of one widely advertised nostrum for arthritis and rheumatism.

advertising has led the dupe to buy it as a cure or a remedy for a serious ailment and thus critically delayed his seeking more sensible treatment.

Face to face with the awesome power of mass advertising, the argument over whether the American citizen is capable of safe self-diagnosis and self-medication is academic. On one side, the better part of medical science declares that self-medication is a "dangerous and undesirable practice, and it is incumbent upon all the health professions to work diligently toward its eventual elimination from the American scene." Against this attitude are those who hold that "anyone has an inalienable right to take his own medication." The cost of this inalienable right is more than $1,000,000,000 a year—for medicine we don't need. This is the best confirmation we can cite for Osler's oft-quoted statement: "The desire to take medicine is perhaps the greatest feature which distinguishes man from animals."*

Science and the sensible protest. The AMA maintains an investigatory body to uncover the quacks and inform the proper authorities. Considering the size of its operating budget, it is performing a miracle of civic aid. The AMA's campaigns to educate the public, in which it is joined by the National Better Business Bureau and bolstered by various Federal and state law-enforcement bodies, are admirable. The books and periodicals that expose the remedy rackets are also helpful. (There have been enough of these in recent years to fill a library, but not one has been on the best-seller lists as long as some of the quackery books.) The expenditure of so much energy has paid off. The public is more knowing, more aware of the quacks and the frauds and swindles they pull.

* Sir William Osler (1849–1919), renowned British physician, who in his day was highly ridiculed for another contention: that men should retire at sixty.

But if these educational campaigns have alerted us to beware of the quack, they have also made us more critical of the medical profession, the drug laws, and the enforcing bodies. The AMA cast the first stone a hundred years ago, but it has never convinced the public that the medical profession is without sin, its Hippocratic (some spell it "hypocritic") oath notwithstanding.

When the American Medical Association and the Food and Drug Administration get together for their annual powwow (which they call the National Conference on Quackery in Medicine), they have, ostensibly, one aim in view: to find preventive medicine against quacks and medical frauds. Attending are representatives from state and Federal health departments, medical groups, and drug companies. It would be hard to find a more eminent body, and its aim is one every sensible American should applaud. Exhibited at a recent meeting were examples of quack medical devices that ranged from a tiny tourniquetlike band designed to improve male potency to elaborate dial-, buzzer-, and light-studded panels—some with dials connected to nothing—for diagnosing and treating ills. There were cancer cures, breast enhancers, vibrating couches, hair restorers, a variety of sex aids, and a score of books written to promote one type of cure or another.

But though this august body shook its concordant head over these frauds and fakes, the discord among its separate members was symptomatic (as they would say) of grave disorder within the body itself. Though the FDA constantly hopes to tighten and amend existing laws, the AMA has always been wary of any Federal legislation. There is the fear that regulation of surgical, therapeutic, and other devices might interfere with a doctor's freedom as a medical practitioner.

The drug company delegates, naturally, had their own

pitch to protect, and it didn't always coincide with the thinking of the AMA and/or the FDA. The drug manufacturers' answer to Federal antitrust and monopoly complaints is that they spend almost $2 on research for every $1 they make in profits. Some of the big companies may spend years and many millions to perfect a new drug, only to have the formula for it stolen away from them by a small shyster outfit or a foreign company. At the moment, Italian pills made with stolen formulas are knocking the bottom out of certain antibiotic markets. Thus drug prices are still controlled by a highly competitive market.

With the voices of vested interests making so much noise, it is often hard to hear the tune of public benefactors they are supposed to play.

If one reads the daily press and the AMA's own *Journal*, he will be both confused and confounded. Along with all the exposés of charlatans and quacks, volleys of criticism have been fired at legitimate medicine for years, and resentments have multiplied. The following charges are heard over and over. The medical profession constantly and carefully covers up the mistakes of its members ("Doctors bury their mistakes"). Doctors keep you coming for injections at $5 and $10 each, when a $1 bottle of medicine would serve the same purpose. Doctors charge whatever the patient can pay. Surgeons perform unnecessary operations and charge high fees, which they frequently split with the referral doctor.

Whether such criticisms are justified or not is not the point. The point is that there is a very indistinct line between the quack who never saw the inside of a medical school and the charlatan who did. And considering the fact that the Hippocratic oath is rapidly disappearing from American medicine (of eighty-four leading U.S. medical schools, only twenty-one still use some form of the classic oath), one must question the morals and motives of every MD in practice. The AMA does.

From the now defunct New York *World-Telegram and Sun:* "A demand that medical societies get tough with doctor-racketeers was considered today by the American Medical Association." The demand came from the president of the AMA, in an address before a state medical society. The speaker blasted doctors who charge "exorbitant fees," declaring: "Medical societies would have to expel only a few racketeers and the practice [of overcharging] would stop. When the public realizes the profession will not tolerate chiseling, the standing of the profession will be enhanced immeasurably."

Fee splitting and kickbacks are frowned on by the AMA too, but only fifteen states rule fee splitting illegal. Several of *The New York Times,* Los Angeles *Times,* Chicago *Tribune,* and San Francisco *Examiner* clippings, all filed under our heading "Kickbacks," offer a good cross-country sampling of the constant battle being waged over this disgraceful practice. For instance, for taking kickbacks, the licenses of 9 Brooklyn physicians were revoked and those of 263 others were suspended for periods ranging from one month to two years in what *The New York Times* states was a "collective action unprecedented in the annals" of New York medical law.

In the aftermath of this scandal, the AMA's *Journal* reported that the New York Academy of Medicine said: "The practices referred to [kickbacks] are, in the opinion of the Academy, entirely contrary to the Hippocratic oath."

Doctors who lie in court have long been targets of an AMA drive. Bernard D. Hirsh, chief of the AMA law section, spoke strongly on this point (quoted by the Chicago *Tribune*): "It is appalling that medical specialists are often selected not because of their skill as doctors but because of their ability as convincing medical witnesses." It was "even more appalling that there is a small but nevertheless significant number of mercenary physicians who are willing to dispense colored or exaggerated and even false medical testimony to either side for a fee."

As a result of this kind of high-level chastisement, more than a thousand community "medical juries" have been set up. If you think your doctor has overcharged you, bungled a diagnosis, or acted like a boor, all you have to do is present your complaint before one of these tribunals. You may not get a rebate on that high-priced appendectomy, but you will get justice, because these community grievance committees have established a reputation for fairness.

Perhaps little can be done about the pharmaceutical advertising that floods doctors' mail. There was a time when the drug factories owned secret formulas and exclusive rights to manufacture certain pharmaceuticals, and any doctor who wanted to use them had to buy them from that house. The only advertising was a notice to the doctor that the product was available. Federal action, fair-trade laws, and a few lawsuits broke up these monopoly situations. With everybody or nearly everybody making the same thing, advertisers devised different trade names for the same product, and price became an object of advertising importance. When the line had to be held on prices, some manufacturers resorted to gift tie-ins, premiums such as nylon luggage and electric can openers (for doctors' wives, we hope), with the purchase of so many bottles or vials or ampules of this or that.

Honest physicians everywhere will resent the implication that any doctor would accept a premium of any kind from a drug house in connection with the administration of medicine. But there is ample evidence that it does happen—and frequently. And since it is the consumer, the patient, who pays in the end, is he not more entitled to the premiums than the doctor?

Some of the illnesses suffered by the FDA might be more difficult to diagnose. From an occasional glimpse of the inner workings of this powerful body, we venture to say that the most serious ailments are dissension in the ranks, timidity of FDA prosecutors, and intimidation of administrators. According to testimony supplied by a retired drug inspector (as quoted in a recent issue of *Saturday Review*): "There appears to be a definite policy on the part of the Administration to treat the big manufacturers of foods and drugs with care and to be much more severe with small manufacturers. . . . The same holds true with respect to M.D.'s in comparison with osteopaths, chiropractors, and others who do not have the blessing of the AMA. The Administration is extremely reluctant to bring charges against an M.D. for proven violations of the law with regard to prescription drugs but willingly prosecutes other medical practitioners."

A consumer lawsuit and its attendant publicity can have a more disastrous effect on a drug company than the lenient fines and sentences handed down in FDA prosecutions. Thus, the fear of adverse publicity acts as a powerful deterrent in preventing violation of the FDA laws. Yet the FDA never uses this as a threat or a weapon.

Though the technical personnel seem to be men of intelligence and integrity, too often administrators are opportunists. "The policy of the Administration seems to be to discourage all initiative on the part of field personnel and to reward mediocrity, apathy, and even, on occasion, downright chicanery," the former drug inspector said.

The wonder is that any quack is ever convicted. Medicine and man's constant search for health have always offered the greatest field for the perpetration of fraud, the cultivation of quackery, the success of swindling. Occasionally, today, by dint of much sleuthing, documentation, and patient investigation, the AMA or the FDA exposes some of the more blatant frauds. A few are brought to trial. But for every charlatan exposed, there are hundreds who go their devious ways to popularity and fortune unopposed. If there is any moral to this sorry tale, it is that in this world it's every man for himself, while the quacks take the hindmost.

8

THE $1,000,000 HAYRIDE

THERE are probably no greater contradictions in the world than American attitudes toward money. And though the contradictions are legion, one might loosely group them under two opposing money mores: the money-is-the-root-of-all-evil doctrine and the work-like-hell-and-make-all-you-can philosophy. The first, obviously, is remnant puritanism, the natural descendant of envy and a cousin of penury. The second is motivated by our acquisitive itch, subsidiary to the basic instinct for survival. Our interest at this point lies less with the contradictory schools of thought than with the neutral zone between them.

Whatever your convictions, you must agree that the only middlemen who profit from both sides are the bankers. "The root of all evil" is the commodity in which they deal, and their customers are the avaricious, the covetous, the mercenary, and the penurious among us who think of themselves as the frugal, the economical, the thrifty, and the prudent.

This position gives banks the enviable control of the socioeconomic elements of the nation and thus the greatest responsibility for our financial health and growth. Any criticism, therefore, would seem impious, for our banker friends tell us banks enjoy greater popularity today than ever before. Banks give more services today, and there are more banks. Bank depositors and deposit totals are up also, but we question whether faith and trust have enjoyed equal growth.

Banks, banking methods, and the entire system of handling money have changed little over the years since money was invented. Machines now do the work of the counting-house lackeys, and the good gray bank facade has given way to more attractive architecture, but Ben Franklin would have no trouble finding his way around today or getting a loan.

Thus, it would appear to the objective observer that banking is out of date. In an age when science has revolutionized so many methods, manners, and morals, banks as a means for handling money are not advanced much beyond the horse-and-stagecoach era. Automation may speed up the handling as the volume of business increases, but it won't materially change the system.* Proof, of course, lies in the fact that the illegal ways of getting money from a bank have not changed either. New protections, new precautions are constantly being devised to stop the embezzler, the forger, and the robber, and still *banks lose more money than any other business in the world*. And more of this loss is through embezzlement and forgery than through holdups and burglary.

Indeed, if statistics mean anything to an intelligent swindler, then the easiest way to get money out of a bank or any other business is by embezzlement. Embezzlement, the in-

---

* Post offices suffer from similar antiquation, and though automation may replace a few men and jets may speed our mail on its way, science has not devised a better medium of communication than the letter.

side job, apparently is most popular and most productive. Statistics (admittedly inaccurate*) show that for every $1 taken in a holdup, $67.50 is taken by employees. Even check passers and forgers, though their take is greater than that of bank robbers, hardly compare in finesse and finance with the inside swindlers.

It's all a matter of intelligence. The brute robber, depending on his gun and a brain little noted for intelligence, is certainly not in a class with the check specialist. And the bad-check artist, whatever his specialty, can't hold a candle or a dishonest buck to the astute manipulator of company books or bank ledgers.

Thus we must consider robbery, however well performed, beneath the dignity of our present work. Brilliant maneuvers like the Brink's holdup and the recent Great Train Robbery in England might disprove our point, except that these were planned and executed by highly intelligent people, considerably above the cut of the average bank robber or payroll pincher. The successful swindler is a man of many parts, as we shall show.

Just how much is lost by banks each year is a figure pretty hard to pin down. Of all the subjects researched for this book, we found it most difficult to get inside information on banks and their operations, especially data involving their losses of money.

The newspapers chronicle the robberies and the million-dollar embezzlements, but little publicity is given the countless petty swindles that occur every day. One of the nation's greatest banks, with hundreds of branches all over the world, averaged one and a half robberies a week, for a total loss of $175,000 last year, but its losses through bad

* Confidential figures circulated among ABA banks confirm our general statements, but totals, which must include losses by non-member banks and those banks not reporting, are estimates based on newspaper accounts.

checks, bad employees, and bad management made that figure beggarly. Anyone who has had trouble getting money from a bank by legitimate means should see how easy it is and always has been for the smart swindler.

One of the earliest records we have uncovered is Achan's dishonesty when he attempted to defraud Joshua (banker for the Lord) out of "a beautiful mantle from Shinar, and two hundred shekels of silver, and a bar of gold weighing fifty shekels" by burying them in the earth inside his tent. This was more a swindle than a robbery, since Achan secreted these spoils of war before they were counted by Joshua's accountants. Such an inside job would be termed an "embezzlement" today and doubtless was then, for the modern term for the act—"to embezzle"—is related to an ancient word for "imbecile," the idea being to imbecile someone, that is, to enfeeble someone financially by cheating him.

Though there were money changers, and therefore swindlers, in biblical times, the term "bank" comes not from the system but from the bench, or banca, on which the changers sat in Roman times and on which they bounced the metal to hear its ring. The first banks as we know them were strongly guarded houses where gold and silver money was kept in safety for depositors, who were given receipts, the first bank notes. Since these actually represented money in safe care, they were negotiable and frequently circulated widely before they were redeemed. The only difference between that system and modern banking was that the bankers did not use the money. They merely charged a fee for guarding it.

Real banking started with the moneylenders of Florence. Toward the end of the fourteenth century, the business had become so lucrative that there were seventy-five to eighty moneylenders or private bankers in the city, which was considered the fiscal capital of the civilized world. So successful were they that they were involved in the financial affairs of every country in Europe.* Thus they were vulnerable to any large borrower, such as King Edward III of England. When he reneged on his debt to two of the most important banking houses, those of Bardi and Peluzzi, they were bankrupt. The default, in effect a monstrous swindle, nearly ruined Florence as a banking center. It was years before it recovered. And six hundred years later, the Florentines still think "Englishman" is a synonym for "fraud."

Five New York City banks and one Long Island bank were bilked out of $221,000 by a gang of international swindlers operating in Latin America and Europe. The U.S. Postal Inspection Service provided us with the details (the gang's operations involved tampering with the mails). Interpol, the international police organization, was alerted, and one ringleader of the gang was arrested in Davos, Switzerland. A woman member, who rifled one New York bank account of $20,000, was tailed across Europe before she was apprehended.

The gang's operations centered on the New York bank accounts of a number of wealthy families in Brazil and Argentina. Members of the gang intercepted bank statements and other mail passing between the banks and their Latin-American customers at post offices in Buenos Aires, Argentina, and São Paulo, Brazil. When a large account was discovered, the gang photocopied the useful information, including the depositor's signature, and sent it to accomplices in Paris, Brussels, and Zurich. There, bank accounts were opened in the name of the wealthy Latin-

* The Medici family became the most famous moneylenders of Florence, and reminders of their power remain today in the three balls we use to signify a pawnshop. The sign had its origin in the Medici coat of arms.

American depositor and the signature of the depositor was forged to a letter instructing his New York bank to transfer a specified amount of money to the European account. When this was done, the money then was taken out by use of the forged signature.

The Postal Inspection Service said the amounts involved ranged from $5,500 to $40,000, usually withdrawn from the European accounts within a day or two after the money was deposited. In the case of the $40,000 withdrawal, the bank discovered later that the depositor had only $26,000 in his New York account, leaving it $14,000 overdrawn.

Again, a letter was received from Zurich bearing what appeared to be the signature of a São Paulo depositor. It was an urgent request for a transfer of $9,000 by cablegram to a Swiss bank. The swindlers drew it out of the Swiss bank the next day.

A Long Island bank received a request to transfer $10,000 to a woman in Brussels. Four days earlier it had received a $14,400 check from the depositor to be placed in his New York account. While waiting for this deposited check to clear, the Long Island bank, having no foreign department, asked a New York City bank to transfer the $10,000 to Brussels. The New York bank happened to be one of those previously burned by the swindle and suggested caution. Investigation turned up the false nature of the Brussels request and, subsequently, full disclosure of the gang's operations.

The only people who best these outside operators, as we have said, are the embezzlers, the inside jobbers. And they have been doing it for a long time.

EMBEZZLEMENT: THE INSIDE JOB

The first emigrant party to cross the continent and enter California, in 1841, contained among its members one who called himself Talbot H. Green. He appeared on the scene at the start of the trip with a mysterious chunk of "lead." Throughout many misadventures and terrible hardships on the trail, he managed to hold on to the "lead."

Ten years later he had become one of San Francisco's most liked and trusted businessmen. Wealthy, respected, and married, he was proposed as a candidate for mayor, and San Francisco's Green Street was named for him. At that point he was publicly and dramatically denounced as being really Paul Geddes, a defaulting bank clerk who had deserted wife and children somewhere back East. The chunk of "lead" obviously was the bullion he had embezzled. Coals to Newcastle and gold to California, indeed! The moral, if one should point to it, is that embezzlers should not become politicians. The professions may be analogous, but the spotlight of public opinion isn't.

The style of bank architecture common in this country for years was one of the biggest psychological swindles ever perpetrated on the public mind. Sometimes called "Bank Gothic," it was mostly Bank Greek and never completely original. Architects engaged to design a bank were told to "make it look solid." And since the prime models of stability were Greek and Roman structures, as exemplified in the nearly imperishable architectural remains of those civilizations, bank designs were invariably warmed-over versions of their solid features. Adapting these massive features to the thirty-five-foot front on Main Street was the extent of the imagination and originality involved. And the swindle, of course, lay in the appearance. For the solid and safe façade covered human beings, and while it might inspire trust, the people it housed were only human. Thus, in effect, the façade was a psychological swindle, and the billions lost in bank failure through embezzlement and poor loans made it the principal accessory to that fact.

What with all the publicity attendant upon embezzlements by bank employees, the wonder is that anyone would trust a bank with his money. Hundreds don't, obviously, so the con man is playing a new game called "Trap a bank embezzler." There are many variations, naturally, but this case is typical. The con called an elderly lady depositor of a St. Louis bank and told her he was the president of the bank. He feared, he said, that employees had been tampering with the widow's account. He asked her to come down to the bank and draw out $2,000 while he watched the facial expressions of bank employees to see whether any showed fear. The "bank president" said he would meet the widow at her home after the trip to the bank. He would then take back the $2,000 for redeposit. He sent a taxi to pick her up and had it wait at the bank to return her home. There the tall distinguished, gray-haired "banker" took the money and gave her a phony receipt. She hasn't seen him or the money since. Little old ladies, depositors in the New York area, were taken for $20,000 by this swindle during February, 1965. What the total for the year in the nation was is anyone's guess.

"Automation, modern architecture, and Federal controls are all recent banking improvements designed to give greater surety and better service," bank ads claim. If the public believes that bank safety and service are better than ever, then no one should disillusion it. One should point out, however, that a system theoretically perfect in the prevention of peculations would render it immaterial whether a clerk were as honest as Cato or as great a thief as Fagin. Though improvements have been made in the banking system since the Medicis, the system still depends for its success upon the honesty of those who are involved in it. Thus swindlers will be envious to know that embezzlement and inside fraud still cause banks to fail and depositors to lose fortunes every year.

And, amazingly, nothing new or original in embezzlement methods has been used by defrauders for the last one hundred years and more. Banks still classify all embezzlements under seven general heads about as the Bank of England did 150 years ago: misappropriation of funds before they are recorded; misappropriation of income; manipulation of expenses; tampering with the bank's or customer's assets; acting beyond the authorization of the management; forging instruments or making fictitious entries; irregular bookkeeping entries.

Tellers who fail to put through deposits and officers who fail to purchase securities with funds left by customers for that purpose are guilty of the first type. By misappropriation of all or part of the money before records are made, or without making records, they can, under ideal circumstances, make pretty substantial hauls.

Service charges and profits on securities and income from loans and mortgages are typical incomes that may be taken by dishonest bank employees.

Manipulation of expenses might include overstatement of interest paid on deposit accounts and interest rebates on loans and mortgages—in a word, padding.

Tampering with assets includes substituting notes of

insolvent makers for negotiable notes, substituting counterfeit bills for good, wrapped washers for coins in the vault, and so on.

Making unauthorized loans to directors, officers, and employees; making loans on worthless collateral; and cashing checks known to be uncollectible are typical of the fifth and most common classification. The biggest hauls are credited to this type of embezzlement.

Forgery of various bank forms and making fictitious entries are tricks the inside swindler learns from the pros on the outside. And "irregular bookkeeping entries" covers a multitude of swindling aids.

The daily press is full of examples to illustrate every category. The extent of the embezzlement (*i.e.*, the size of the haul) is limited only by the funds available; otherwise, the size of the bank has nothing to do with it. A classic example of the small-town-bank embezzlement occurred recently in a tiny (population, 267) town in Nebraska. Bank examiner F. H. Pochop, making a routine visit, had just exchanged greetings with the bank's ninety-three-year-old president, when there was an explosion in a back room. Arthur Walford, seventy-three-year-old cashier, was found dead on the floor, a shotgun beside him.

The cashier was described as a "pillar of the community," a "much respected" widower who regularly sang in the choir of the United Presbyterian Church, and "the last man in town to do anything wrong." But a single check of the bank's books convinced the examiner that there were "large sums unaccounted for."

That was an understatement, as it turned out. Eventually the total shortage was figured at $468,000. It began in the Depression days of the 1930's. The bank began covering checks for hard-up farmers and ranchers who didn't have sufficient funds on deposit.

By shifting money from liquid accounts to cover the discrepancies and by the preparation of bogus ledger sheets whenever an examiner was expected, they managed to cover their irregularities for thirty years. Concealment was easy because the bank rendered account statements only at the specific request of its depositors, a practice as outdated as the elderly president's Model-A Ford.

A large bundle of bogus checks found hidden in the vault implicated so many "pillars of the community," it nearly collapsed. The guilt was pretty evenly distributed.

THE SHRINKAGE SWINDLE

Back in the 1930's, when the little Gresham bank began its peculations, it had several excellent examples to emulate. There were dozens of bank failures in the aftermath of the stock-market debacle. The managers of the defunct banks truthfully said that the crash of their banks was due to the stock-market crash and the shrinkage in security values. There is no doubt about that. It was the market collapse that wiped out the banks' security values and caused their failures. It also made possible the revelation of what was going on behind those "solid façades." If the market had not collapsed, there is very good reason to believe that the banks would have gone ahead, and, of course, the managers would have continued to ply their grafting activities unmolested and with the approval of their boards. But they would have been grafters nonetheless.

The unquestioned leader in this field was Roger Caldwell, head of Caldwell and Company, an old established investment banking house in Nashville, Tennessee. Founded in 1876, it rose to be one of the largest, if not the largest, in the South.

Affiliated with Caldwell was financier James B. Brown of Knoxville, Tennessee. Brown was president of the National Bank of Kentucky and of the Knoxville *Herald-Post*. Another confederate was Colonel Luke Lee, former U.S. senator from Tennessee, owner of the Memphis *Commercial Appeal*, the Nashville *Tennessean*, the *Evening Tennessean*, and the Knoxville *Journal and Tribune*. Lee was the dynamic and colorful character of the era who attained a kind of seriocomic national notoriety during the First World War, when he concocted a scheme to kidnap the Kaiser. He was a member of the Federal Reserve Bank for the Nashville district.

Under Caldwell's domination was a group of powerful banks in Tennessee, Kentucky, and Arkansas. Backed by the financial resources of these institutions and dozens of smaller affiliated banks, Caldwell and Company embarked on a widespread program of expansion, during which it got under its control industries and financial concerns of all sorts, including banks, security companies, insurance companies, newspapers, and manufacturing establishments.

In June, 1930, the banking house formed a holding company and began shifting interests, crossing and crisscrossing concerns whose combined assets were more than $615,000,000. It was the juiciest financial melon ever grown in the South. By fall it was ready to harvest.

No one knows to this day where all the money went, but by the middle of November, 1930, Caldwell, crushed under a load of vast imprudences, was forced into a receivership. It was the signal for one of the most disastrous series of bank failures that the South has ever known.

Immediately the important banks with which Caldwell was associated were closed. The National Bank of Tennessee, the Holston Union Bank of Knoxville, and the Liberty Bank and Trust Company shut their doors. Next day a run started on the Hermitage Bank in Chattanooga because of reports that it had lent heavily to Caldwell. In Knoxville three other banks had to be hurriedly merged and supported to save them from actual ruin.

Within the week the shock waves hit banks in Kentucky and Arkansas. More than seventy banks in Arkansas were either suspended or closed completely. In Kentucky eleven large banks were closed through their association with the wrecked National Bank of Kentucky. Even banks in Ohio and other adjoining states were affected. And before the debris had finally settled, nearly two hundred banks had felt the shock.

More than $615,000,000! Again one wonders what happened to all that money. No one knows. Caldwell was convicted for "certain irregularities" in the swindle. After receiverships and bankruptcies, some of the firms affected reopened. The rest of the record is buried under time and several tons of paper.

Easier to prove is the fact that embezzlers ply their profession today with the same finesse and financial gain. The following quotations are from the "Eighteenth Report by the Committee on Government Operations" of the Eighty-eighth Congress, published February 20, 1964:

In 1962, two banks not insured by the FDIC [Federal Deposit Insurance Corporation] were closed because of large losses caused by dishonest employees; the embezzlement losses of three banks exceeded the amounts of their bankers' blanket bonds by about $815,000, but they were fully insured through having the "million dollar umbrella" coverage; i.e., $1 million employee dishonesty in-

surance in excess of blanket bond coverage; and four banks
without such umbrella coverage had infidelity losses of
about $920,000 in excess of their basic blanket bonds,
which losses they were able to absorb, without being
forced to close.

Over the past 5 years, 12 banks insured by the FDIC
have been closed as the result of defalcations: 8 were
State-chartered banks not members of the Federal Reserve System, 1 was a State-chartered Federal Reserve
member bank, and 3 were national banks.

The American Bankers Association reported that in
1964, "there were 118 embezzlements of $10,000 and over
with aggregate reported losses of $11.2 million. Six banks
closed as a result of unprofitable deposit, lending, and investment practices and other acts. The question of employee dishonesty, in at least three of these cases, is under
investigation by interested authorities and remains to be
resolved." Defalcations, according to the report, totaled
862, of which 744 were less than $10,000, averaging about
$3,000 each. There were 926 holdups and burglaries, with
losses totaling $4,514,000.

If this is all that Congress and the ABA know about
bank embezzlement, it's a poor summary to bring our story
up to date. Some of the details contributing to those reports
would be more enlightening. They might also change some
popular concepts of human nature in general and of swindlers in particular.

THE SWINDLING SAMARITANS

For instance, no one could have imagined that Mrs.
Wallace P. Geiger, fifty-eight, was capable of swindling the
Sheldon (Iowa) National Bank out of $2,126,859, one of
the largest amounts ever taken in this country's banking
history. Wasn't she known as the Good Samaritan of the
community?

The New York Times, in a dispatch, quoted a local
resident as saying that "although Mrs. Geiger had no children of her own, she had 'many, many children. All those
she has helped, and their children are her children,' she
said. 'It would take every page of an entire day's newspaper
to print the good this woman has done. She never took any
credit or sought any praise.'

"The Reverend Thomas Hutman, her pastor at the First
Congregational Church and a friend for twenty years, said
that Mrs. Geiger 'has always been a leader in giving to any
good cause.'

"As finally disclosed, one of the good causes was the establishment of the Northern Biochemical Corporation to
produce enzymes for animal feed. It took about $900,000
and fifteen months to make it Sheldon's major industry.
Providing jobs for 125 people (from a start with 4) in a
town of 4,251 was one way of causing a lot of good, to say
nothing of the national prestige it brought the community.

"Mrs. Geiger and her husband were members of promi-
nent old families in this northwestern Iowa community. She
was assistant cashier of the Sheldon National Bank, a

member of its board of directors, and the daughter of W. P. Iverson, eighty-three, president of the bank for forty-five years. The old man also was a popular local druggist. Wallace Geiger was in the hardware business." They lived in a large two-story brick house, considered by many "the best in town," but they entertained little and did not live ostentatiously. They were active in the local business community and devout church people. The bank, a financial bulwark for half a century, was a member of the FDIC, with total assets of $1,995,000, and depositors' accounts were insured up to $10,000. How, then, could this nice little old lady have swindled the bank out of $2,126,859 and caused such tremendous losses to so many?

We have no commentary on the lady's morals, but Federal examiner Edward J. Kail, Jr., and F. E. Van Alstine, U.S. District Attorney, explained how they arrived at that total. Mrs. Geiger had helped by keeping over the years a running total on adding-machine tapes of all embezzled funds. Also, she readily admitted that she had been taking money from the bank for forty years. Royal L. Coburn, general counsel for the FDIC, told how her embezzlement worked. He said that it was a simple and efficient method. According to a *New York Times* report, "Her system had been to remove from the bank's files from time to time the records of a number of individual accounts showing deposits amounting to the sum embezzled. These records were hidden in the basement of the bank, where Mrs. Geiger could get them if a customer made withdrawals or additional deposits in an affected account. Thus, bank examiners, in their periodic checks, found that deposits recorded in the bank's files jibed with the institution's assets. The files of more than four hundred accounts were removed from bank records by Mrs. Geiger, according to Coburn."

The FDIC covered the small depositors, but those like

the Big Four Cooperative Processing Association (soybeans), with $100,000 on deposit, and the Farmers Co-op Elevator, with $50,000, suffered. The biggest casualty (after the bank) was the Northern Biochemical Corporation. Harold E. Kistner, Jr., thirty-five, president of the company, was indicted on a dozen counts of aiding and abetting Mrs. Geiger in her embezzlement.

With the Sheldon, Iowa, bank failure before him as an example, Eldon L. Job, fifty-nine, president of the little Community National Bank and Trust Co. of Knoxville, Iowa, committed suicide and left a note in which he admitted embezzling more than half a million dollars. He did it with forged notes.

Harry William Voorhees, a sixty-three-year-old widower who lived with his grown children, was the $139-a-week president of the National Bank of Livingston Manor, New York. He was a highly regarded member of his community.

The New York Times came up with this story. Voorhees' bank was small, with only six employees, and sometimes the president took over the duties of a teller. On such occasions, he had withheld cash from depositors, according to the Federal agent investigating the case. Voorhees was always on hand in the periodic or surprise audits by examiners from the FDIC. When questions arose, Voorhees covered the shortage by embezzling from another account at random. As his manipulations became more involved, he refused to take a day off or even leave the bank for lunch for fear of discovery. He hid hundreds of bank papers, ledger cards, statements, and passbooks in the bank's basement.

Then one day the banker tripped and broke several bones. He hobbled to work, but after two days he was forced to enter the hospital. That day an assistant cashier, snooping around in the basement, found thirteen cartons crammed with bank papers hidden behind a furnace.

Such examples have wised up examiners. They are beginning to note whether the banks they examine have a compulsory vacation requirement. An embezzlement of any size requires the constant presence and attention of the swindler for the juggling of the records; thus, large embezzlements are usually perpetrated by officers who do not take vacations. Indiana some years ago established a requirement of two consecutive weeks' vacation away from the bank, and there was a noticeable reduction in embezzlements.

"The misapplication of bank funds and making false entries in bankbooks" covers a multitude of swindles under the general heading "embezzlement." That's approximately what the judge said when he sentenced Elsie Houck Stone, fifty-seven, for embezzling funds from the First National Bank of West Plains, Missouri. She was the trusted vice-president of the bank, at a salary of $470 a month, which in the Ozarks in the mid-1960's wasn't peanuts. Nor, for that matter, was the $318,000 she embezzled.

From these examples, one might assume that small banks offer the biggest opportunities for the embezzler. Actually, the only difference between the small-bank swindle and the big-bank swindle is the simplicity of the operation. Small-bank embezzlements are easy to carry out and simple for the examiners to prove. Large banks, with many employees, offer the same opportunities, but the swindles are more complex.

For instance, while some of the above cases were getting headlines, Federal files were running over with other bank frauds not so simple to unravel. One of these concerned the Capitol Hill State Bank of Oklahoma City. There, several employees were charged with embezzling $1,562,000 and using part of the money to buy controlling interest in the bank.

U.S. Attorney Robert M. Morgenthau said the scheme was "the most flagrant and serious misapplication of bank funds by bank officers to come to official attention." In addition to embezzlement, a Federal grand jury charged the three bankers with mail fraud, wire fraud, and inter-state transportation of stolen property. The scheme in-volved a dummy bank, chartered by the Bahamian govern-ment to do business at Freeport on Grand Bahama Island. The "bank" was a $50-a-month rented room, bare of furniture or records, and the only "deposits" were the se-curities and cash transferred from the Oklahoma City bank.

There are no character traits that typify the embezzler. Who would have thought Mrs. Geiger was capable of em-bezzling?

Or take the example of a successful young man on the way up. On the very day he was to be honored by the American Institute of Banking, he was arrested and charged with embezzling about $20,000. He had been named an outstanding student of the Institute for 1960–1961. He had completed work for three Institute certificates and was to receive three awards at a banquet that night.

Then, too, the age of a bank may invite trust and create an air of stability, but that is really all it is—air. A 136-year-old London bank, which collapsed in December, 1964, owing millions of pounds, is the best—or worst—example. The bank was small by London banking standards, with a capital of only £275,000, but it had always enjoyed a high reputation and never once in its long history let its clients down. Then one of its employees embezzled £100,000, and in an attempt to recoup this loss, some big loans were recalled and found to be insolvent.

It was the worst blow to banking's image* since the Americans George and Austin Bidwell and two accomplices defrauded the Bank of England out of £200,000, about $1,000,000. They did it with forged notes and except for one small slip (dates were inadvertently omitted on two of the artfully forged notes) might have gotten away with it. As it was, the Old Lady of Threadneedle Street got the fright of her venerable life and succeeded in recovering only about half her loss. What happened to the other half a million dollars? Only the Bidwells or their accomplices could say, and they have never talked.

We have wondered why embezzlements are nearly always reported in good round figures. Banks don't do business that way, as anyone knows who has made a 1¢ mistake in his monthly tally. A $62-a-week Brooklyn bank teller employed by the Kings Highway branch of the Commercial Bank of North America, accused of having embezzled $46,249.56, denied in court that he had taken that much. "The amount is about right," he said, "but I can't understand the fifty-six cents. I never took any change."

With all the bank holdups being pulled off these days, one wonders how many are simply conspiracies to help bank tellers avoid embezzlement indictments. Hugh J. Degnan, twenty-nine, of Cliffside Park, New Jersey, tried it. He arranged for an accomplice to approach his window

---

* The loan associations that specialize in loans on real-estate and building and construction projects are the banking industry's biggest competitors. They also contribute to banking's image. Depositors (called "members") are covered by the Federal Savings and Loan Insurance Corporation (FSLIC), a twin of the FDIC. It also insures deposits up to $10,000. But since this is such a specialized field for swindlers, we have included the loan associations in our chapter on real-estate swindles.

and present a note reading: "Gun in hand. Give me money." The man fled with a bag containing, according to Degnan, $83,903. Actually, the FBI reported, the bag contained only $25,000. The more than $58,000 that wasn't in it was scattered around half a dozen racetracks, and Degnan had thought up this ruse to cover his swindle.

The Federal Deposit Insurance Corporation, which insures individual bank deposits up to $10,000, is not infallible either. Two sharp operators milked the First National Bank of Exeter, Pennsylvania, of nearly half a million dollars. As soon as the FDIC discovered the loss, it stepped in and announced that the usual deposit payoff would be made within ten days. Meanwhile, probably because one man was also president of a local labor union, the government, through its Controller of Currency, froze the bank's deposits. It was a maneuver not used since bank failures in the early 1930's. The action "irritated" the FDIC, according to a spokesman for the latter, and the resulting hassle almost obscured the man's getaway. As it was, he made it to Washington. He was carrying travel brochures and enough cash to take him anyplace, in any style to which he wanted to become accustomed. He explained that he was planning to go to South America "just for a vacation"—from the warring government factions, no doubt.

Inevitably the superlatives in swindling must be credited to California. Top grades go to one man, who in five years rose from a bankrupt plumber to a prosperous businessman, was convicted recently of embezzling $3,714,610 from the Long Beach (California) National Bank. The U.S. attorneys prosecuting the case said it was one of the biggest single embezzlements in American banking history.

The topper was the recent scheme to defraud the great (875 branches, $10,000,000,000 in capitalization), California-based Bank of America of $20,000,000. The alleged mastermind was an Austrian citizen who maintained an import-export business at his home in Manhattan. He had several accomplices. The scheme involved the use of the bank's secret international cable code. According to the FBI, one man sent a cable in the name of the Bank of America to the Banco do Brazil in Rio de Janeiro ordering the transfer of $20,000,000 to another's account. The swindle came so near succeeding that bank officials are still touchy about the details.

One should not infer from all this that embezzlement is on the increase. Banking associations continue to announce annual increases in all types of bank swindles, but these increases jibe with the growth in banking services and deposits. Any excess in number and amounts of embezzlements over normal growth figures might merely be an indication of stricter audits. The congressional report mentioned previously says: "The supervisory agencies suggest that the increase in reported defalcations is largely due to the increased use of audits and internal controls. The full extent of actual embezzlements can never be known; they can be measured only after they are discovered, and vast amounts may go undiscovered for years, or forever."

Most losses from crimes against banking institutions (banks and building-and-loan associations), in recent years at least, have been absorbed by commercial insurance or surety bonds, by stockholders' funds, by the FDIC, or, in the case of B&L associations, by the FSLIC. While such protections generally shield depositors, the losses fall heavily on the operations of the banks involved, rendering them less able to provide maximum service to the community at reasonable cost. Although insurance protection can prevent a particular loss from being disastrous to the bank involved, it spreads the burden of the loss over the whole banking industry and, ultimately, over the banking public.

As losses increase, insurance rates must rise. All suffer when funds that should serve the community must be paid out in insurance premiums made higher because of covering the losses resulting from crimes.

This is no plea for stricter laws, however, or for more Federal control of banking practices. Rather, it is our suggestion that the American banking image is what it is and ever shall be, with or without laws, so long as the system remains antiquated and the human element dishonest. It is this combination that most encourages bank swindling.

Obviously, there's more bunkum in banking than meets the eye. The reports, news accounts, and ABA records of bank swindles are only those the examiners expose or the banks themselves volunteer. What of unreported, unexposed, uninhibited swindling? Like the iceberg, eight-ninths remains below the surface.

Not all banks are insured against embezzlements and swindles, and not all swindles are reported. Even those few defalcations that are reported to insurance companies and the police are not channeled through to any central statistics-gathering point. The total dollars taken from banks every year would be such a fantastic figure that no government agency would want to be responsible for announcing it. It is a skeleton best kept in the back of the vault. Its rattle might shake the foundations of our most cherished monetary mores. It might also spoil a good thing for the nation's swindlers.

SWEET CHARITY

In this world, as any big-time con knows, money is the easiest thing to get, a good idea the hardest. Put another way, one can always sell a good idea, market a new gadget, raise money for a fresh attempt to solve an old problem, or simply sell a novel service.

Anyone who has tried to launch a new charity racket will agree. Given an idea of sufficient emotional appeal and the American public on which to exercise it, the charity swindler can roll up some fantastic figures. We shall cite a few examples, but first a hurried look at the average American in community action, for he is the key to the swindle.

Alexis de Tocqueville, more than a hundred years ago, expressed amazement (in his *La Démocratie en Amérique*, 1835) at how the American combines strong individualism with "an attitude toward community action that knows no counterpart in the world." This critique is valid today, only more so.

Today our vaunted individualism may be frustrated and hemmed in by a more populous and more complex society, but these hurdles have not dulled the individual's desire for self-fulfillment. Indeed, the disadvantage of being "one of the faceless mob" may be the whetstone that puts the edge on leading personalities. Obviously, also, involvement in community action is total fulfillment for many people. It is not difficult to get enough volunteer workers to put in enough time and effort to put over any community project provided the volunteers can feel that the "cause is just" or that they are "doing some good in the world."

This is self-fulfillment of the highest caliber. It is not important that the project or the cause may have little actual merit or monetary value to anyone but its promoters. It is important that millions of Americans daily raise themselves to heights of personal satisfaction unattainable in anything else they could do. The millions voluntarily engaged in the promotion of some national charity or church or community-welfare project prove the point. They also form the base on which this country's most extraordinary rackets build ("nonprofit" and tax free) monolithic empires.

Let someone announce a drive for funds to erect a shelter for homeless dogs and in no time at all enough money is collected to build a palace—except that the palace isn't built, and the dogs are lucky if their hunger pains are ended in the gas chamber of the SPCA. So what happens to the money?

Charity in the United States, in these last years of the swindling sixties, is a fantastic business, the nation's fourth largest industry! In round figures, $11,000,000,000 will be taken from many pockets and put in a few—all in the name of sweet charity. Considering the tremendous staff of fund raisers it takes to raise $11,000,000,000 a year, and the even bigger staff it takes to spend $11,000,000,000 a year, it is surprising that anything much is left for charity. Not much is.

Time was when the annual Red Cross drive was all we ever heard about. The local YMCA and the Boy Scouts and maybe a church would put their hands out too, but they were neither important nor importunate. Now every city and town has a long list of charities (more than seven thousand in Los Angeles), and in the places where they have not combined their annual request under a single Community Fund, the competition for the donor's dollar is unbelievably frantic.

There has always been some doubt about the ultimate good that charity accomplishes. And who benefits more, the giver or the recipient?* The answer is that neither the giver nor the recipient benefits more. The real beneficiary is the man or the organization through which the charity fund is channeled. Only in direct charity, where no middleman is involved, can one be sure of benefits to the giver and the recipient. But who in today's world enjoys such a direct benefactor-to-beneficiary role? Hardly anyone, for who today would do for love what is easier to pay someone to do for profit? Besides, with the Internal Revenue Service in cahoots with the charities, one's personal charity isn't easily tax deductible.

The wise ones quickly saw the potential in this situation and realized long ago that all they needed was an idea that would "touch the heartstrings" of the people. Thus were organized the professional charities. They depend on sentiment more than gullibility, and they frequently spend more on fund raising and "organizational expenses" than they give to charity.

Thus the fine line, if one exists, between a legal charity and a charity swindle is only a license. Their common ground is the philanthropic field, wherein ideas are all-important. A good charity dodge can be the basis for the easiest swindle in the world—and one of the most profitable. Charity feeds a million swindlers.

Philanthropy in the United States grows faster than the economy as a whole and faster than the personal earnings

---

* There are some historic analogies here. For example, at one time "charity" and "whore" were interchangeable.

of private givers. It is a racket that thousands of hustlers, masquerading as solicitors, work to their great financial gain in every conceivable manner. Indeed, if all of every dollar given in the name of charity had reached the spot it was intended for, the word "charity" could long ago have been written out of the language. Enough money has long since been contributed in charity's cause to lift the millstones of need and misery from this nation for all time.

Generally, the charity buck is divided into three portions, with the smallest third reaching the intended beneficiary. Frequently, where donations are solicited by a professional fund raiser, this third may become only a tenth, or disappear entirely, for it is the charity swindler's axiom that charity begins at home.

In the community or local fund-raising scheme, the key man in this racket is known as the promoter. He assumes all responsibility for the success of the project. He confers with the executives of an organization, the deacons of a church, the heads of a lodge, the officers of a veterans' group. He glibly explains how his efficient organization will ensure the success of any drive for funds, assures the committee members that they will be relieved of all worry and labor, and exhibits numerous letters from other societies that are highly complimentary about his ability and honesty.

The fund raising may include an entertainment, a dinner, a ball, or all of these together, and the promoter takes over the duty of the ticket sale as well as the publication of a program in which advertising space is sold. The latter is usually worked on a 50-50 basis after all expenses are deducted. These include solicitors' commissions of 50 per cent on all advertising plus the cost of printing, telephone bills, and incidental charges. The same arrangement is made for the ticket sale.

Special stationery is provided for the drive, and credentials—usually letters signed by the society's executives—are given to each solicitor. The committee also supplies to the promoter a list of prospective advertisers, ticket purchasers, or large contributors, and permission is always asked, and genially given, to use the name of those behind the movement to aid solicitation. The promoter works the racket from his own office, located near the society's headquarters, and soon surrounds himself with a staff of solicitors who specialize in this particular species of charity.

Every charity swindler acquires his own private sucker list when he moves into a community. He knows those people who are charitably inclined and the various propositions they fall for. Some will give liberally to Catholic affairs, others invariably donate to Jewish drives, while still others will dig deep for the Protestant cause. He may have a list of people who are patriotic and will kick in the minute the flag is waved or a collection of names that will assure the success of any drive where the kiddies are concerned.

Donors may also be influenced by some big sociological or catastrophic event. A local solicitation recently uncovered shows how one charity was designed to cash in on the Harlem riots. We'll call it Special Book Promotions and it solicited funds with the stated purpose of making books available to needy families in Harlem. The organization's representatives stated that it was a nonprofit enterprise and that they were contributing their time "free" for the benefit of the so-called Negro Committee. A little investigation disclosed that it was a profit enterprise; that it was started by two young brothers, who operated out of their home in an eastern city, and that 50 per cent of the money collected was kept by Special Book Promotions—the rest was "overhead" and "costs."

The promoter, once a proposition is signed up, has little

to worry about. His first tap will be the pushovers on his particular list. In this he will follow Benjamin Franklin's advice: "In the first place, I advise you to apply to all those whom you know will give something; next, to those whom you are uncertain whether they will give anything or not, and show them the list of those who have given; and lastly, do not neglect those whom you are sure will give nothing, for in some of them you may be mistaken."

Today the bulk of this work can be done over the telephone, in a "boiler-room" setup similar to those used by stock promoters.*

Once he has had a little experience on the community level, the ambitious con is ready for the big-time national charity. Now ideas count, for he is not selling a local product within a localized market, and he knows that the success of any idea depends on his organization. The American Association of Fund-Raising Counsel says: "There is no effective economical way of raising substantial sums from large numbers of givers save through a professionally *directed* organization of *volunteer* workers" [the Association's italics]. The loner, unable or unwilling to operate through an organization of volunteer workers, must contact large numbers of givers by a more direct method.

The National Association of Veterans Employment Councils (the bigger the name, the bigger the emotional impact) mailed out two and a half million cheap pens in a nationwide fund solicitation on which the returns expected

---

* The "boiler-room" setup is described in more detail later, in its more popular stock-promotion use, but the telephone man working a charity racket can exercise much more pressure in his pitch. His plea is made in the name of local big shots, the welfare work of the charity is known, and the pitch is tuned to win friends and influence consciences. Intimidation may also be included in his bag of tricks.

were about a million dollars. Of this the NAVEC contracted to pay out $898,575 to a Chicago direct-mail concern. Anything left over went to the NAVEC. The main offices were in Washington (always a good address for veterans' rackets), and they admitted receiving $3,131,963 in two years. Of course, this wasn't all gravy—some of it had to go for pens.*

Anyone can create a charity organization. A taxicab driver in New York City created the bogus Fifth Avenue Cancer Fund. His Fifth Avenue address was a mail drop that cost him $8 a month. Most of his donors were fares who were touched by his pitch.

Women who dress themselves in religious habits, or good imitations thereof, can be seen in every town around Christmas and Easter. Most of these are just can shakers, and their daily take is probably less than $100. Occasionally, however, one encounters a Bessie Hamilton. Blessed old Bessie isn't around any more, but in her day she was top con with the nun bit. She was in no sense a copyist, aside from the nun's habit she affected. On the contrary, she was an originator. Her methods were bold and imaginative. In the garb of a nun she seemed to have a magic touch when she talked to men with money. When she and her crew swept into a city, everyone with money felt her touch. And when she left town, she virtually floated out on a river of the green.

At one time, Bessie's pitch was for a Bessie Hamilton Home for Epileptics. To our knowledge, the only "home" her collections supported was a magnificent dwelling on Chicago's North Shore. It was near the present *Playboy* headquarters and, for its time, more sumptuous than that

* We have one of them, and we didn't write this chapter with it, or even this line, so this wasn't a very big expense.

fabulous pad. Later she cut the name to, simply, Hamilton
Home. By then her "charity" was so well known (or her
donors assumed it was, which is the same thing) that she
had only to make an appearance, flash a few letters and
credentials in a banker's face, and walk out with checks
up to $50,000. No one ever thought to check up on the fate
of the epileptics all this money was supposed to be helping
or even to question the pretty nuns who represented the
"founder." The really big donors or the particularly difficult ones were handled by Bessie herself.

Chicago May, a notorious contemporary with her own
bag of tricks, once told a reporter friend of ours that she
suspected Bessie of blackmail in some of her biggest hauls.
If this was true, then Bessie was not above enticing an
occasional sucker who thought it worth ten grand to seduce
a nun.*

Those who lack the imagination to originate their own
ideas need only to set themselves up as "fund raisers" and
sell their services to established community organizations.
A smart operator showed how easy this trick can be
worked. He contracted to raise money for the Reverend
Benjamin Franklin Johnson, who conducted a community
center for the Metropolitan Baptist Church at 400 Bergen
Street, Newark, New Jersey. The fund raiser painted glowing pictures of the wonderful things the reverend could do
with a practically unlimited flow of contributions. He
then mailed out appeals in the name of the Community
Services Fresh Air Fund. The minister got the air, and
the operator got the fund.

The Rehabilitation and Hospital Fund of the New York

* In a recent legislative committee investigating ways of curbing
swindlers in religious garb, one respectable senator voiced the
opinion that "a religious habit is something you just can't go
behind under the present law."

County Council of the Marine Corps League contracted with fund raiser Joy Gottesfeld to stage a charity ball at the Statler Hotel: Miss Gottesfeld's share, 60 per cent; the League's share, 40 per cent, with the League to pay all the expenses of the ball out of its share. This is the average deal that any organization can expect to get from professional fund raisers. The end result, money actually available to the intended beneficiaries, is about as questionable as any result obtained by the unlicensed fund raiser.

The inevitable finally occurred. Sooner or later all the good causes were going to be taken up (how many miseries are there?), so the idea boys had to dream up the ultimate: a charity organization to help the charity organizations. The first announcement came in a news release from Cleveland, headquarters for the group: "A new move to protect generous-minded Americans from being mulcted by racketeers operating in the name of charity has been made by the National Conference on Solicitations, Inc." It distributed a booklet entitled "Safeguard for Givers." By this means, it hoped to arouse public interest and, incidentally, to secure (financial?) support from Chambers of Commerce across the country.

In addition to curbing dishonest solicitors, the Conference confessed that "something must be done to reduce the multiplicity of campaigns." With some 52,000,000 volunteers collecting $11,000,000,000 from 187,000,000 Americans for 230,000 philanthropic causes, that could be called an understatement. As is this: "Contributors are almighty tired of being faced every morning with a flood of campaign mail, barraged with pledge cards at the office, greeted at home by a parade of door-to-door solicitors, and asked to serve on countless committees."

"The public may soon be sickened by all this," said one of the Conference members.

The public found its voice in a recent editorial by Shana Alexander in *Life:*

> Something flinty has been happening to my heart. I no longer feel compelled to buy Girl Scout cookies from the children staked out in front of my supermarket, and when pennies, plastic key rings or even Easter seals turn up unbidden in my mailbox, I feel very little guilt at dropping them in the wastebasket. I have not yet set fire to an orphanage or kicked a beggar downstairs, but I do invite the malevolence of the gods by tearing up Worthy Cause chain letters—three in the past month.

What our favorite columnist disliked most about the way the billions are garnered was:

> . . . the recurring feeling that I am being hustled. I automatically resist being trapped or tricked into a position where I cannot gracefully say no. Some of the fund-raising practices which annoy me are the IBM-style pledge cards which note last year's donation and automatically demand more. Is failure to escalate a crime?

Several million givers think so, obviously, else why do the charities play this note so often? The crookedest swindlers we know wouldn't take a more unfair advantage of their gulls. They call it "pulling a little con-con" (from conning the conscience, no doubt).

There is a theory going around that this play on the public conscience probably gets its start in the guilt feelings brought on by some economic condition. The record shows that the Depression of the 1930's loosened up people's purse strings* and that charity rackets thrived as never be-

---

* Those who had purses? No, those whom the Depression had hit hardest. About 68 per cent of the funds raised for charity during the Depression years came from the pockets of those least able to contribute. Today 78 per cent comes from individual donors, the rest from corporations and foundations.

fore. The nation's Community Chests, a dependable meter of the American philanthropic urge, amassed 50 per cent more in 1932 than in the best predepression year. Donations to other charities not feeding at the communal trough increased in proportion. The word "charity" became the motivating factor on the nation's conscience, and the slogan was "Give Till It Hurts."

Manipulators of the public conscience will have to think hard to beat the idea dreamed up by the group that put over a new hospital in the mid-west. The group started with a mailing of two thousand new $1 bills, which they asked contributors to match. In less time than it took us to dig this item out of the *Daily Blab*, the promoters of this one had pyramided their $2,000 to $630,000—all of which they pocketed. It would be helpful if we knew a few percentages here. For instance, what was the return per thousand dollars mailed out? A famous optimist once said that 95 per cent of the people are honest, which we doubt, but the operators in this particular case must have figured that the percentage was in his favor.

Running down that story, we came across one about a self-ordained priest who rented out nun's garb to women at $2.50 a day and lived very well on such rentals. He let the women keep all they collected above that amount, and they did very well too. A really enterprising young fellow could build up a pretty nice harem with such a racket.

We don't consider blackmail in any form a swindle. Solicitors who pose as police officers or police officers who pose as honest cops to raise funds for a police benefit or policemen's ball or to sell advertising in some book or program are not above using pressure. Whatever it is, a hint, a suggestion, or an outright threat, it all amounts to the same thing, and in our book we call it blackmail.

Nor do we have much respect for the con who can't

originate his own swindle but depends on another charity racket to make a buck. One imaginative type we heard of collected a quarter million tons of used clothing from donors in the New York area. He told the donors the clothing would be sold for the benefit of Athletics for the Blind, Inc. He sold the clothing in foreign markets for a tidy sum, but the benefit was his own.

The newspapers from which we culled hundreds of examples of charity swindles in no case ever completely covered the stories. This was no fault in reporting, nor was it a lack of space. Newspaper policy generally limits coverage to the known facts or at least to those facts which the paper can substantiate in case of suit for libel. The independent investigator or researcher is not so constricted. He can "read between the lines" all the missing parts of the story. Only if he should attempt to publish the complete story would he be subject to the same restrictions imposed on newspapers and their reporters. In such case, however, he has many advantages over the reporter and the day-to-day coverage of the story. He enjoys the benefits of objectivity, detachment, and time. From the perspective afforded by the latter, he can see the whole picture, not just the day-to-day pieces. With a little judgment, he can use enough of the whole to publish a condensed facsimile.

California, land of grapes and wrath, is having fun with another kind of charity swindle at the moment. Individually it's not much of a swindle, as swindles go, but on a statewide basis it amounts to several million dollars annually. It is the trickery going on in the state's welfare rolls. One young female in our own county is drawing monthly support for eleven children, all hers, though she is not married. The taxpayers are a little annoyed at having to subsidize another man's pleasure. But, then, you could probably top any story we could tell, for every state has this same problem in greater or lesser degree.

Our neighbors in New Mexico report that even married couples are separating and declaring desertion so that they can get on the welfare rolls. Judge Robert Gardiner Wilson, a longtime critic of welfare-agency administration in Massachusetts, said he would like an investigating commission to examine welfare rolls to see whether it is possible "to effectively purge the rolls of fraudulent cases." Commenting on this, a Boston welfare worker said, "This is a whale of a big thing—this welfare. It can be criticized from just about any angle." Donors don't mind giving $11,000,000,000 to charity every year, but they hate like hell to see their taxes used up in the same swindle.

That very frightening letter you got from the Cancer Cytology Foundation of America, Inc., was an original idea of George R. Bryant, owner of Promotional Mailers, Inc., of Englewood, New Jersey. The $340,000 he raised on this mailing was split nicely—$24,000 to the CCFA and $316,000 to George. We hope he also got part of the $24,000 for all his hard work.

Sucker lists obviously are the stock-in-trade of direct-mail outfits. Any swindler can acquire lists of people in a thousand different categories, for several large firms now do a profitable business compiling and selling them.

Since there are a number of ways in which nearly everyone can legitimately write his name or word his address, each way can be used as a key to determine how one's name gets on the sucker lists. We used this key and tested it. A couple of years ago, we subscribed to a popular magazine and gave our name and address, both spelled a certain way. We checked this one off on our list of variations and never used it again. In the past twelve months, under that name and address, we have received 189 pieces of junk mail, a ball-point pen with that name printed on it, two neckties, three boxes of "cards for every occasion," a box of "hand-painted" printed Christmas cards, miniature auto-license tags for our key chain, a packet of foreign stamps, a box of cheeses, and a sample of dried beef—all accompanied by or followed up by letters soliciting funds for every human misery imaginable. And this was only one name and address.* How much of this was fraudulent is anybody's evaluation and the Post Office Department's headache. However, we shall not object. Though junk mail poses some problems in waste disposal, we enjoy it. We also know that whenever one receives an item in the mail that one did not order, no matter what the sender says or threatens, one need neither pay for the item nor send it back.

Any big-time con knows that money is easier to get than good ideas, but ideas for swindles aren't hard to come by when they hinge on public faith, hope, or charity—not the least of which is charity.

---

* There are many ways of getting on a sucker list, but subscribing to a magazine is one of the most prevalent. We haven't found any publication that won't sell its subscription list. Could the magazine publisher be considered an accessory before the fact? And does such sale of one's name constitute a breach of contract and an invasion of privacy? Several cases now pending in the courts are based on the fact that the telephone and the telephone directory have become the tools of pitchmen and swindlers and may also constitute an invasion of privacy.

9

NO LIMIT

THERE is an old adage to the effect that there are two principal ways to create wealth. One is by investing in real estate, the other is by buying stocks. It follows, obviously, that the biggest swindles have been in these fields. We shall recount now how the big swindles were perpetrated in the past, show how they operate today, and suggest some guidelines for the swindler with the guts to play in this no-limit game.

Our text for this sermon should come from the Bible, for nothing equals it as a source of historic swindles. The race of man is hardly established in Genesis before Jacob swindles his father-in-law out of stock—sheep and goats—and his brother, Esau, out of his inherited real estate. Were we to revere anyone as the patron saint of swindlers, most certainly Jacob would be our choice. And if Jacob's swindles were justified "in the eyes of the Lord," cannot subsequent swindles be absolved from wrong by the same expedient? If not, then heaven has been robbed of several million adherents in the centuries that have passed since then, for swindlers have never ceased to swindle. And though the gimmicks used have been as infinite as the stars, real-estate swindles and fraudulent shares have continued to this day to rake in the biggest hauls.

It would be tedious to list all those which historians have recorded, even those in the million-dollar class, and take more space than we have to make our point. It will expedite our story, therefore, if we skip a few millennia and start with the stock promotion that set the pattern for the last two centuries.

THE SWINDLER FROM SCOTLAND

The best Scottish jokes have always been those that portrayed the penurious, and over the years "Scotsman" and "stingy" have become synonymous. We have no desire to change tradition or immemorial usage, but we suspect that the Scots themselves are the main promoters of the legend. Do they push the legend because it is a cover-up for a trait more Scottish than simple stinginess? By playing up the lesser of two evils, do they thus hide the greater?

Any student of history knows that Scotland's heroes for the most part were generous and magnanimous where their wealth was concerned, noble and openhanded in their dealings with their fellow men. Only rarely was there one who verged from the straight and narrow, and when he did, it was to his credit that he was not satisfied with mere penuriousness. Indeed, the outstanding example might well be called the father of stock swindling. Certainly the scale of his operation should entitle him to such an honor.

John Law was born at Edinburgh in 1671, the eldest son of a prosperous goldsmith and banker. He began his apprenticeship in his father's business when he was fourteen, and by the time he was seventeen, he had acquired an extraordinary facility with figures and banking methods. He had also acquired considerable vanity about his dress, a great many feminine admirers, and several envious males among his acquaintances.

Upon the death of his father, he went to London to see the world and to let the world see him. Rich, handsome, and gallant, he soon became the darling of London society. His banking experience and his keen mathematical mind were the foundation on which he now built a reputation as a shrewd gambler. His excesses, however, got him into numerous costly escapades and one nearly disastrous love affair. A jealous suitor challenged him to a duel, which he accepted. Unfortunately, Law killed his opponent and was immediately arrested for murder. He was found guilty and sentenced to death, but a little bribery and some careless jailers enabled him to escape. He fled to the Continent, and the reward posters described him as aged twenty-six, six feet tall, well built, and dark complexioned (*i.e.*, "tall, dark, and handsome").

He wandered about Europe for the next several years, devoting his days to the study of banking in various countries and his evenings to augmenting his income in the gambling houses. What he did with his nights would have made a good story too, but he was extremely circumspect about his many love affairs.

John Law was living in Paris in 1715, when le Grand Monarque, Louis XIV, died and the Duke of Orléans became Regent. Though the King had been the greatest autocratic monarch of France, his reign of seventy-three years the longest in European history, and his court the indisputable model for all the lesser princes in Europe, his extravagances and wars had left his country nearly bankrupt. For John Law, gambler and financial wizard, this history and this circumstance were most opportune. He had long been a gambling friend of the Duke and a frequent participant in the Duke's scandalous orgies. He now became the Duke's adviser on finance.

Law's first idea was a quick solution to stave off bankruptcy. France's troubles, he said, were simply due to a shortage of gold and silver. What the country needed was some kind of currency to take the place of metal. Paper money, he said, was the answer. Establish a bank and issue paper money and the paralyzed industry and agriculture of France would prosper again. This scheme Law was permitted to put into effect—and, sure enough, prosperity, on paper, soon became apparent throughout the land.

Riding the crest of this boom and his resulting personal popularity, he proposed another plan. "My bank," he wrote the Duke, "is not the only nor the greatest of my ideas." He proposed to "produce something which will surprise Europe by the changes which it will produce in favour of France . . . increase the population to thirty millions, and the King's revenue to three hundred millions." Law's grandiose plan was to create a company to colonize and exploit France's holdings in America. Then known as the province of Louisiana, it stretched for three thousand miles along the Mississippi River and included the present states of Louisiana, Mississippi, Arkansas, Missouri, Illinois, Iowa, Wisconsin, and Minnesota. The company, which came to be known as the Mississippi Company, was created by royal letters patent and granted a monopoly for twenty-five years.

Law began his promotion of the new project at once. He needed vast capital resources, so he devised a scheme to issue shares in the company. It may not have been the first stock promotion of its kind, but it was the first of its size. Law issued pamphlets and prospectuses that depicted the Mississippi lands as loaded with gold and silver, abounding in agricultural potential, and lush with beautiful Indian maidens. He secured the appointment of a governor for Louisiana, who, in 1717, laid the foundations of New Orleans,* named in honor of the Regent.

However, few Parisians could be attracted to life in the wilderness, and fewer peasants were interested in giving up the relative security of serfdom for the unknowns in a faraway land. He managed to enlist a few colonists, but most of his "volunteers" were felons released from prison for the purpose.

Law had less trouble selling shares. By a series of shrewd maneuvers and the consolidation of all France's overseas trading companies—the East India Company, the China Company, and the Africa Company—followed by a monopoly on coinage and the control of taxes, the price of shares rose quickly from a par value of 500 livres to 10,000, then to 15,000 and even 18,000 livres.

The frenzy of buying and the national hysteria that accompanied the rise had no equal before or since. Wall Street at its most frantic was less than a passing zephyr by comparison. Servants sent to sell their masters' shares at a specific price found the market doubling, pocketed the difference, and set themselves up as brokers. Coachmen, waiters, bootblacks, prostitutes, and cooks became rich overnight, and a few, wiser than most, turned their paper profits into hard cash. A peasant pyramided his meager savings into a quarter of a million dollars in a week of sharp trading, spent his profits for a cartload of silver and

* The only concrete and lasting result of Law's fantastic swindle.

gold in bars and plate, covered the load with straw and cow dung, and quietly drove himself and his fortune to Belgium. Traffic in the streets of Paris became so congested, it came to a standstill on several blocks and remained so for weeks.

Even the late Louis XIV himself had never been more popular than John Law. Peasants and princes alike badgered him for a few shares in his company. One highborn lady, the mother of the Regent, wrote to a friend: "Law is so run after that he has no rest day and night. A Duchess kissed his hands before everyone, and if Duchesses kiss his hands, what part of him won't the other ladies salute?"

History records only estimates of the total sales of Mississippi stock, but it probably exceeded $840,000,000 before the bubble burst in the summer of 1720, two years after the venture began.

Meanwhile, back in England another big stock promotion was in the making. The British, as usual, were learning no lessons from their neighbors' folly. Their bubble was fully as big a swindle, but it took longer to blow. And whereas John Law had alone hypnotized the bankrupt and debauched French court into creating his vast swindle, the English divided their swindle among several ringleaders.

The scheme originated in the mind of Daniel "Robinson Crusoe" Defoe in 1711. Defoe, a sometime pamphleteer, part-time economist, and full-time dreamer of utopian ideas, sold the idea to his benefactors as a way to pay off the government's £10,000,000 debt. Defoe had always been fascinated by South America (Crusoe's island was located off its coast), and he reasoned that fortunes could be made in trading there. Why not organize a company, call it the South Sea Company, and sell shares to raise the necessary capital? Why not indeed! It was such a good idea that the Chancellor of the Exchequer pushed through Parliament a bill setting up the "Company of Merchants of Great Britain trading to the South Seas and other parts of America." The first block of shares was given to the government's creditors to pay off the big debt.

But there was no trading with South America. And even though King George I became governor of the company and his mistress one of its most substantial stockholders, the project floundered for some half-dozen years.

About this time the wind from across the Channel brought news of the bizarre swindle John Law was putting over on the French. That wind blew Britain's South Sea Bubble to dizzying heights. The South Sea Company offered its shares to the public, requiring only a small down payment and thus originating margin buying. England went mad. Aristocrats, country gentry, intellectuals, servants joined in the orgy of speculation.

But the South Sea promotion was not the only bubble in the British air. Hundreds of smaller swindles were organized along the same lines, and these prospered in the general frenzy of stock promotion. The range of these ran from the logical to the ludicrous. Advertisements offering shares in "a company to advance the manufacture of wool . . . which will employ all the poor of Great Britain" or in "a company to carry on the trade of the Royal Fishery" seemed logical, and entire offerings of shares in such companies were sold out within a day or two, as were those of others set up to trade with Russia, with Africa, and along the Barbary coast. The wits of the day, untouched by the general hysteria, began to advertise the wildest imaginable schemes—projects to "import jackasses from Spain to improve the breed of British mules," to "manufacture perpetual-motion machines," to "facilitate and expedite a more cleanly way of emptying" the privies of England, and, prophetically, a company to "melt down sawdust and recast it in boards without cracks or knots." All these were fully subscribed the moment they were offered. Even a scheme to promote a secret company whose product was as yet unknown found takers and made its originators a handsome profit.

The South Sea Bubble and Law's Mississippi Scheme proved the one important dictum recognized by every master swindler: the size of the swindle is limited only by the dimensions of the swindler's imagination.

MORE HYSTERIA THAN HISTORY

A gold rush, a silver strike, or an oil boom has certain psychological features about it that are of particular interest to every swindler. The mining community and the gusher town are small concentrations of men with more gambling spirit than one might find anywhere outside a casino. The professional gambler who knows how to handle his cards or even the crooked craps expert finds the pickings in these places generally good, especially after paydays or after a big strike.

But the big-time swindler out to make a million knows that his pickings in such places are pretty chancy. He might acquire the mining or oil rights to a parcel of land and by some shrewd wheeling and dealing pyramid it to a handsome profit. He might even salt a mine or squirt a little oil into a dry hole to boost his take, practices more common than the public might think. But all these together do not add up to much in the eyes of the big-time stock promoter out to make an easy million.

This man knows something about gold rushes, silver

strikes, and oil booms that only other swindlers and a few academicians are aware of. It is the psychological effect that the rush, the strike, or the boom has on the rest of the world. He knows that the footloose and fancy free, who can physically participate in a gold rush or similar expenditure of time and effort, represent a minuscule part of the total population. It is only the effect that these few create on the rest of the nation that has any value to the swindler. The highly contagious fever generated by the few becomes an epidemic when it reaches larger segments of the population, thus creating a climate especially efficacious for stock promoters.

The widespread sale of fictitious oil stocks that followed petroleum discoveries in Texas, Oklahoma, and California in recent years was preceded by swindles inspired by the Klondike gold rush of 1897–1899. And the antecedents of these, of course, were the pioneer promotions that followed the California forty-niners.

The mining booms that hit California, Colorado, and the Klondike resulted in waves of swindling. Indeed, there were several years around the turn of the century when swindlers took in more than the Federal Treasury. One of these, by no means the greatest but one of the few who had extraordinary influence on the Western mining boom, was George Graham Rice. He was the reporter, you remember, who made and lost a fortune touting horse races and whom we last mentioned in Chapter 3.

Rice's activities after his racetrack fiasco provide a composite picture of the typical swindler of an era that influenced all later times and stock promotions. He was well grounded in all the nuances of fraud, and he knew that every man "is a member of a race of gamblers."

With the last few hundred dollars he had salvaged from the Maxim & Gay debacle, he bought a ticket to California and a few months later found a job as press agent for a mining promotion in Goldfield and Tonopah, Nevada. It was the first time mining stock was promoted nationwide by modern promotional methods. The money that soon made Goldfield the "greatest gold camp on earth" came from investors outside the state. Though the state's history doesn't say so, George Graham Rice was directly responsible for bringing into Nevada tens of millions of dollars for local investment and for the development of the state's greatest mineral resources. The ads he placed and the publicity stories he sent out made him the pioneer of all the great Western promoters that have followed.

Rice's News Bureau, as he called it, soon became the state's publicity agent. He enlisted the services of several competent newspaper men, who turned out a daily flow of human-interest stories, mining news, and advertising copy. Rice himself seems to have been sincere. He said: "I became imbued with the idea that investors who put their money into [Nevada] stocks were not only going to get an honest run for their money, in that the mines were going to be developed and many would make good, but that the opportunity for money-making, if embraced by the public at that time, would earn a great reputation for the man who educated the public to a full understanding of the situation."

But what Rice didn't appreciate, despite his experience with racetrack gamblers, was the enormous power of publicity. His simple little human-interest stories, accounts of new strikes, and production reports* created a sort of nationwide hysteria. More than two thousand mining com-

* During one six-month period of operation, the Mohawk mine of Goldfield produced $1,000,000 a month. A million dollars in mine shares and cash changed hands nearly every night in Tex Rickard's Northern Saloon and Gambling House.

panies were incorporated throughout the nation, not one of which had any real foundation in Nevada mines and not one of which made money for anyone but their promoters, who cleaned up more than $350,000,000 in a three-year period. No such swindle could have been accomplished without Rice's press-agentry, however sincere and honest.

Probably as good an example of his artistry as any was his efficient publicizing of Bullfrog, a mining camp set up two years after Goldfield. When the Bullfrog boom was still young, former United States Senator William Morris Stewart, an octogenarian and out of a job, traveled from Washington, at the expiration of his term, to the Bullfrog camp. There he hung out his shingle as a practicing lawyer. Immediately Rice's News Bureau secured a photo of the venerable lawmaker and composed a story about his fresh start in life on the desert. The yarn appealed so strongly to Sunday editors throughout the country that Bullfrog got for nothing scores of pages of priceless advertising in the news columns of all the big-city dailies. Their old files disclose the popularity of such stories.

The senator built a home, one full-page story said, on a spot where, less than a year before, desert wayfarers had died of thirst and coyotes had roamed. The interior of the house on the desert was minutely described. Olive chintz curtains protected the bearded patriarch from the burning rays of the sun as he worked in his study. Old Florentine cabinets, costly Byzantine vases, and matchless specimens of Sèvres filled his living room. Silk Persian rugs an inch thick decked the floors. Venetian-framed miniatures of former Presidents of the United States and champions of liberty of bygone days graced the walls. Costly bronzes and marble statuettes were strewn about in profusion. And the name of Bullfrog exuded from every paragraph of the story, along with the names of various other camps and mines located in the vicinity.

The only part of the story that had any resemblance to truth was the fact that the senator had set up practice in Bullfrog, on a spot where a man could still die of thirst and coyotes still roamed. His home (and "study") was a tent over a dirt floor.

Elinor Glyn, the famous English novelist, was riding the crest of her popularity after the publication of her sensational *Three Weeks* at about the same time that Rawhide's history began. Rice's crew reasoned that nothing would attract more attention to the camp than having Mrs. Glyn visit it. Certain mutual friends happened to be in San Francisco at the same time that Mrs. Glyn visited there. At Rice's suggestion, they persuaded her to visit the wild desert mining camp, on the pretext that she could pick up enough "local color" there to write another *Three Weeks*.

Mrs. Glyn and her party arrived in Rawhide after a thirty-eight-hour journey by rail and auto from San Francisco. Meanwhile Rice's men had set up a number of "exhibits." The first was a gambling house, where she saw a real game of stud poker as played on the desert. Six players were seated around a table, coatless and grimy, their unshaven mugs twisted into strange grimaces. All appeared the worse for liquor. Before each man was piled a mound of ivory chips of various hues, and alongside these rested a six-shooter. From the rear pocket of every player, another gun protruded, and each wore a belt filled with cartridges. The game was well staged.

One man, with eyes more bloodshot than those of the other players, shuffled the cards and dealt a hand to each.

"Ten thousand dollars," loudly bet the first player.

"I'll call that," drawled the next one, "and go you fifteen thousand."

"Raise you!" cried the next, and before the jackpot was played out, $300,000 in chips had found its way to the center of the table and four men were standing up in a frenzy of bravado with the muzzles of their guns pointed at one another. At that point the visitors hurried out. Immediately there was the sharp report of guns (fired at the canvas ceiling), followed by the sound of scraping chairs and violent scuffling. A moment later two stretchers, carrying the "dead," passed along the street, where Mrs. Glyn and her escorts stood with drooping chins.

Mrs. Glyn had hardly recovered from this act when she was taken for a walk through Stingaree Gulch. The lane was lined on both sides with dance halls and brothels, and the famous authoress saw all of it.* Many parts of it were to crop up later in *The Career of Katherine Brush, This Passion Called Love,* and *It* (the movie of which starred Clara Bow, who later retired and moved to a ranch not far from Stingaree Gulch).

By such manufactured nonsense, Rice created more basic atmospheric material, Western characters, and wild plots, later to be mined for movie and paperback Westerns, than Mark Twain, Bret Harte, and all the other reporters before him. And this was the skillful way Nevada mining

---

* Rice's scribes saw a chance here for bombast. This bit appeared in all the Eastern papers the following week:

The wasted cheeks and wasted forms of frail humanity, as seen last night in the jaundiced light that was reflected by the crimson-shaded lamps and curtains of Stingaree Gulch, visibly affected the gifted English authoress. They carried to Mrs. Glyn an affirmative answer to the question, so often propounded recently, whether it is against public morality to make a heroine in *Three Weeks* of a pleasure-palled victim of the upper set. It was made plain to Mrs. Glyn that her heroine differed from the Stingaree Gulch kind only in that her cheeks were less faded than her character.

stock was promoted. That some mining corporations were legitimate and profitable to the stockholders was only the grain of truth in a sand dune of swindles. Nevada, the Silver State, was born of a mineral discovery, and mining has always been so much a part of the state's life and history that its people still speak a language compounded of mining and money terms. The state's total mineral production is quoted in billions, and the swindles based on the state's good name take more each year.

THE BIG MILKERS

Nevertheless, stock selling in America was a sporadic business before 1919. The first mushrooming in this field occurred during the early part of that year, and for the next ten years something new to the public, the selling of corporate securities, became a national phenomenon. About $50,000,000,000 worth of new securities were sold, of which half were fraudulent—more than $2,000,000,000 annually being mulcted from the gullible public.

Such a fabulous season of swindling was accomplished via three major channels of merchandising: the United States mail; personal solicitation by salesmen (who were more knowledgeable in high-pressure salesmanship than in high finance); and the first use of "boiler-room" tactics. All these approaches are in use today, with the additional advantage of extensive advertising in all media. And all, including advertising, are available to the swindler who may also be in the favorable position of stock manipulator.

Should he be in some position of control of a company's stock and its manipulation through these channels, he can milk the corporation and its stockholders of every penny.

In the 1920's, the big names in this operation were the promoters who had the reputation of financing corporations that were in poor financial condition. They bought up large blocks of a company's stock, then watered it down with an overissue of new stock, which they sold in national campaigns. The individual swindler in this racket was necessarily a man of many parts. His genius was evident in his knack of surrounding himself with competent men as assistants. His method was to open a luxurious office and a large training room for salesmen. In the latter he could accommodate several hundred applicants daily, and his classified advertisements brought in a steady flow. He did not seek experienced security salesmen; indeed, his ads specifically asked for men who had no previous selling experience.

The applicants were first given a pep talk and told that after two weeks' training they would be able to go out and average from $100 to $300 a week income (in a day when $35 a week was top salary for a salesman). In subsequent meetings, which were always conducted by experienced con men, trainees were told this was their real opportunity not only to become wealthy but to help all their friends and relatives to share in the wealth of the nation by becoming stockholders of prosperous corporations. There would be an advantage, of course, if the salesman himself owned some of the stock. The trick worked, for the public was already softened up. It had been educated to purchase Liberty bonds during World War I, and the postwar industrial boom had created popular interest in better living standards.

Office overhead, advertising, and the salaries of a few key people were the promoter's only expenses. The stock cost was minimal—usually just the printing bill, for the certificates rarely were worth more than the paper they were printed on. And since he had no intention of refunding any money or declaring profits on any shares, he could afford to pay high commissions. His net was at least 50 per cent and often as high as 75 per cent of the sales.

Some of these brokers processed as many as five hundred new salesmen every week, most of whom bought shares in the companies they were sent out to promote, and very few of them failed to make additional sales to their families and friends. It took only a few months to bankrupt some companies, but since the supply of suckers never seemed to run out, the promoters were always on the lookout for new corporations to milk. The smart ones didn't even bother with established companies. They made up their own, the fancy names exceeded only by the fanciful brochures and prospectuses used to advertise their nonexistent mines, oil properties, factories, and the fabulous profits awaiting anyone who invested in them.

It was not a new racket by any means, but its popularity during this ten-year period engendered several new terms that have since become common in the fraternity of stock swindlers. "Mooch," of ancient derivation, came to be the word for the gullible prospect, the inexperienced purchaser of securities. It was derogatory in all its connotations. It found its way into the slang dictionaries a few years later with a different definition, and today it has many other meanings, but a mooch was an easy mark in the early days of big stock swindles. The "coxey" made the first pitch. Usually he was a smart kid "working his way through college." He was satisfied to make a $50 or $100 sale. The "reloader" or "loader" was the high-pressure salesman who worked the sucker lists. The inexperienced investor who had already purchased some worthless stock was this man's meat. He reloaded the mooch with more of the same old stock through an assortment of tricks. In particularly difficult cases, however, he would call in a "superloader," or "dynamiter." The sucker who got by this supersalesman was either broke or dead. His pitch was a work of art.

"Mr. Jones," the dynamiter would begin, "may I speak to you confidentially? I am one of the directors of the corporation in which you own some stock. I'm not a salesman. I just dropped by to meet you because our president feels that our stockholders are all part of our great big prosperous family. He just wants you to know that the company is in favorable financial circumstances and is earning profits far in excess of what we had anticipated."

The dynamiter then produced what he called the company's financial statement. It had several pages of colored graphs, all the lines of which started at the lower left-hand corners and ran off the upper right-hand edges. "You will note, Mr. Jones," continued the salesman, "that your stock is now worth twice what you paid for it. The president has asked me to personally thank you for your investment in the corporation and for helping it to reach its present financial success."

Whatever the mooch had paid for his stock, it was money to him, and he was pleased to hear that he had been helpful and, of course, that he had doubled his investment.

Then came the hook. "We'd like to show our appreciation," said the dynamiter. "You've helped us—now we'd like to reward you. The board of directors has agreed to let you have additional shares of stock at the original cost per share." When the dynamiter pointed out that the mooch was really paying only four bits for a buck, the mooch generally swallowed the bait.

When an investor instructed a crooked broker either to

buy or to sell shares, the investor received the usual confirmation sales slips, but the orders actually were not executed. That is how the term "bucket shop" originated. It meant that the broker would bucket the order; that is, he would buy and sell the stock against his own client. The broker's books would show, under the same date, the stock sold and purchased, or vice versa.

The "boiler room" got its start about this time too. As a means of selling large quantities of stock to large numbers of moochers, it had no equal then, and no one in Wall Street has invented anything to beat it today. The bucket-shop broker set aside a large room in his office building and fitted it up with from ten to twenty telephones. And since the most effective calls were long distance,* it was important that this room be soundproof. In those days, that meant no windows and no circulation of air. The room must have been stifling, and it is no wonder that when the telephone salesmen completed their day's work, they were steamed up and boiled out.

The boiler room is used today to sell many other products besides stocks and bonds, but the pitch hasn't changed much. About the only thing that has changed is the comfort quotient. Boiler rooms today are air-conditioned. And boiler-room salesmen who peddle worthless stock are swindling the public out of about $150,000,000 annually. Boiler-room swindles in other commodities and services, including fake charities, are running about twice that.

The decade ended with the stock-market crash in the autumn of 1929. There were a few months when the adverse publicity, the widespread panic, and the near hysteria put a damper on legitimate brokerage houses, and even the

* One can imagine the effect of a call "direct from Wall Street" to a farmer in the Midwest or a small-town merchant in New England.

bunco bond boys had their troubles. Then someone discovered that such a time was ripe for crackpot ideas—and the more crackpot, the easier they were to sell. One, which made several million dollars for its promoter, will illustrate the point.

A promoter in California thought of the scheme of building a factory to manufacture glass caskets. After gathering around him a staff of hotshot salesmen and circularizing thousands of prospective investors with a fancy prospectus, his dynamiters followed up with personal calls. California was filled with dupes who had come looking for the Promised Land, and so for a couple of years the promoter had all he could do just to cover the state. Later he branched out until his operation covered the nation.

The brochure extolled the manufacturing methods "in our own factories, with glass of a patented process." The caskets could be manufactured for about one-fourth the cost of wood, brass, or copper caskets. Further, they could be sealed so tightly that once the deceased was buried, the body would not decompose. Another advantage of the glass casket, assumed but not pointed out, was that it could be seen through should the bereaved want to arrange periodic exhumation.

That was only one of a thousand and one different ideas that brought their promoters millions in the decade before World War II, and this despite increasing restrictions imposed by the SEC. The security swindlers suffered very little during the Depression years. Nor, for that matter, did the big "legitimate" stock manipulators, board chairmen, and corporation presidents.

For instance, the officers of Bethlehem Steel Corporation struggled bravely through the Depression like this. In 1928 they paid themselves more in bonuses than they paid in dividends to all the common stockholders. Charles M.

Schwab, chairman of the board, received a salary of $150,000. He drew the same wages in 1929, when the company income was $42,242,980. By 1930 the Depression was under way, and the company income was cut in half. Schwab's salary, however, was increased to $250,000. In 1931 the company income was only $115,745, but Schwab's salary was still $250,000. The punch line came in 1932, the bottom of the Depression, when Bethlehem Steel lost more than $19,000,000, but Schwab again drew $250,000. The officers of several hundred large corporations suffered a similar fate.

An ex-convict by the name of Philip Musica posed as F. Donald Coster and gained control and then the presidency of the famous old drug firm of McKesson & Robbins (established in 1833), and by a long series of manipulations, forged inventory reports, and promotion of false companies, he swindled the drug firm out of millions. It was deception and fraud on a scale that was unequaled for the times.

The 1938–1939 edition of *Who's Who in America* contains this entry (our asides in brackets): "COSTER, Frank Donald [Philip Musica], corpn. official; *b.* Washington, D.C. [Naples, Italy], May 12, 1884 [1877]; *s.* Frank Donald and Marie (Girard) C. [Antonio and Maria]; Ph.D., U. of Heidelberg, 1909 [Elmira Reformatory, same year] . . . ; *m.* Carol Jenkins Schiefflin . . . 1921 [Carol Jenkins Hubbard, 1926]." There follows a long list of clubs and affiliations, in none of which did he hold memberships as claimed. The paragraph remains in the old volume today as the most lies in the shortest space.

Musica, alias Coster, organized several fake companies to deal in alcohol (which he cut and rebottled and sold to bootleggers as "Scotch, straight off the boat") and ballooned the stocks of these to fictitious heights. Some of this stock figured in his trade for control of McKesson & Robbins. Once in the saddle as president there, it was no trick at all to establish fake subsidiary companies and warehouses in name only all over the map. Out of this setup, within the period 1927–1938 and with faked Dun & Bradstreet audits, he took $10,000,000. It was a neat profit for Philip Musica, whose ornate Long Island mausoleum bears this enduring alias, a reminder of the swindle: "F. Donald Coster, 1884–1938."

SEC: SWINDLERS' EAGER CONFEDERATE

Stock swindlers thoroughly conversant with the shenanigans that are standard practice in Wall Street know that few things have changed in that greatest of gambling casinos. The exchanges, despite Security Exchange Commission regulations and their own more severe self-supervision, are still run by people. And whenever the human element is involved, there are anomalies. Many practices of the past are still available to the swindler. The New York Stock Exchange's highly touted regulations for self-policing are easily circumvented. And no one in the know believes that the small stockholder, despite his numbers, has created a "democratic capitalism"; he has only helped create the fallacy that speculation is not gambling.

Among the other fallacies maintained by the exchanges are these: that the stock market is a major force in creating new industries; that stock prices rely solely on the laws of supply and demand.

Actually, the SEC has been a boon to stock swindlers. In an attempt to close the wide-open market that brought on the 1929 debacle, the "truth-in-securities" act was passed in 1933, the "full-disclosure" act followed in 1934, and a mass of legislation came fairly regularly thereafter—all of which have had their accompanying publicity and public applause. The total effect of these measures has been to create such a sense of (false) security that even the most obvious stock swindle seems an aboveboard venture to the average gullible investor. This may sound like a fantastic theory, but how else can one account for the rise in stock swindles or the increase in swindlers' take since the SEC began "protecting the public interest"? According to one big con in the game, "SEC approval of a stock issue, whether stated or intimated, is the best damn gimmick for selling stock you ever heard of."

Even suckers already wised up to the three-M requirement of good stock can still be sold with phony figures and beautiful prospectuses. The first of the three M's, of course, is *money*. The swindler's statements of the company's financial structure show that there is enough money in the treasury to carry the firm's main project through development to marketing and profits. Whether or not that is a fact is not important. The gullible's faith in anything printed is a common phenomenon that the swindler considers his principal asset.

Management is the next most important part of the promoter's pitch. It is not difficult to get big names on the board of directors, good engineers (for oil and mining-stock promotions), and officers' names that ring with ability, substance, and integrity.

The third part of the pitch or the prospectus portrays with some logic the *merchandise* to be manufactured or sold. Crackpot ideas may have been profitable a few years ago, and in certain areas still are, but the average prospect today has been educated to look for these three M's, and the swindler's pitch takes this into consideration.

MO: MODERN OPERATORS

The newspapers, never willing to give the Devil his due, said master rogue Lowell McAfee Birrell bilked his stockholders out of "at least $14,000,000." If the truth were known, the total would probably be nearly twice that. Of course, he never got it all—no swindler ever does who operates on such a wholesale basis—but considering the inscrutable maze of his stockholdings, in an empire that included oils, paper, gas, airlines, insurance, and chemicals, he very easily could have milked them for $20,000,000.

Birrell's MO was not as complicated as the press would have you believe. He simply acquired the assets of good companies and either sold them outright or transferred them to other companies where only he could get at them. In the course of such manipulation, he was not above issuing a little extra stock—say, three million shares when the company had only forty-three thousand (e.g., Swan-Finch Oil)—and disposing of the lot by scattering shares among many different agents here and in Canada. It's done every day on Wall Street. Still, few have the courage to attempt anything like that which Master Birrell did so smoothly. Who was Birrell, and how did he get that way?

Lowell Birrell came from the same pocket of the nation that produced the late astronaut Virgil Grissom, such artistic lights as Red Skelton, Phil Harris, Cole Porter, Hoagy Carmichael, merchant Bernard Gimbel, and, in an earlier day, writers George Ade, Theodore Dreiser, and James Whitcomb Riley. He had the advantage of being born in a small Indiana town, (population, 465) and being the son of a poor ($900-a-year), hard-preaching Presbyterian minister. Advantage? Is not a poor-but-honest beginning the traditional springboard to success? Years later, Birrell was to say, "I decided early I wasn't going to be poor."

He was a brilliant student. At only twenty-one he got his doctor of laws degree with one of the highest academic averages, a remarkable feat, since he had had to work his way through school. It also earned him a place in the well-known New York law firm of Cadwalader, Wickersham, and Taft.

Birrell distinguished himself as a shrewd lawyer, then turned to business and formed his own company. It was only a matter of months before he was the owner of several fabulous residences, among them a twelve-hundred-acre farm in Bucks County, Pennsylvania, complete with tenant farmhouses, old stone mansion, pool, lake, and well-stocked bar. Here he entertained such guests as Serge Rubinstein, the playboy stock rigger and currency juggler, who probably taught him some of the trickier tricks of the trade.* And bandleader Paul Whiteman, a neighbor, liked him. Thus, quite aside from the millions he mulcted from his numerous companies, Birrell was the epitome of all those talents necessary in a man of the world and in the traditional Horatio Alger hero. He made good in his chosen profession.

One of Birrell's contemporaries and undoubtedly his

* The frequency and the size of Birrell's parties made them an excellent market for $100-a-night call girls, one of whom told us that Birrell bought them by the gross (no pun).

competitor in this field was Alexander Guterma. About the same time that Birrell was hitting his peak, Guterma's empire of phony ownership was worth in excess of $25,000,000. Guterma, however, had reached this pinnacle over a longer and more devious road, so devious that despite all our inquiries, it remains more clouded than clear.

One thing everyone knew was that at the top of his career, he headed three multimillion-dollar corporations listed on the New York Stock Exchange, a Wall Street record. In this position he ruled a major auto-parts factory, a large Hollywood movie-and-television studio, a national radio network, one of the nation's oldest makers of household cleaning compounds, a brokerage firm, and he owned enough cattle, oil, and uranium stocks to make him a big wheel in these fields. At this point he was asked to explain his phenomenal success. "It was all accomplished," he said, "by a goddamn genius."

Guterma was a corporate genius, true, but he was also one of the cleverest financial pirates who ever cruised the Main, or Wall Street. He said he was born in Irkutsk in eastern Siberia, the son of a general in the Czar's army. Judging from his accent, he probably spent some of his formative years in Brooklyn. There are records and newspaper accounts that describe him as being one jump ahead of the law in such unlikely places as Tientsin, Shanghai, Manila, and Honolulu, and somewhat in that order, before he came to the United States.

By 1956 Guterma had acquired control of United Dye & Chemical; Bon Ami, a manufacturer of household cleansers; and F. L. Jacobs, an auto-parts manufacturer. All three were listed on the New York Stock Exchange, a fact that Guterma's public-relations man used to impress the investing public with the financier's business acumen. According to some of the disgruntled stockholders, the man from Siberia milked these companies of $5,000,000 in corporation assets in a two-year period. No figures were ever made public regarding a score or more smaller jobs he pulled off, but the Mutual Broadcasting Company was his next big one. No figures are available for that one either, but one deal he made as president of the corporation got a lot of publicity in the press at the time.

Dominican dictator Generalissimo Rafael Leonidas Trujillo was frantically casting about for a new image. The thousands he had murdered and the millions he had squeezed out of that little Caribbean republic were beginning to disturb his sleep. He was spreading small fortunes among American writers in an attempt to convince the American public that he was a benign elder statesman, father of his country—were not some five thousand bridges, monuments, buildings, roads, babies, and the national capital named in his honor?—and not the murdering swindler he really was. We recall the regret with which we had to turn down an offer that his *sub rosa* ambassador Porfirio Rubirosa made us in those halcyon days. But Guterma, as head of Mutual Broadcasting, had a better medium of public relations than any book we could write. He made a deal with *sub rosa* Rubirosa that involved the dissemination of nice news about the old dictator and $750,000 as the first payment. Guterma flew down to Ciudad Trujillo (the name has since been changed back to Santo Domingo), signed the contract, and returned to New York with the cash in a satchel, all within a few hours. It was probably the biggest cash swindle in the shortest period of time on record.

Guterma and Birrell were both part of what *Fortune* magazine once described as a "kind of demimonde within the U.S. financial community," a little-known world of fast operators who can swindle a corporation out of a million dollars while the timid ones hide behind their façades of honesty grubbing for a buck. With men like Birrell and Guterma romping through American finance like the James boys on a spree, it's pretty hard for most writers to make their books sound like exposés and not sour grapes.

Subjects for additional study should include the contemporary club members Gerardo A. Re, kicked out of the American Stock Exchange for "bilking unsuspecting investors of untold millions of dollars"; Edward Mortimer Gilbert, who milked the Memphis hardwood firm of E. L. Bruce of enough to attempt a raid on Celotex and earn the *nom de pirate* "timber wolf of Wall Street"; San Francisco's Virgil David Dardi, who, through United Dye & Chemical and in association with Lowell Birrell, gypped some three thousand stockholders of $5,000,000 and involved an improbable cast of Las Vegas gamblers, Wall Street respectables, and well-known swindlers; and Billie Sol Estes and Anthony De Angelis. The latter two are such giants in the racket, we think they deserve greater kudos than we could give them here.*

SILENCE IS GOLDEN

Among those swindlers whose job it is to influence public opinion, publicize a character or a company, create images, advertise a product, and/or sway large masses of

* Norman C. Miller gives Tino De Angelis the coverage he deserves in his *The Great Salad Oil Swindle* (New York: Coward-McCann, 1965).

citizens to their (the swindlers') profit, the subtle hint, the innuendo, and the suggestive silence are tools most powerful.

Of these, silence is by far the most ingenious. The manipulation of a silence so evocative that it motivates the public to fantastic action favorable to the swindler's cause demands a talent not common to the average man. When that cause is the promotion and sale of stock, of whatever quality, this image maker's tool—silence—is put to its ultimate test. The Windfall story is most exemplary. It may also be one of the best examples of how to make a million dollars in sixteen days.

Financial page readers will be familiar with the squabble concerning the Securities Exchange Commission and the Texas Gulf Sulphur Company. The SEC accused certain "insiders" (in a civil suit) of Texas Gulf of being dishonorable if not unlawful. This legal battle is making news if not history. What with the principle of free enterprise already at stake in this country, we suspect that this is more than an ordinary case. And since we have already shown our own bias where business principles are concerned, it would be useless to protest our equitable position. This, then, is the background for the Windfall story as we interpret it.

Timmins, Ontario, in 1963, was a bleak little mining town clinging to the desolate, muskeg-covered land some 350 miles northwest of Toronto. It was near there, on a cold and blustery day in November of that year, that prospectors working for Texas Gulf brought up the first cores of the fabulous ore body that lies beneath the muskeg. It is now known to be one of the biggest and richest bodies of ore ever discovered, estimated to be more than sixty million tons of high-grade copper, zinc, silver, and lead, evaluated at about $2,000,000,000.

At that time, however, since the cores had not yet been assayed, it was imperative that no word of the strike leak out. The cores looked promising, but until an assay could determine some facts, Texas Gulf officials were not about to put themselves in the position of creating false rumors. It was good business for them, on the strength of the untested cores, to secure as much of the surrounding acreage as possible. Some of the insiders purchased stock. It was their gamble and their money. It would have been considered shady practice to have started any rumors or let outsiders, even the rank and file of stockholders, in on the secret, for had the assay shown negative results, their purchase of stock would then have been a swindle.

The secret was kept for five months, but their sound reasons for concealing the news of the big bonanza were questioned by the SEC. There are always a few disgruntled gamblers who gripe when they are not let in on a big thing. Strangely, they are the first to yell "gyp" when they gamble and lose. Some who didn't get in on the ground floor of this one went to the SEC, which went after Texas Gulf insiders. Others, better sports or better businessmen, profited by the strike in their own way. While Texas Gulf was quietly gobbling up all the acreage on the perimeter of its holdings, another outfit had just as quietly acquired a few acres adjoining the Texas Gulf property and overnight became the talisman of tens of thousands of investors. Its long-shot name was Windfall Oils and Mines, Ltd.

The story of Windfall's manipulations began in April, 1964, when Mr. and Mrs. George MacMillan bought a parcel of claims adjoining the Texas Gulf property. The parcel had by accident been overlooked by the Texas Gulf surveyors. The price: $100,000 plus 250,000 shares of Windfall. George was the president of the company, but Viola was the promoter. And what she doesn't know about Dominion mining business is hardly worth knowing. Mrs. MacMillan is one of the industry's best-known figures; for twenty-one terms, she reigned as president of Canada's Prospectors and Developers Association.

As one account told it, the first thing Windfall did with its claim was to bore its own hole through the muskeg, but with a little more fanfare than its neighbor Texas Gulf. Meanwhile, with the Texas cat out of the bag and the SEC chasing it, public interest in Windfall's claim rose to fever height.

Barrons, a business publication, reported that on July 4, George MacMillan chipped two samples from the drill cores and pocketed them. The following day he ordered a halt to the drilling. The drill cores were packed into boxes and taken to Toronto in the MacMillans' station wagon and stored in the garage of their home. There the cores remained for the next nineteen days.

During this period, speculation concerning the cores' contents turned the market into a circus. Whereas Windfall's operation out on the muskeg had been no secret, every action now was. Secrecy now became the tool of manipulation. When trading began on Monday morning, July 6, Windfall opened at $1.01, some 44¢ above its Friday close. A flood of buy orders had accumulated over the weekend, and by the time the exchange closed that day, about one and a half million Windfall shares had changed hands at prices ranging up to $2.

Windfall stock traded wildly all week, at one point reaching a high of $4.25. By July 31, some 13,387,000 Windfall shares, worth more than $36,000,000, changed hands in nearly 57,000 trades. The MacMillans showed a trading profit on their own shares of $1,455,928, more than $1,000,000 of that in sixteen days. Who could have kept a secret more profitably? Of course, the action taken by the MacMillans did not violate any Canadian laws.

NOT SO REAL ESTATE

The earliest method of transferring land is lost in the antiquity of the law. Some of its history is apparent in the English method of transfer of a thousand or more years ago. It was then called livery of seizin (leave or permission to seize and legally take possession). If it was a large tract, there was a symbolic pageant with the definite purpose of ensuring the just delivery and acceptance of the unique and immovable land. As the pageant proceeded, the neighbors were called to witness the transfer and to make sure that justice was done. The new owner was taken to view the land and escorted upon it, where he was clothed with the robes of ownership (investiture). The person presently seized of the land would hand to the new owner a twig or a clod of earth to symbolize the transfer. The neighbors would know whether the man in possession (the seller) was truly seized of the land, and they could verify the seizin of the new owner. Fraud at any stage of the transaction was rare and difficult.

Today the delivery and acceptance of a written instrument replaces the clod of earth, real-estate agents act for the neighbors, and fraud is more often a part of the transaction than one might think.

The first real-estate swindle in America for which we could find any record was the so-called sale of Manhattan Island to the Dutch in 1626. It might even be called the first double-play swindle. We recall the historical pablum we were fed, and looking back on it, we don't think we completely swallowed all of it even then. Certainly, in light of our recent researches, we figure the Indians were swindled. Maybe you were fed the same and had the same reactions.

Peter Minuit, you remember, was sent by the Dutch West India Company to establish a trading post in the New World. The Dutch knew that the French and the British already had established beachheads in the area, and they had no intentions of being left out in the cold and the Atlantic. They also suspected that neither the French nor the British would be pleased at the establishment of a Dutch colony amidst their newfound lands. And the Dutch, being smaller but smarter, knew they didn't have the strength to resist intervention by either nation. Consequently, they resolved to make their colonization as legal as possible by purchasing Manhattan Island from its occupants.

It was a noble thought, but Minuit's 60 guilders' worth of knives, axes, cloth, and beads for all of Manhattan, even unimproved, always seemed to us like a monstrous swindle. And having always considered ourselves akin to underdogs, we resented the way the poor Indian was pushed around. It wasn't until we dug a little deeper into history for this chapter that we discovered that another swindle was involved.

The Indians who sold Manhattan Island were bilked, all right, but they didn't mind. The land wasn't theirs anyway (they were just weekenders over from Brooklyn); it belonged to the Weckquaesgeeks,* who had occupied the island long enough to have squatters' rights.

---

* How the Dutch got "Manhattan" out of that, we don't know —but we're grateful.

A lot of real estate has changed hands in the 340-plus years since then, and it is anybody's guess how much fraud was involved in the deals.

THE BARON OF ARIZONA

Arizona was bypassed for years. Prospectors, settlers, and city makers rushing westward to the utopias of California and Oregon paused only long enough to replenish their water tanks at the occasional oases or followed trails that purposely avoided the "arid waste" that was Arizona. California became a state in 1850, Oregon in 1859, but Arizona was not even organized as a territory until 1863, and of all the thousands who rushed westward, not enough people settled in Arizona to make a state of it until 1912.

New Mexico suffered somewhat the same neglect, even though Santa Fe, the oldest capital city in the United States, had been a trading and government center for centuries. The territories of Arizona and New Mexico did not begin to grow until about 1880, when emigrants headed for the booms farther west, decided this was far enough, and began to put down roots in the hot sand and the sunbaked trading posts. They discovered that the meager streams could be diverted to irrigate the desert and make it bloom and that the dry and sunny villages' could become meccas for the unhealthy. Prospectors drifting back from failure in the gold fields of California discovered rich lodes of ore in the rugged mountains. It was a time for the establishment of law and order and the adjuncts of civilization such as public utilities and newspapers.

The *Arizona Gazette*, founded in 1880, soon established itself as the ears, the eyes, and the voice of the people. It continues today as a powerful voice in the state, but it is no longer unique. It has competitors that speak for some of the people some of the time. Still, its old files are an inspiration to read, and some of the swindles it uncovered are thrilling to follow. The biggest invariably had something to do with real estate.

The most fantastic of these concerned the Peralta Claim, one involving land that encompassed twenty thousand square miles of territory in Arizona and New Mexico, an area larger than the states of Massachusetts, Rhode Island, and Connecticut combined. The first news break appeared in the summer of 1883. Don James Addison de Peralta-Reavis, it began, had come to claim his inheritance, the Peralta Grant, or La Baronía de Arizonac. This grant was given by King Ferdinand of Spain to his warrior kinsman Miguel de Peralta on December 20, 1748, and "I, the living descendant of Don Miguel, am here to take possession of my lands and all that exists upon them."

The territory encompassed by this grant included all the land in the counties of Apache, Gila, Graham, Maricopa, and Pinal. And these counties, everyone knew, contained the townships of Casa Grande, Florence, Globe, Pinal, Silver King, and Tempe, as well as the entire city of Phoenix.

One can imagine the shock waves that rolled over the territory after this announcement, the disbelief, the ridicule, the fear, the question mark behind every deed of land within the boundaries of the *baronía*. If the baron's claim was valid, everybody who owned one square foot of land in that area would be dispossessed. The land, with all its improvements—homes, buildings, farms, banks, mines, railways, and factories—would become as a kingdom, subject only to the Federal government of the United States, and every inhabitant a vassal to Don James, the Baron of Arizona. However, he never gave himself such an Americanized title; it sounded more authentic to use the full-flowing Spanish—Don James Addison de Peralta-Reavis, Barón de Arizonac, Caballero de los Colorados—and more mysterious.

The panic and the furor, as reported in the *Gazette*, built up to a historic confrontation between the baron and his lawyers and provoked a mass meeting of citizens in Phoenix. The wonder of it was that it didn't turn into a lynching party; that it didn't says a lot for the baron. He was suave, handsome in a patrician way, elegantly dressed, and obviously aristocratic. And in stating his case, he was firm without hardness, superior without condescension. There was not the slightest hint in anything he did or said that was cruel or cunning or deceitful. The people of this barony must pay him their assessed tribute, in rents or purchases, or find themselves on the street. That was the law, and he had all the proofs necessary to substantiate his claim and answer any questions.

A committee was formed to investigate Don James and examine his documents and to find out what could be done to protect the citizens' rights. There followed several weeks of intensive study by the committee, with weekly progress reported in the *Gazette*. All the documents exhibited by the baron were checked out by the best obtainable authorities and were pronounced authentic. The proof piled up, until another mass meeting was held, which the baron addressed.

His manner was courteous, his speech refined, and what he had to say was delivered with a slight Spanish accent, the words like music. The crowd was lulled into an acquiescent mood. "Ladies and gentlemen," he said, "I am dis-

turbed more than you are to have to tell you that I must
pursue my claim, that justice must be served, but I will do
everything within my power to make the burden easy on
you."

And then, with a show of genuine reluctance, he gave a
detailed account of how, long ago, the Spanish kings re-
warded their deserving *caballeros* with huge grants of land
in the Nuevo Mundo. He reminded them that Arizona and
New Mexico were once a part of Mexico and said that
when the grant was made there was no thought that someday an English colony would spread this far. He paused to
unroll a large map that showed plainly the surrounding
grants, with Peralta in the middle. Besides the counties,
towns, and farms, he said, his claim also included the Silver
King mine (whose output was running about $5,000,000
annually) and the right-of-way occupied by the Southern
Pacific Railroad.

He concluded in a voice that seemed to be tinged with
genuine sorrow: "I regret, ladies and gentlemen, but I must
inform you that all these cities and towns and all the improvements thereupon are my property."

The investigations became more intense and ranged farther afield, and it soon became evident that the baron had
many influential friends and supporters in high places.
Among them were Robert G. Ingersoll, the "Great Agnos-
tic," and former U.S. Senator Roscoe Conkling. They were
convinced that his documents were authentic and his claim
valid, and with this backing he persuaded the California
empire builders Charles Crocker and Collis P. Huntington
to finance his campaign to establish his title.

The committee sent emissaries to Washington and then
to Spain and Mexico City. In the end, after the most exacting research, its conclusion was that the King of Spain had
made the grant to Miguel de Peralta in 1748, as claimed;

the Spanish Inquisition had confirmed it; the viceroy of
Mexico had acknowledged it; and the heirs of Don Miguel
had a right to it. The only question was whether the present
pretender was a descendant of Don Miguel and also
whether he was the only living heir.

The baron produced intricate and detailed genealogical
tables that proved beyond question that only *two* descendants remained. And who was the other? Thereby hung another tale. "In the course of my investigations to see if any
other descendants remained," the baron said, addressing
the committee on the occasion when this question came up,
"I discovered that a female descendant of Don Miguel gave
birth to twins in 1859. One of the twins died, the other
grew to maturity. Her name is Sofia Loreta Micaela."

While the gentlemen of the committee sat stunned with
this news, the baron excused himself. He returned in a
moment, leading by the hand a very pretty Spanish woman.
"Gentlemen," he said, "may I present my wife, La Baronesa Sofia Loreta Micaela de Peralta-Reavis."

What with all the investigations and the hundreds of
proofs that had to be run down, it was nearly a year before
the baron had firmly established his claim. The citizens
began to pay tribute on the property they had thought they
owned; the Southern Pacific bought a quitclaim for $50,-
000; the Silver King mine paid him an installment of
$25,000, with a promise of further payments. He even
pushed a claim against the U.S. government for $50,000,-
000 for land the government had given several hundred
homesteaders. Thousands of small owners scraped their
pots and poured their savings into the swelling stream. Don
James had become the richest and the most powerful man
in the West. He collected millions in tribute and spent it
like a prince. He invested huge sums in mines and industries and real estate outside his own domain, and he bought

palatial homes in St. Louis and Washington and Mexico City and Madrid. His carriages, when they passed through the streets of these cities, always attracted large crowds, for it was a show of royalty. He lived and he traveled like a king, and he ruled his Arizona barony for a decade.

But the applause, the acclaim, and the tribute were not given him without complaint and lingering doubt in the minds of many of his subjects.

The *Gazette* suspected fraud, but it never risked a hint. However, it did continue to report on the investigations being carried out by a qualified detective. He had been sent abroad to examine the documents in the archives of Spain and then was sent to Mexico City. Little evidences of forgery began to show up. One day, while looking at what purported to be Peralta records, he held one of the pages up to the light to see the ancient writing more clearly. It was dated 1759. Suddenly his eyes popped, for the sheet of parchment bore the watermark of a paper mill in Wisconsin!

It was the big break in a long series of disclosures that rocked the Southwest and particularly the Barony of Arizona. It was soon proved that Miguel de Peralta had never existed, that the genealogy of his descendants was the concoction of a vivid imagination, and that all the documents in the archives of Spain and Mexico and the baron's hands were forgeries of the highest caliber. It was the most fantastic land swindle and doubtless the most brilliantly conceived and successfully executed in the history of American real estate.

James Addison Reavis had not one drop of Spanish blood. He was born in Missouri, and he was a Confederate soldier in the Civil War. He discovered, by trying, that he could forge his captain's handwriting—so well that he could make out his own passes. Soon, for a fee, he was forging passes for other soldiers. Some such activity may have led to his early discharge, because before the end of the war, he was working as a streetcar conductor in St. Louis. He continued to practice his penmanship in his spare time, and when he felt that he had attained some proficiency, he opened a real-estate office. He forged titles to property that were so well done he was never discovered. He had an honest face, a glad hand, and an ingratiating smile. Nobody ever suspected him of duplicity.

There was a lot of talk in St. Louis in those days about the fabulous opportunities "out West." Reavis went as far as Santa Fe, where he got a job in the newly opened land office of the U.S. government. Recent treaties with Mexico had caused many old land grants to come under question, and it was the job of this office to sift out the true claims from the false.

That office held the key to a fabulous future for a man willing to study old records, familiarize himself with history and geography and noble Spanish families. Reavis was fascinated, and he learned fast. He studied the tricks that fraudulent claimants used and the methods they used to prevent detection. Little by little, he amassed a fund of knowledge the equal of which no one in his day could match.

Meanwhile, he also studied Spanish, mixed socially with the aristocratic Spanish families of Santa Fe, and in time he acquired a patina of Spanish character.

His big task lay still ahead. For a year or two he traveled to Mexico, South America, Portugal, and Spain, where he visited monasteries and church and government archives. Step by patient step he changed old records, tampered with ancient writings, and substituted whole pages of forged records where necessary.

Once he had created his character with such meticulous

care, his next step was to find his *baronesa*. She was a waif named, simply, Carmelita, whom Reavis found working as a slave on a poverty-stricken ranch. Reavis became her Pygmalion. He gave her a name, a family, a veneer of culture, and inspired her to become the queen of his domain.

From that point on, he made history—and such a mess of Arizona land claims that even today citizens of the Grand Canyon State curse his memory. We think they are neglecting a fabulous opportunity: the exploitation of a character as extraordinary among men as their Canyon is in geography. Tourists, suckers for the fantastic, would eat it up.

LAND BARONS TODAY

The best titles ever acquired for land in the United States were those handed the homesteaders by the Federal government. Not only did the homesteader have to earn his title by "proving" the land, it was the first claim ever granted on that particular parcel. There were no previous grants, no previous owners—except the Indians, and they didn't count.

But the Homestead Act had about run its course by the 1920's, and during the Depression of the 1930's, the parcels of land still remaining in the government's grab bag were going begging. They couldn't be given away like the hundreds of thousands of fine acres already doled out because the remaining pieces were inaccessible, unproductive, or underwater.

The Depression may also have depressed the pioneer spirit, which had been the prime motivation behind homesteaders. Further, the national economic condition stimulated and speeded up the great population shift from rural to urban environments that began with industrialization in the 1890's. Nevertheless, the desire for land remained a constant if submerged motivation, inhibited only by economic factors. It was still a good climate for the real-estate swindler.

By far the most overworked and universally employed device used by land swindlers was the "free"-lot scheme. It didn't originate in the 1930's, in the 1920's, or even in 1717, when John Law blew his Mississippi Bubble, but in spite of its antiquity, it was and still is a sure money-maker. The swindle is pulled off several times in every generation and at least once in every locality. The best description of its MO can be found in some of the old warnings issued by the National Association of Real Estate Boards (NAREB). The swindler's lots, said the NAREB, were not free. The happy winner of some lottery, the simpleminded soul who solved a picture puzzle in a newspaper advertisement, and the gullible citizen who fell for the tale that he had been chosen for this award because of his prominence in the community all paid for their prizes in the end. An old NAREB bulletin described the swindle thus:

> The most prevalent method of extracting money from excited "winners" is to charge them for the "cost of searching the title, drawing the deed, making the transfer," etc. The collection of these sums, varying from $14 to $68 and more, gives the good-hearted promoter ample profit for his trouble. In most cases of this kind . . . the "incidental" charges were more than the value of the land.

> For example, in one case . . . the land was bought for $20
> an acre, cut up into six or seven lots per acre, and "given
> away" for $39 title expense, per lot.

The free lots were and still are located in remote places
where the land was worthless. Such "prizes" were and still
are often of peculiar size or too small on which to build
under existing building ordinances or on remote deserts
or underwater.

Winners who go to the trouble and expense of inspecting
such property are always disappointed and easily prevailed
on to switch their holdings. The salesman for the promoter
is so very sorry that the prize happens to be in such a
poor position, but by special arrangement with the boss, he
can give the winner credit for the poor lot on another and
better piece of land. "Switching" takes skill, and frequently
it is the promoter himself who takes charge of this important phase of the swindle.

If the "free" lot is too small, invariably it happens that
the adjacent lot is for sale. The gull is delighted. He thinks
he is pretty lucky to get part of the strip for nothing and
cheerfully antes up the price of the other lot. It is not until
he tries to build on it or puts it up for resale that he learns
that water, streets, and public utilities may not be available
for the next fifty years.

Key men in organizations of this sort are the ad writers
and the brochure-bunco artists. Men who can turn a
phrase, twist a truth, and contort a cliché are in great demand. A glance at any of the advertising put out by such
firms as Molly Cameroun Associates (a fictitious name for
an outfit with wild acreage in Florida and a vast desert piece
in Arizona) will disclose some neat turns, twists, and con-
tortions.

If the property being advertised is twenty miles to the

nearest town and the same distance to a lake in the other direction, the bunco brochure says: "Located between town and lake." Taxes are a big headache to most people, and most of these developments are unincorporated communities with only county or state taxes on real estate, so the brochure reads: "No city taxes." "Zoned and restricted" is another neat phrase that can mean anything but probably means nothing. "Member of the Chamber of Commerce" means, simply, that the promoter paid his dues. "Water available" creates a good impression but doesn't mean anything, since the available water may be the other side of a mountain forty miles away. And "within an hour's drive of large city facilities," of course, depends on one's skill as a racing driver and the use of a souped-up four-wheel-drive jeep or swamp buggy. "Congenial neighbors, schools, hospitals, churches, theaters, shopping centers" must always be used but never qualified by any statements of how far away they are. And, naturally, such words as "planned," "projected," "scheduled," "contemplated," "under construction," and "proposed" are the hooks on which a lot of bait can be hung. The subtle lie by omission is an art form of extraordinary convenience to the real-estate swindler.

One of the best gimmicks to boost interest in worthless land or to boom a lagging subdivision is to spread the rumor that a new industrial enterprise is projected by some large corporation, a dam or reservoir is planned, or the development of a big power project is contemplated. Several thousand acres of Arizona and Nevada sand near the great Hoover Dam project were predicted to "bloom" with irrigation, but the only things that bloomed were gigantic swindles. At least two of these were the financial parents of some of the largest and oldest gambling layouts in Las Vegas today.

The really big promoters are not above an erroneous quotation or two. When Muscle Shoals was being projected, Henry Ford was quoted as saying: "I will employ one million men and build a city seventy-five miles long at Muscle Shoals." Lesser promoters cued in their own: "Muscle Shoals, the Pittsburgh of the South," "Greater than Detroit," "Another Chicago," and so on. Acres that cost $20 were split up into six lots that sold for $5,000 a lot. After thirty years, some of these acres can still be bought for $20.

Even philanthropy in real estate can be profitable. Only the biggest wheels know what happened to property values along New York's East River when the United Nations buildings went up. Surrounding property that was only a jump ahead of "run down" when the Rockefellers gave the site increased in value to more than offset any loss incurred in the gift.

But this is a trick used everywhere, by states, by counties, by cities, by individuals, and there is nothing really illegal about it. So it has no place in our book, except that the same gimmick can be used to make a really big haul, such as the Florida Boom of the 1920's. It is pretty difficult to tell a slimmed-down version of a voluptuous story, but Florida as a subject for storytelling has always been like that. From its beginning as a mere dream in the doddering mind of Ponce de León to the year 1915, when the land speculators and subdivision promoters began to turn that dream into cash, Florida has been synonymous with dreams of youth and beauty and voluptuous femininity. But the state does exist and the illusions do become real for the "right" people—those people who saw the state the land was in and made the most of it; they knew all that green stuff wasn't jungle—some of it was U.S. currency.

The boom took about ten years to build up, but the

frenzy that really shook the state occurred mainly in 1925–1926, when about $7,000,000,000 worth of real estate changed hands, most of it underwater. Whole communities were "developed" and sold even before they were outlined on drawing boards. Advertisements in Northern newspapers extolled the wonders of living in Florida, America's tropical paradise. And the people believed and the people came and they invested. A few communities were developed, and some of these rode out the collapse of the bubble, to lead the state's comeback a few years later, when a less frenzied, more cautious population began to move in. The suckers who bit in the first boom were middle- to upper-income people. The waves that have been sweeping over Florida for the past two decades, as the common man was coming into his own, have been from the middle- and lower-income brackets. Most of these are the retired and the young people who find employment in Florida's burgeoning industries. Still, the land sharks forage today exactly as they did in the boom days of the 1920's. Their pitch is the same, and the gimmicks they use to hook the suckers have changed only in color and sex appeal. Today there seems to be more of both.

Those eager-beaver operators who would enjoy a little homework in this subject should read a publication by the Eighty-eighth Congress (1964) on "Hearings Before the Subcommittee on Frauds and Misrepresentations, etc."* We can excerpt only a few of the paragraphs pertinent to our account:

> Some old techniques . . . appear to have long lives. The subcommittee has learned in recent days, for example, that the "free lot" gimmick is still with us. Individuals

* Available in three parts from the U.S. Government Printing Office for $1—the best one-spot investment any real-estate operator could make.

still receive letters informing them that they have "won" lots. They are then asked to pay the costs of closing the deal. In the cases we have heard about, these "costs" are almost $150.

The senators, caught in the squeeze play between voters and vested interests, hedge a little on their estimates of the annual take in this field. They think that "the entire industry is worth about $700 million annually."

A witness before the subcommittee conceded that there is a definite increase in two types of promotional advertising—the "investment" and the "retirement" types:

> The exposés of earlier promotions revealed that lack of physical improvements on many subdivisions makes habitation difficult at best, and impossible at worst. Now we find that stress being placed either on holding the land as an investment for resale later at a profit or buying it now, so that when retirement age is reached the land will be paid for and ready for occupation.

The "investment" promotions were said to be purely speculative, and the "retirement" approach can be good or bad, depending on the honesty of the subdivider and his ability to make good on his promises.

One witness, sketching the history of land frauds in Colorado, outlined the swindler's advantages today:

> History, verified by the often overlapping and cloudy titles on record in many recorders' offices, tells us that land promotions in the West are not new. In fact, the records indicate that as early as 1870 land promoters were luring immigrants from Russia, Germany, and other countries with promises of rich farm lands, stoutly built cabins, and other blandishments which often were found to be nonexistent. Land speculation was rampant during the Gold Rush, fabulous sums being paid for urban sites in once-booming areas that are now just ghost towns.
>
> Today's fraudulent land promoter has a much different

atmosphere in which to work. He has the means of communication—newspaper, radio, TV, direct mail, and
gatherings of people—by which he can quickly reach
large numbers of the population. He has easy credit
facilities, which make it easy to secure agreement to purchase. The maze of overlapping jurisdictions, antiquated
laws, conflicting interests, indecision, all combine to en-
able him to operate his scheme with more than an even
chance that he will escape penalties of law. Added to all
of this is a growing segment of the public who believe
they can get something for nothing.

Aggressive nationwide promotion of Colorado land for
home and recreational sites began in 1954, when a Florida
promoter optioned large areas of mountain land and
began a widespread direct mail "bait" advertising barrage
to lure prospective purchasers to the site. As the cash
success of his promotion became evident, some salesmen
spun off from this promotion to form their own developments, and the mountains and the mails were littered with
advertising of cabin sites. Today, the great majority of
these original promotions are deteriorated areas, or have
reverted back to their natural state, and thousands of
people who eagerly paid for community recreational living
in the mountains have given up hope of either recovering
their money or seeing their dream come true.

By 1961, land operators had recognized Colorado as a
"sleeper state with a great potential," and within a matter
of weeks, twelve subdivisions were offering "free" lots at
state fairs, garden, home, and auto shows, the World's Fair
in Seattle, and other public events throughout the nation.
People were invited to "register" for a drawing, and everyone who did "won" a lot, for which they had to pay up to
$49 for "closing costs," "title," and so forth. At the open-
ing night of the Texas State Fair in Dallas, seven thousand
people registered for and "won" "free" lots offered by one

Colorado promoter. By mail and personal-contact sales-men, "winners" were advised of their good fortune and were offered the opportunity to buy additional lots at prices ranging from $395 upward. Some of the lots had cost the promoter nothing but an option to buy. By the mid-1960's, Colorado was no longer a "sleeper state." It bustled with a wide variety of wildcat real-estate pro-motions.

The MO of most of these promoters began with the little card the suckers signed at the fair or at their church social. The first follow-up to this was a letter that began: "Con-gratulations, you have won," and the pitch that followed was bound to make anyone feel lucky. If the gull didn't send in his money for the so-called free lot, there was an-other follow-up, which usually clinched the deal. Once he was hooked on that one, he was "let in" on a proposition to buy the adjoining lot. One operator unloaded two thousand acres, each cut into six lots, for an average profit per acre of $1,000.

An operator in Texas skips the card. He buys his sucker lists and makes his main pitch in his first letter: "Congratu-lations. You have been selected to receive a homesite for $95. This is offered in lieu of advertising," and so on. Any-one who takes the time to investigate may find that the homesite is a lot only twenty feet wide or located in an impossible gully or on a sandbar. The promoter's out is another pitch: he'll give you a $95 discount on a lot in a better location, the price of which may be $1,500 or more. One fellow used cocktail parties and boiler-room tactics to promote a Florida site in the middle of an Everglades swamp.

When discussing or advertising improvements and facili-ties, promoters are generally vague. They build their pre-sentations on the area's recreational facilities, climate, and beauties of nature. Pictures of skiing, fishing, wildlife, and scenic beauty were used in the Colorado promotions as though these were on or adjacent to the property, when in fact they were probably miles away. Drinking water is described as "easy to get," or it is said that "artesian wells abound in the area." There are references to "proposed" golf clubs and "projected" lakes and "planned" schools, churches, shopping centers, and so on.

A witness before the Senate's subcommittee, describing Oregon's promoters, stated that the success of land speculators in that state depended on three points: (1) keeping distance between the purchaser and the land and selling sight unseen; (2) devising sales contracts designed to fit everyone's pocketbook—a low down payment and low monthly payments with low interest rates; and (3) the use of misleading advertising.

An example from those presented by this witness, one familiar to us, will illustrate how the Oregon operators operated. From all over the United States, from Hawaii to Maine, came answers to the colorful advertising of the Harney County Land Development Corp., whose offer of acreage in "Beautiful Lake Valley Oregon" was ambitiously described as "The Greatest New Investment Opportunity in the West!" Since this promotion was mainly by mail and the promoters did not anticipate much actual inspection of the property before purchase, they could and did stretch a few points.

So-called Lake Valley was heralded as "one of the last great unspoiled areas of the West! A paradise for sportsmen! Healthful outdoor living! Hunt! Fish! Swim! Find new happiness in this sun-drenched wonderland where your investment dollar buys unlimited pleasure!" One-acre tracts were offered for $395—$5 down, $5 monthly, including 6 per cent interest.

The land, we happen to know, was formerly used for seasonal cattle grazing and has a cash value of $5.60 per acre on the county assessor's rolls. The assessor's records also indicate that the assessed value is 25 per cent of the appraised value. The "lake" is mostly dry alkali most of the year, and the nearest good hunting and fishing are fifty miles away. The scenery is good, if you like unbroken vistas of dry sagebrush (we wonder where they got the photographs for the brochure), and no one knows where the water table lies—it could be a hundred feet down, or it could be halfway to China.

However, since this is a no-limit game, some idea of the potentials involved should be illustrated with further examples. There are literally hundreds of really big operations. Most were organized by men who came up through the ranks by operating many of the lesser swindles covered herein. Most of them either own or control large direct-mail-addressing outfits or big boiler-room setups. They specialize in barren desert land, remote mountain acreage, or swampland. They easily gain temporary possession by option or simply by contracting to pay the owners something in the future. Options on a thousand acres for $1 down and $1 a year are not uncommon.

The big boys in this racket operate mainly in California, Arizona, New Mexico, and Florida, where large parcels of wasteland are still available. And those companies mentioned above as typical have at one time or other controlled not only acres but hundreds of square miles. One such outfit, for instance, acquired, as just one item in its stock-in-trade, 175 square miles in one county in Florida. At 640 acres per square mile, that's 112,000 acres. If they were cut into six lots per acre and given away as "free" lots with a "closing" fee of $50 or sold for $300 an acre as "ranchettes,"* the take would be $33,600,000. Of course, that figure would be the gross. But assuming that half of it had to be spent in advertising and operating expenses, still the net would be a pretty fair profit for a two- to five-year campaign.

Any swindler who is wary of mail-order selling or who has had some warning from the Post Office Department can set up his own boiler-room operation by installing a telephone. For a flat monthly fee, the boiler-room operator can make unlimited long-distance calls anywhere in the continental United States. The fee is $2,475 a month for each telephone. How many telephones are leased on this basis in New York, Miami, Los Angeles, Phoenix, and other centers for boiler-room operations is a figure not available from the telephone company. However, it must be a good proposition for many operators, for we know of several who lease as many as twenty telephones on this basis.

When you figure that these telephones are kept busy around the clock, with three shifts of salesmen, who together can average $18,000 in sales daily, the $50,000 monthly telephone bill doesn't seem so big. And what do the salesmen make out of it? Ads in the classified help-wanted columns of newspapers in boiler-room towns say that telephone acreage salesmen make up to $25,000 a year. All one has to do to find out the size of the operation is to ask, in answering the ads, how much commission is paid and how many other salesmen are in the same boiler room.

It takes real know-how to sell land that is under several

* Californiacs, clinging tighter to the state's Spanish background, call them "ranchos," a hypocrisy if not a subtle swindle in itself, for the Spanish *rancho* usually meant several thousand acres, not just a little homesite.

feet of water. "Swamp swindlers," they call them in Florida (and "sand swindlers" peddle the desert wastes of California and Arizona), and it is a name that goes way back. The operation, however, has changed a little in recent years. Florida real-estate booms of the 1920's roped in buyers that were pretty well off financially, as we have said. Installment buying—low down payments and low monthly payments on long-term mortgages—was not a common practice forty years ago. Underwater-homesite deals used to be a national joke. The sale of underwater property as "homesites" is taboo today under Florida and Federal laws. But swamp swindlers have developed a new commodity that is safer and just as profitable. They still sell lake bottoms, swamps, and jungles, but they represent the land not as homesites but as "investment acreage."

What happens when a buyer tries to inspect his property? Getting back to the Senate's subcommittee, we can repeat what a Florida official said:

> I spent almost two days, using a slow plane and a four-wheel drive, radio-equipped jeep, to try to locate a certain parcel [for a buyer] in a development called University Highlands, being sold by a corporation named Firstamerica Corp., located approximately ten miles west of Daytona Beach in a dismal swamp.
>
> After two days of some of the roughest riding, we had to give up, as it was impossible to penetrate deep enough into the swamp to a point which we had spotted from the air.

The parcel had been sold to a woman from Syracuse, who had intended to use it as a homesite for a house trailer. It wasn't even usable as a site for a houseboat.

If you haven't yet been approached by real-estate swindlers or have not received any of their colorful brochures or been told by telephone how lucky you are, then you don't get any mail and you have no telephone. If you would like to see for yourself how the land sharks operate, just let them know you are interested. Immediately you will get the picture—in full, flaming color, with words to match. You'll be thrilled with spectacular pictures of snow-capped mountains backing up a pretty valley or new factory buildings surrounded by palm trees and landscaped gardens. There will be girls, girls, girls in every seductive pose imaginable, and you wonder what the hell they are selling anyway. Streets filled with beautiful homes and playgrounds for every age level are part of the pictorial pitch. It is the greatest show on earth. Don't miss it. Barnum at his best was never as good as the poorest of these.

One of the witnesses appearing before the subcommittee summed up the Senate's problem this way:

> It has been said many times by people in high places that only fools buy land sight unseen. If this is so, then we are . . . mainly concerned with protecting fools from themselves.

Every lawmaker since Moses has wrestled with this problem, and no one has solved it. Can anyone protect a fool from his own folly? What are the odds that today's Senate can, or tomorrow's?

Good gambling odds against it, say the swindlers.

Swindlers' Glossary

Angel The person supplying the money in any big gamble with no guarantee that he will get it back.

Arsonist An incendiary, a torch, a firebug.

Badger game A swindle in which the victim is placed in some compromising situation with the swindler's female accomplice (posing as his wife or sister) and then blackmailed.

Barker The spieler, the talker, in a short-con game.

Beef A complaint.

Big con A big confidence game or a trick, usually with an elaborate setup, whereby the swindler realizes big money.

Boob A victim or dupe.

Booster A shoplifter.

Bucket shop A stock-gambling place where stock is sold on margin for future delivery, which is rarely made.

Bunco A confidence game or swindle.

Cannon A pickpocket.

Capper An outside man who works for a gambler, one who brings in the suckers.

Century A $100 bill, a C-note.

Check kiting Passing a check whose amount has been fraudulently raised; a check bearing a forged signature; a check without funds to cover it.

Chump A sucker.

Clip artist A swindler.

Cold deck A deck of stacked cards dishonestly introduced into a game.

Color A miner's term for a trace of gold. A mine that shows color could have been "salted" (which see).

Con One who specializes in confidence games.

Con game A confidence game, a swindle.

Flush Having plenty of money, well heeled.

Folding money Bills, green stuff, scratch, loot, dough, hay, swag, chips, sugar, cabbage, lettuce.

Forger A check passer, paperhanger, paper man, check kiter, scratch man.

Front money Money put up to lead a sucker into a swindle.

Gaff, gimmick Any device, method, or system used by a swindler to trick a sucker.

Gaffed dice Crooked dice.

Goldbrick Any confidence game in which a relatively worthless "brick" is sold as solid gold or the real thing; a fraud or confidence game in general.

Grand A thousand dollars, a G-note.

Grift To steal.

Grifter A thief.

Gyp artist A swindler.

Haul The swindler's take or profit; also called loot, gravy, cut, dough, swag.

Hay Money, chips, dough, sugar, cabbage, lettuce.

Hooked Swindled.

Hotel prowler One who specializes in stealing from hotel rooms.

Jug Usually a jail, but among old-time cons it meant a bank.

Lam To flee hastily.

Laying paper Passing worthless checks, paperhanging.

Layout The swindler's paraphernalia; also called a setup.

Lemon A worthless or unprofitable swindle; a victim of a confidence game.

Lush A drunk or heavy drinker.

Mark A prospective or an actual victim of a confidence game.

Mob Any gang of crooks.

Money machine A confidence game involving a machine represented as capable of making money or of raising the value of money.

Nut The sum total of expenses.

One-spot A $1 bill.

Paper Checks, securities, marked cards.

Paperhanger A bad-check passer.

Patsie A dupe or victim of a swindler.

Pennyweighter One who steals jewelry and small objects by substituting a worthless item for a valuable one.

Phony Counterfeit money; a package of paper with good bills on the outside.

Pigeon The dupe or victim of a confidence game.

Pigeon plucker A swindler.

Plant Usually a detective stationed to watch for con men in action or vice versa.

Poke A pocketbook or wallet.

Rap A complaint, a beef; a criminal charge.

Salesman A swindler's advance man who makes the first contact with the mark.

Salted Fraudulently enriched. A salted mine is one where mineral evidence has been placed to hook the sucker.

Score To pull off a swindle; the proceeds from a swindle.

Shapes Dice whose sides have been altered to favor the swindler.

Shill, shillaber A swindler's assistant who poses as one of the crowd. He may be permitted to win in a short-con game in order to rope in the suckers.

Short-con A confidence game in which little preparation and small stakes are involved.

Smack A fraudulent coin-matching game.

Spieler The person who does most of the talking in a con game.

Spring To release from jail on bond.

Steer joint A crooked gambling house; a swindler's layout.

Steerer A confidence operator who first approaches the intended victim; also called a salesman.

Store A fake layout or setup to inveigle suckers; also called a joint.

Sucker From the swindler's standpoint, any person not engaged in some swindling activity; also called the fall guy, sap, pigeon, dupe, gull, easy mark, boob, chump, egg, customer (*i.e.*, the victim).

Thimblerigger A shell-game operator.

Touch The victim of a swindle, a sucker.

Trick A swindle. To "pull a trick" is to swindle.

Trim To swindle, fleece, gyp, clip, beat, cheat.

Wildcat Usually an independent oil swindle; a far-out swindle.